PLAYING FOR AUSTRALIA
THE FIRST SOCCEROOS, ASIA AND WORLD FOOTBALL

PLAYING FOR AUSTRALIA
THE FIRST SOCCEROOS, ASIA AND WORLD FOOTBALL

TREVOR THOMPSON

First published in 2018 by Fair Play Publishing
PO Box 4101, Balgowlah Heights NSW 2093 Australia
www.fairplaypublishing.com.au
sales@fairplaypublishing.com.au

ISBN: 978-0-6481333-7-7
ISBN: 978-0-6481333-9-1 (ePUB)
© Trevor Thompson 2018
The moral rights of the author have been asserted.

All rights reserved. Except as permitted under the Australian Copyright Act 1968 (for example, a fair dealing for the purposes of study, research, criticism or review), no part of this book may be reproduced, stored in a retrieval system, communicated or transmitted in any form or by any means without prior written permission from the Publisher.

Design and typesetting by Retta Laraway, Looksee Design.

Front cover photo: captains of Newcastle and China, Clarrie Coutts and Lee Wai Tong, Newcastle v China 1923. Newcastle won 7-2. From the original manuscript by Harry Hetherington, 'History of soccer in Northern NSW, Sydney and South Coast' by Northern NSW Soccer Council. Held at Newcastle Region Library..

Back cover photo: captain Mile Jedinak holds the Asian Cup trophy after the final, Australia v Korea Republic, 2015. Australia won 2-1. Getty Images

Thank you also to Poppy Fogarty, Kay Hunter and Peter Lukeman for photographs from the personal collections of Harry Millard, Tom Traynor and Ernest Lukeman respectively.

All inquiries should be made to the Publisher via sales@fairplaypublishing.com.au

A catalogue record for this book is available from the National Library of Australia

Disclaimer

To the maximum extent permitted by law, the authors and publisher disclaim all responsibility and liability to any person, arising directly or indirectly from any person taking or not taking action based on the information in this publication.

CONTENTS

Introduction 1

1. Australia's International Roots
   Thinking Outside the Box 1863-1920 5

2. The Game Begins
   Australia and New Zealand 1922-1923 22

3. The Chinese Connection
   Australia's First Contact With Asia 1923 29

4. Lee Wai Tong
   Asia's Greatest 45

5. Empire Cousins
   The Canadian Tour 1924 52

6. The Gods Themselves
   England and Australia 1925 59

7. East Indies and the Philippines
   Asia, Europe and Colonial Football 72

8. The Boom Goes Bust
   Australian Soccer Stretched to Breaking Point 1927 83

9. Set Sail for Asia
   The East Indies and Singapore Tour 1928 98

10. Have Ball Will Travel
    Travelling Players, Australia and the Football World 113

11. Tom Traynor and Ernest Lukeman
    Australia's First Leaders in Asia, 1928 120

12. New Ambitions
    Growth and Big Ideas in Australia and Abroad 130

13. Return to Java
    The East Indies Tour 1931 141

14.	The Australian Championship Interstate Nation Building 1928-1936	149
15.	Maurice Vandendriessche Australia's European Advocate	155
16.	The Asian Championship The Far East Games, 1913-1934	164
17.	Cruising the Pacific New Zealand and New Caledonia, 1933-1936	171
18.	Asia in Berlin China and Japan at the 1936 Olympics	182
19.	Japanese Glory, Korean Shadows The Tangled Emergence of Japan and Korea	190
20.	The English Rollercoaster The Death of the English Tour Dream, 1934-1938	198
21.	Asia in Paris East Indies and the 1938 World Cup	213
22.	India Steps Out The Bengali Tour of 1938	220
23.	Palestine and the Gathering Storm The Tour from the British Mandate in Palestine, 1939	231
24.	Australia's Early Stars Australian International Players Before World War II	241
25.	Where Do We Go Now?	250
	Acknowledgements	261
	Author Bio	363

INTRODUCTION

On a warm Sydney night in January 2015, Australia's captain Mile Jedinak held a silver trophy above his head to the deafening acclaim of fans who had just witnessed the Socceroos become the champions of Asia.

A goal from James Troisi rewarded persistence and a piece of magic from Tomi Juric on the goal line just outside the penalty area to create a chance out of nothing and a 2-1 extra time victory over South Korea. The crowd of over 76,000 erupted. The Australian festival of Asian football that was Asian Cup 2015 ended with the jubilation of home fans celebrating the Socceroos scaling their highest peak to be continental champions.

Australia's women's team, the Matildas, had already become Asian champions in 2010 and Western Sydney Wanderers had reached the summit of the confederation's club football beating Saudi Arabia's Al-Hilal 1-0 over two legs in the Asia Champions League final. There could be no longer be any doubt that Asia offered paths to glory for football in Australia. For Australians, the slogan of the Asian Football Confederation rang true. The Future is Asia.

Less well recognised is Australia's Asian past. In a 16 year spell between the world wars, Australia hosted or went on five long Asian tours. Nearly half of Australia's 109 games against foreign opposition were against teams from Asia. Asia played a key role in the development of Australia's national team in its first two decades and Australia played a significant role in Asia.

There was never any conscious decision to detach from British roots to embrace an Asian identity, and any suggestion of that kind at the time would have been seen as bizarre. The reverence for all things British was plain in Australian life, and in football, the authority of English opinion and the position of the Football Association was unassailable.

However, the experience of the decades between the world wars showed that England could not, or would not, guide Australia to the world stage, while new friends in Asia demonstrated that alternative paths to progress were available. Could Australia navigate a course which respected its cultural roots in Britain while recognising its sporting and geographical realities in Asia?

The new football cultures of Asia were also wrestling with the problems of getting established and working out how to connect to the wider world, and engagement with Australia was part of their thinking. Asian approaches to international life proved to be far more successful.

By the time Asian teams reached the Olympic and World Cup big stages, Australia's national team life was slipping in to disrepair. There was no meaningful competition, no real plan for the future, and the credibility of touring opponents was being openly derided.

The value of playing internationals at all was under attack. The Anglo-Australian relationship had failed to satisfy Australian ambitions, but a new model for international football yet to take shape. Why did this happen?

The Australian football story also includes fabulous games, euphoric moments, star players and largely unacknowledged great characters. China's Lee Wai Tong, arguably Asia's greatest football figure, twice toured Australia as a player and terrorised local defences with his devastating scoring power. Huge crowds turned out to see his team play.

On tour in Java, Australia played against one of Europe's top forwards, Dutchman Bep Bakhuys, as well as the man who became the first Asian player to walk on to a World Cup pitch, Achmad Nawir. Other early stars from Asia lined up against Australia, and European internationals Maurice Vandendriessche and Willy Stejskal came to play club football in Australia. Prague side Bohemians even adopted the kangaroo as their club emblem after their Australian tour.

The Australian scene produced a top class British professional as early as the 1890s in Jimmy Jackson, while Sydney's Arthur Savage had already played for England when he started agitating for association football in Sydney in the late 1870s.

At home, Judy Masters emerged as a highly talented domestic star, Charlie O'Connor breezed into the Australian side as a teenager and stayed there for nearly a decade, while the likes of Jimmy McNabb and George Cartwright established a proud Australian tradition of always having a high class goalkeeper.

Australia's football story stretches back more than 150 years through the presence of Australians at the birth of the modern game in England but Australian players knew through direct experience of football's global reach. In matches from top international level to social friendlies, they played against teams from all continents.

This book looks at the emergence of Australia's national side in the context of Asian football progress, comparing Australia's experience with other nations in the Asia Pacific region. It gives an account of big matches, tournaments, and key players on and off the field in Australia and Asia.

Australia's soccer landscape was eventually transformed by waves of European migration after World War II which created new clubs and competitions and swept away an Anglocentric establishment unable to deal with change.

This book examines the time before that revolution, a time of first contact with teams and individuals from all over the world. It was the 1920s and 1930s which first raised questions about whether following English ideas was really in Australia's interests and whether FIFA, Asia, or other non-British ideas offered some kind of alternative.

Australia's link to the story of football is the longest in the world outside Britain and deserves more attention.

The football people who first tried to establish an Australian national identity in the most international of sports deserve our respect.

1.
AUSTRALIA'S INTERNATIONAL ROOTS
Thinking Outside the Box 1863-1920

Right from the very start, Australia's football life had an international pulse. Even though the gap between the first knockabout games and the first international match was nearly 50 years, and even though the first competitive international was still another 34 years on from that event, football - soccer - was always a sport standing with one foot in another land.

Australian football's struggle to celebrate its international dimension, to develop an identity for the Australian public and for its national team, and to find a role in the world game, has been a constant feature of a story which has evolved over a century and a half.

Leave aside the countries of the British Isles and Australia emerges as the country with the longest link to the world football story. Within Britain, Australian figures were present at the formation of the Football Association, the first exhibition matches under F.A. rules, the first international matches of the 1870s, and the 19th century growth of the Football League.

The Football Association, the game's first controlling body, was formed at the Freemasons Tavern on October 26, 1863 after a series of meetings of football clubs, universities and others involved in running football teams of one kind or another.

The very first meeting included a representative from the Blackheath Football Club, Frederick Henry Moore, one of the club's founders in 1858 who had also been captain of the team for five years.

Fred Moore was born in Western Australia in 1839 but left the west for Melbourne and then London while still a teenager. He worked for Dalgety and Co. in London and was sent to work for the company in Dunedin, New Zealand, in 1864 followed by appointments in Invercargill, Launceston, Christchurch, Sydney and Melbourne. He died in Hobart in 1934.

Moore was most definitely an advocate of the Rugby rules and Blackheath, one of the founders of the FA, split from the Association ranks to become one of the founders of the Rugby Football Union. Nevertheless, Moore was an Australian voice at the table when the historic meetings took place between the groups we now see as soccer and rugby as they tried to hammer out a set of laws for the games collectively referred to as "football."

In 1867, the FA arranged an exhibition match in an effort to promote the Association and its Laws of the Game. The match would be Surrey and Kent playing against Middlesex. Charles Craven Dacre lined up for Surrey.

Dacre was born in Sydney in 1848 and moved with his family to Auckland in 1859. Like many boys from well to do colonial families, he was sent to England to further his education. He attended Clapham Grammar School and played football with London Athletic and Clapham Rovers. He played cricket for Surrey.

He was the kind of man who succeeded at any sport he turned his mind to. He was awarded a medal as the best all round sportsman while studying at the Royal Agricultural College in London and after completing his education, returned to New Zealand. He was a champion rower in Auckland, he was a founder of the Takapuna Jockey Club, a prominent yachtsman, played rugby for Auckland and played a significant role in establishing football in that city.

In the 1920s, his nephew Ces Dacre played football and cricket for New Zealand against Australia.

The great Charles W. Alcock was the creator of both the F.A. Cup and international football. He began the tradition of England versus Scotland matches in 1870, but it is only the clashes starting in 1872 that are generally regarded as properly constituted "A" internationals.

In the fifth of these events in March 1876, a big crowd turned out at Hamilton Crescent in Glasgow to see the home side score three first half goals to beat England 3-0. In goal for the English

The oldest national team photo in world football, the English side to face Scotland in Glasgow in 1876. Sydney born Arthur Savage is sitting on left of the picture, one of the first ten international goalkeepers.

was another Sydney born man taking part in some of the great seminal events in the history of the game, Arthur Henry Patrick Savage.

Arthur Savage was the first Australian international in any football code.

He was another young man sent to England for a better education. He was the son of the chief surgeon of Port Jackson who had settled in the colony of New South Wales after first travelling to Australia as ship's doctor on a convict transport ship.

He also went to Clapham Grammar School and played for its old boys team Clapham Rovers and then Crystal Palace, a side not connected to the modern club of the same name. He went on to study at the Royal Naval College at New Cross, an experience which gave rise to his later football pen name, Novicrucian.

The year after his sole appearance for England, Savage returned to Sydney and wrote letters as Novicrucian to the *Sydney Morning*

Herald extolling the virtues of the Association game and referring directly to his big match.

He drew attention to the fervour of the crowd, noting "despite the rain falling in torrents at intervals and the ground being half under water, there could not have been less than 40,000 spectators on and around the ground." Other accounts have the crowd figure at half that number.

Savage attended the meeting in Sydney which established the Wanderers club and played in the celebrated match in August 1880 between the Wanderers and the boys of Kings School at Parramatta Park, the first properly documented game. He is the first international player ever to take the field in Australia.

Savage dropped out of the organised football world and pursued his career in the military where he was a highly popular officer who served in the Australian contingent in the Boer War. He retired with the rank of Lieutenant-Colonel in 1904 and died in England the following year.

One of the Kings School boys who played in the Parramatta match was Granville Ryrie, later Major-General Sir Granville Ryrie, head of the Australian Imperial Force. He also served in the Boer War and in World War 1 was prominent in the Australian Light Horse charge which captured the town of Beersheba. Ryrie was one of the mourners at a memorial service for Arthur Savage in Sydney in 1905.

By the 1890s, England and Scotland were supporting booming professional leagues. The first Australian player to come to prominence in this vibrant scene was Jimmy Jackson. Born in Cambuslang, Scotland, he came to Australia as a two year old when his family emigrated to work in the coal mining industry of the Hunter Valley.

He played for Hamilton and Wallsend and was selected for the representative team of the North - the Hunter region - against the South - Sydney, alongside his brother Alexander. The match was refereed by Jack Logan, the man who would head Australia's first national association. Jackson returned to Britain as an 18-year old and was signed by Glasgow Rangers before joining Newcastle United.

His most successful phase was with Arsenal. Jackson was part of the team which launched the club for the first time to Division One in 1898 and went on to become captain of the team.

Jimmy Jackson was the first home grown player to leave Australia to become a professional overseas. His son James was also a prominent player who became captain of Liverpool. A man of deep religious convictions in keeping with the family's strict Methodism, he was known to all as "Parson" Jackson.

Jimmy Jackson's nephew was the cricket prodigy Archie Jackson, son of Jimmy's brother Alexander. Young Archie played cricket for New South Wales at 17 and outshone his batting partner Don Bradman when he made 164 on debut for Australia against England at the age of 19, at that time the youngest player ever to score a Test century. His cricket career was curtailed by tuberculosis and he died in Brisbane at the age of 23.

John Cuffe was born in Timbrebungie, Dubbo, in the central west of New South Wales in 1880 and made a name for himself as a cricketer in Brisbane and Sydney before playing for New South Wales against Queensland on Boxing Day 1902. He left Sydney for England where he played twelve seasons of county cricket for Worcester, his left arm spin taking more than a hundred wickets in two seasons and cracking more than a thousand runs in three separate seasons.

He was also a stalwart full back for Glossop in the second division of the English Football League making 282 appearances over ten seasons. He had no football profile in Australia, but the fact that he could play at a good level for so long in England starting at the age of 25 certainly implies many others could have done the same. At Glossop, he was a team mate for three years of Ivan Sharpe, founder of the Football Writers Association, and Fred Spiksley who became one of the great coaching innovators in continental Europe.

Sharpe became a prominent journalist and gave the first live radio commentary of an F.A. Cup final in 1936. He was a strong critic of England's failure to properly engage European football and one of few prominent figures to back the case of countries like Australia in the between wars battles over amateurism and 'broken time' payments. Spiksley was an England international who coached teams to national titles in Sweden, Mexico and Germany.

Cuffe's occasional cricket captain at Worcester was R.E. "Tip" Foster, the only man to have been captain of England at both cricket and football.

'Tip' Foster and John Cuffe played together for Gloucestershire against the touring Australian cricketers in 1905. A year earlier, the former England captain played football in Australia against two state teams. Foster scored a massive 287 on debut for England in the first cricket Test at the SCG and England went on to regain the Ashes in a 3-2 series win. When the serious cricket business was completed, the English squad agreed to play two football matches on the way home.

Foster scored a hat-trick in a 7-0 thumping of South Australia at the Adelaide Oval, and netted another in a 3-0 victory over Western Australia at Fremantle Oval. The Reverend Henry Foster, father of seven sons including Tip who played cricket for 'Fostershire', was the form master of Australia's football advocate Arthur Gibbs when he was a pupil at Malvern College.

When the Melbourne adherents of the football cause met at Young and Jacksons Hotel in March 1883 to form a club, they decided to call the new body the Anglo Australian Association Football Club. The club set about organising inter-colonial matches against New South Wales to be played in Melbourne in August.

The *Argus* in Melbourne published a letter calling for trial matches to be played with a view to sending a team to England. Anglo Australian secretary John Teare wrote to the *Argus* to say "there is not the slightest doubt that if Victorians played the same game they would be a match for British teams."

Correspondence shows a favourable response in London to Australian suggestions of a tour to Britain in the mid 1880s, with plans for matches reported to be under way. A later report in *The Referee* refers to F.A. President Charles Alcock's report that "there is every hope of their having a great success, especially as it is proposed to include two or three aboriginals in the Australian team."

The F.A.'s own history of the organisation, published in 1953 to mark its 90th birthday, notes that Alcock read a letter from the Anglo Australian Club to the Football Association Council in November 1883 and that Alcock wrote in reply to express "the gratification of the F.A. Committee at the development of the Association game in the Colonies."

The book's author, Geoffrey Green, cites this event as the beginning of the F.A.'s life as an international administration, "that, in effect, was the birth of F.A. relationships overseas, relationships that were soon to multiply and spread in various directions."

The first big push for an English tour of Australia came in 1901 when Arthur Gibbs, representing Australia and New Zealand, went to London to make the case directly to Alcock. Gibbs' pitch was for an amateur team to make the trip. The *Athletic News* report on a reception which heard speeches from Alcock and Gibbs quotes the Australasian representative referring to the 1899 rugby tour saying "We really do not see why the Football Association should not accomplish what the Rugby Union has done."

Gibbs was an Englishman who played for Calthorpe F.C. before emigrating to Melbourne at the age of 23 in 1883. He became secretary of the Anglo Australian the following year and a lobbyist for the idea of an Australian team to go to the old country. He played for Prahran and was captain of Victoria in the inter-colonial matches of the mid 1880s before his work in the insurance industry took him to New Zealand.

There he founded the New Zealand Football Association and held just about every senior administrative position in the Wellington football world. He returned permanently to England in 1906 but still acted for New Zealand and Australian football. He was co-opted to the Football Association Council in 1912 and served as the Australasian representative until his retirement through ill health in 1928.

In 1925, Gibbs recalled the 1901 meetings in an interview noting that "The F.A., particularly the late Charlie Alcock, were very courteous and polite and all that sort of thing but we really did not get beyond the sympathetic stage. The proposal never died, it merely dropped into acquiescent state." Things never got any easier.

Nevertheless, the contributions of Fred Moore, Charles Dacre, Arthur Savage, Jimmy Jackson, John Cuffe and Arthur Gibbs all show how close Australian identities were to pivotal early events in British football, on and off the field, in the late 19th and early 20th centuries.

Australia's first international experience was the six week tour of New Zealand by a New South Wales selection in 1904, with a return trip by the New Zealanders the following year. Gibbs had done much of the groundwork on the New Zealand side of the ditch. Nervousness about over-committing the game's meagre finances persuaded Queensland to stay out of the venture, which would otherwise have seen the first contests for an Australian national team.

Both sides were satisfied with the tours and the birth of a new inter-colonial rivalry, although no more trans-Tasman matches took place until 1922. Crowds for the 1905 Sydney games fell short of predictions but at least the football community had shown that two way tours could be done.

There were reflections on both sides of the Tasman about playing standards and styles. An international football conversation involving Australian experiences had begun and the quality of discussion leapt ahead. There was now a yardstick by which football progress could be measured.

Even these tours though were seen as a prelude to the greater aim of playing contact with Britain. At a send off for the New South Wales squad, the perennially top hatted chairman of the state association, conservative state MP John Nobbs, expressed his delight in seeing a team leaving Australia for the first time and his hope that in the course of a year or two that a team would be sent to England.

Buoyed by the New Zealand trip, another request was made to the Football Association for a team to tour Australia. The annual report of the New South Wales Soccer Football Association reported that a committee had been formed in London to look into the question.

The committee could hardly have been more high powered. It included F.A. President Lord Kinnaird, vice president Charles Alcock, secretary Fred Wall and honorary treasurer Dan Woolfall. The chairman of Manchester City, John Allison, had visited Sydney on business, met local football officials, and was said to have given an undertaking to help build the case for a tour upon his return home.

The big international development in 1904 was the establishment of FIFA, an organisation created with the central aim of coordinating the international development of football. The British Associations were not enthusiastic about this continental push, but joined anyway in 1905 with Woolfall becoming FIFA's second president.

FIFA was eager to include England but inaugural president Robert Guérin found F.A. Secretary Fred Wall less than engaged by the whole idea of European football. In a review of those days written in 1929, Guerin recalled being amazed to find Wall was "completely ignorant of what was happening on the continent and of the importance the game had gained in many countries."

Right from the start, FIFA aimed to stage an international championship and as early as 1906 foreshadowed a competition with 15 European teams in four qualifying groups with winners progressing to semi finals to be played over the Whitsun holiday, seven weeks after Easter, in Switzerland.

The advent of FIFA received no attention in Australia. Like FIFA, Australia craved English involvement, but England, although keen to assert its primacy in the world, did little to demonstrate its leadership in Australia.

The creation of the Commonwealth Football Association in 1911 at last meant there was an organisation with the job of looking after the Australian national interest. The CFA's presence heightened expectations that big time football was on the way. The NSW annual report of that year described the arrival of the new body as "the most important event in Australian soccer history."

The first chairman, the former Queensland and New South Wales representative goalkeeper Jack Logan, told the 1912 Queensland Association meeting the CFA would press for more interstate and international matches. This view was echoed by NSW South Coast secretary Charles Moore who wrote in his local newspaper that a major aim was "to procure a team from the Mother Country to tour the Commonwealth in 1913, failing which a team will be sent home."

Delegates to the CFA's second annual meeting in Brisbane in April 1914 made some big decisions about the shape of Australia's international future. The conference was united in the view that games against British opponents were the peak aim but acknowledged that this was not likely to be achieved in a hurry despite the best efforts of Australasia's man at the F.A. Council, Arthur Gibbs.

They thought that raising standards through interstate contests was the way to go in the meantime, although a plan to hold a carnival in Sydney later that year was shelved.

In other decisions, the conference endorsed the exciting proposal to get a representative Australian team on the field at the 1916 Berlin Olympics and resolved to make every effort to raise funds for that purpose. Two years continuous residence was deemed to be the minimum qualification to play for Australia.

Ten years after its launch raised a deafening silence in Australia, Tasmania moved at the conference for an affiliation with FIFA. However, the conference stuck solely to the Football Association since, it was told, FIFA's 1912 Stockholm congress had in any case declared that stand alone affiliations from the countries of the Empire were unnecessary. Australia was a de facto member of FIFA via England.

They did not know South Africa had joined FIFA independently in 1909 and Canada became a member in 1913. Membership of FIFA at this time started at 50 French francs a year, about ten American dollars.

The Referee reported in 1912 on FIFA's growth to more than 20 members and wondered aloud whether it offered Australia international opportunities. It noted that FIFA's annual report concluded that its members aspired to making it "the greatest organisation for the greatest game the world has ever seen."

The football community became increasingly self conscious about the lack of international action. Cricket and rugby tours were well entrenched so why were the excuses of cost and time away from home a problem for us and not for them?

Before World War 1, Australia had played 24 rugby Test matches against the British Isles, New Zealand, Wales, England and the United States. There had been two British Lions tours of Australia, the first in 1899, and Australia had toured Britain in 1908-09 and the U.S. and Canada in 1912.

Test cricket tours had been in play since 1877. Australia played in no fewer than 31 Test series up to 1912, all against either England or South Africa.

Australia played in 17 rugby league Test against Great Britain and New Zealand as well as other important matches against Maori and Welsh teams. The 1908-09 rugby league tourists in Britain highlighted Australian soccer's alienation from its imagined heartland by playing at some of the game's great venues - St James' Park, Villa Park and Tynecastle, albeit in front of small crowds.

By the time war arrived, Australia had been petitioning England about home and away tours for more than 30 years. They had been spectacularly unsuccessful, and yet, they continued to believe only London could deliver salvation.

In the other sports, Australia was a crucial member of a tiny circle of participating nations. England needed Australia as much as Australia needed England. Otherwise, there was no such thing as international rugby league, rugby union or cricket.

But England had no need for Australia in football. The "home championship" against Scotland, Wales and Ireland was all important and accounted for all but three of the 119 clashes acknowledged by the F.A. as full internationals. Europe was the next focus, and an F.A. tour led by Fred Wall in 1908 took in Austria, Hungary and Bohemia.

An English FA XI played four games on a tour of Germany and Austria as far back as 1899 and a tour to South Africa in 1910 – clearly not impeded by its FIFA membership – yielded wins in all 23 matches, some of them by wide margins. Clubs were now regularly playing friendlies in Europe during the off season and the FA already saw its "missionary" development role as more suited to Empire dominions closer to home than far away Australia.

"British Association" football, as it was still called by many, had comprehensively failed to establish any on-field relationship with clubs or representative teams in Britain. This failure to produce an international life, and sporting validation for Australia on the imperial scale, greatly damaged the game's status and credibility in the broader Australian sporting community.

Where rugby and cricket players knew for sure where they stood in the pecking order of their tightly defined world, footballers could only speculate. Where cricketers and rugby players spoke to their British counterparts as equals, footballers spoke either not at all or presuming they were on a much lower level.

Further afield, some flickering lights from the non-British world hinted at alternative paths to an international future.

Around the time the Commonwealth Football Association was formed, the air was thick with new ideas about organising Australia's international sporting life, including football. Some of the bolder ideas were put forward by people outside the British

Association scene

The doyen of sports administration was Ernest Samuel Marks, chairman of the Amateur Swimming Association and secretary of the Amateur Athletic Union of Australia from 1896 to 1934. He was manager of the Australian team at the Olympiads of London in 1908, Stockholm in 1912, and Los Angeles in 1932.

Marks was also briefly a Lord Mayor of Sydney and was well connected at the highest levels of domestic and international sport, business and politics.

On his return from Stockholm in 1912, Marks called for financial support from governments and the general public for Australia's Olympic effort for the next Games in Berlin in 1916. He pointed to the United States, Britain, France, Germany and the Scandinavian countries as nations pursuing national prestige through sport and said Australia should do the same.

He argued that the Berlin Games would be a great advertisement for Australia and called for preparations for a team of around 70 athletes. In Marks' plan, the biggest single sport representation would be 15 soccer players.

Ernie Marks was the guest speaker at the NSW Football Association annual meeting in March 1913. *The Referee* recorded that he referred to "the vogue of the code on the continent of Europe" and "gave a lucid account of the Soccer tournament of the Olympic Games."

This was most likely the first time an Australian football gathering had received an eyewitness account of an international tournament. Great Britain defeated Denmark 4-2 in the final. All eleven teams taking part were European, although the majority of the bronze medal winning Dutch squad were born in Java.

The Referee report noted "His concluding remarks urged on the meeting the desirability of Australia being represented in Berlin in 1916". This was enthusiastic backing for an Olympic football push from one of the most influential figures in Australian sport.

Whether Marks would ever be able to mobilise government

and public support to amass the pool of money required for his 70-strong squad is debatable. Whether other sports would tolerate football using hard won, all-sports resources to take up more than 20% of the Olympic team places is another question. And would the new national association have the skill to score from this opportunity?

A few months later, Arthur Gibbs attended a dinner in his capacity as the Australasian representative on the Football Association Council celebrating the F.A.'s jubilee. There's no record of whether Gibbs sought to use the occasion to discuss Australian football interests, but if he did, he would have some fabulous dining companions to talk to.

Also at the dinner were the Dutch General Secretary of FIFA Carl Hirschmann, the man who persuaded the British to join FIFA, Belgium's Baron de Laveleye; Danish football pioneer Nils Middleboe; Austrian coaching great Hugo Meisl; and Juan Anderson, the first ever captain of Argentina and one of the six founders of what became the Argentine Football Association.

Perhaps some ideas were exchanged. A few months later, Gibbs passed on a request for a tour by the champion Bordeaux club La Vie au Grand Air du Medoc (VGA Medoc) written by the club's senior figure Henri Gasqueton. The club proposed a tour in late 1914 or 1915 and to pay for it themselves but taking a cut of any profits generated.

Shortly after the formation of the Commonwealth Football Association, a proposal was received for a tour of the USA and Canada. The idea was pitched by the former vice president of the NSW Rugby League, Alexander Knox, who came up with the plan after a trip to North America. The tour would involve matches in four Canadian and nine United States centres. The highlight would be an international competition staged as part of the San Francisco Exhibition, the world's fair.

Knox claimed that American soccer's chief financier Winton E. Barker, linked to the Spalding sports goods company, would ensure that expenses and return fares would be covered. Australia just needed to send a competitive team. This could be used as a springboard for an extended tour to Britain and Europe.

Knox even claimed the proposal had the backing of U.S. President William Taft, who wanted to see a quality amateur team undertake the trip. Although this sounds like far-fetched spruiking, Taft did have his own history with football. As Governor-General of the Philippines in 1907, he donated a silver trophy for a football match commemorating the opening of the Philippine Assembly.

Around this time the Sydney born bookie, businessman and promoter, Con Jones, was the biggest name in sport in Vancouver. He took over a sports ground which became Con Jones Park and involved himself with a group which had just kicked off the Pacific Soccer League, a competition featuring teams from western Canada and the U-S Pacific coast.

Jones pinched the Australian "Don't Argue" advertising signage well known to his countrymen as the logo of Hutton's Smallgoods and used it for his own interests. In Vancouver, the logo and slogan signified the presence of a Jones business, not a branch of Hutton's.

San Francisco's Exhibition didn't take place until 1915 and the grand American tour idea faded and died like so many others. The Pacific Soccer League did sputter along for a couple of years amid spats over access to grounds and arguments over professionalism. It revived in the 1920s but only briefly.

Con Jones Park still became the home of Vancouver football, the only faint Australian imprint on the soccer scene of the west coast of the American continent. On the eastern seaboard, a Darwin man of Chinese descent, Kwang Lim Kwong, was playing and organising Chinese student football in New York and Boston at the tail end of the Great War. He would make his mark in his homeland ten years later as the promoter and manager of the 1927 Chinese touring team.

In Manila in 1913, the Philippines defeated China 2-1 in Asia's first international match, the sole football fixture of the Far Eastern Games which would be the bedrock of east Asia's national team football development for the next 20 years. This tournament too excited Australian Olympic manager Ernest Marks and fired his enthusiasm for a Pan Pacific theatre of sporting contests which did not rely on Britain or Europe for its legitimacy.

The onset of the Great War obliterated all plans for football expansion in Australia. Players signed up to serve in the military and lost their lives. Amid the horrors of the conflict in Europe, men were exposed to the steady stream of matches behind the front lines, or that they saw while on leave.

Quite a few played against good quality British players and European footballers with full international experience. Many more mingled with players and fans sharing a passion for the game.

Conflict threw together people from all over the world with unexpected consequences for football in Australia. Ballarat born journalist Harry Millard cited his wartime experiences with Chinese labourers in France as the genesis of an idea which eventually produced the Chinese tour of 1923. One of those labourers was Kwang Lim Kwong, whose football journey took him to Shanghai, Boston, New York and Australia.

The French international Maurice Vandendriessche, who spent the seasons before the war playing in Sydney and Melbourne, organised matches for Australian footballer soldiers in France. His knowledge of European football and range of contacts in France and Belgium would influence the thinking of Commonwealth Football Association secretary Ern Lukeman after the war.

Vandendriessche was a Sydney contemporary of the Australian star Judy Masters when he played for Northern Suburbs and Masters was at Granville. Masters saw action at Gallipoli and on the French western front and while on leave witnessed football as it was played in England. Other Australian soldiers' impressions of English football grounds and games are sprinkled through wartime newspapers. Australian soldiers sent to the Middle East played football against men from the Egyptian military.

England claimed world leadership in football but did not do much with regard to Australia other than to plant a flag in the ground and claim it as territory. Despite the grumbles that international life in the world's most international sport had yet to be seen in Australia, English leadership was never questioned. The struggle to find an Australian role in the rapidly expanding football world had so far been arduous and, except for a fleeting affair with New Zealand, largely fruitless.

But cosmopolitan seeds were sown and international football would burst into life in the decade after the armistice, with a hitherto dormant Australian team playing more matches in the 1920s than any other national team on the planet.

2.
THE GAME BEGINS

Australia and New Zealand 1922-1923

Australia's decades of international football dreaming had been filled with images of the country's best running out on to the great arenas of England and Scotland to show that we too were worthy exponents of the great game. In 1922, the most recent fantasies might have included an image or two of the grand new Empire Stadium being built at Wembley in north west London.

As fate would have it, Australia's full international debut would take place about as far away from Wembley as it was possible to be, Dunedin, on the south eastern coast of the south island of New Zealand. Before that, warm-up matches would be played around a country giving a warm welcome to their Australian visitors.

In the lead up, Australia's international football team took to the field for the first time in the modest surroundings of Cooks Gardens in the small New Zealand north island town of Wanganui.

On a cold and windy May day, the Australians faced the local Wanganui selection in the first of six matches preceding a clash with New Zealand. Local press reports say around 2,000 spectators turned out to witness the spectacle.

Australia played with the wind at their backs and went ahead when Jock Cumberford lashed in a long range shot, the only goal of the first period. According to an unnamed player quoted in Brisbane's *Daily Mail*, the players were supplied with coffee and rum at half time which was "very acceptable, as although the sun was shining, it was exceedingly cold."

Cooper equalised for Wanganui after the break and the Australians were made to wait until the last seven minutes for a second goal from Cumberford and another from Wilf Bratten to seal a 3-1 result. Australia made a winning start.

We like to think of Aussies and Kiwis as being neighbours,

always in and out of each others sporting houses, but as two football centres they didn't appear to know much about the life of the other at all. Just two weeks before the tour opener in Wanganui, New Zealand's *Truth* wrote "If anyone in the Dominion knows just what soccer the Australians play he has not spoken his mind within hearing of the officials of the N.Z.F.A., nor have they been able to get the straight tip from the other side."

The article goes on to say "So far they do not even know whether the team will go through the country as Kangaroos, Emus, Bunyips, or plain New South Wales - Queensland reps, nor do they know their fancy in bands, stripes, hoops or patches and so have to go canny in picking colours for their own provincial reps. Still, if New Zealand knows nothing of Australian soccer the reverse probably holds just as soundly, for there have been no recent meetings on which to base an argument."

The tour came about more from the work of the New Zealanders than the Australians. It was New Zealand who kick-started the Australians to action to reform their national association after the war to get on with the work required to push for a visit by British footballers to the south Pacific.

An Australian team visited New Zealand in 1904, but as New South Wales. The players were all drawn from that state, but the bigwigs in Sydney would argue that they had all the best players anyway. Even if that were true, the prevailing view at the time held that any national team must draw players from around the country, or at least from more than one state, in order to be regarded as truly representative of the nation. This principle would become a point of great division in later years.

On this occasion, the players were drawn from New South Wales and Queensland, the only states in a position to contribute to the cost of the venture. Players notified their state associations of their availability, and selectors put forward the names they backed for the national squad. Eight players were picked from each state.

The selection process was recognised in the colours worn by these first Socceroos, a kit of light blue shirts with maroon markings.

The Wanganui debut preceded an 8-2 belting of Nelson followed by a 3-0 setback on a mudheap at the Basin Reserve against Wellington. Following that shock, they won matches against Westland 2-1, South Island 4-1 and at Carisbrook in Dunedin, Otago 2-1.

In the first Test, Edward Cook opened the scoring for New Zealand, Bill "Podge" Maunder's equaliser was Australia's first international goal, then Bill Knott and Cook both scored to give New Zealand victory 3-1. The 10,000 fans on hand set a new attendance record for a match in Australasia.

Australia again went down 3-1, this time to Canterbury, before facing New Zealand in the second Test at Athletic Park in Wellington. Cook once more opened the scoring but Bratten's reply secured a 1-1 draw.

Regional victories over Taranaki (6-1), Auckland (4-1) and South Auckland (2-1) prepared Australia for a chance to square the series in the third Test at Auckland's Domain. Fifteen thousand spectators broke the crowd records set by the first two matches.

The Kiwis were too strong, running out winners 3-1. Bratten's account of the tour given to his local paper at Flaxton on Queensland's Sunshine Coast described the match as "soccer at its very best" and more open than the previous two, acknowledging that Australia was "fairly and squarely beaten."

George Campbell and Edward Cook had New Zealand two-nil up inside ten minutes. George Brown pulled one back after half time but the Australians ran out of puff. Ces Dacre finished them off with a late third goal.

Australia strolled to a 5-0 victory over Manawatu in the final fixture of the tour.

Travelling players in both countries dipped into their own pockets to pay for everything from bandages to laundry and tram fares to training but players, officials and fans would all regard the encounters as successes. Prominent matches drew big crowds and a schedule of games which turned a profit. International football was not only a good thing in itself, it produced plenty of public enthusiasm and generated revenue for a sport with little capital.

In years to come, a typical grumble about Australian players was that they were too physical, that they compensated for their limited skills by bullying and kicking their opponents. On this tour, it was the Australians who complained about the aggressive play they encountered in New Zealand.

In particular, they were perplexed by referees' acceptance of barging, bodily charges which were in theory shoulder charges. The Australians were surprised to find the liberal New Zealand interpretation of the laws meant that not only was plenty of contact generally allowed in a contest for the ball, barging was allowed for players nowhere near the ball.

Bratten's description in the *Chronicle and North Coast Advertiser* of the first Test notes that "One cannot say it was an altogether pleasant game as the operation of the New Zealand bumping game gave them an advantage, and the feeling ran somewhat high towards the close of the game. However, no bones were broken ..."

The return leg of this contest in 1923 again reflected the higher status of the east coast states with all Australian players coming from New South Wales and Queensland and all 16 matches taking place there.

New Zealand lost early tour games against Granville and Newcastle but drew with New South Wales and beat Queensland. They were still fancied to do well in the big match at the 'Gabba, the first ever full international match played in Australia.

Australia went ahead after seven minutes when Balgownie winger Tom Thompson back heeled past his marker and swung in a cross which Percy Lennard cracked in off the crossbar. New Zealand equalised in the second half, Ces Dacre knocking in a George Campbell shot deflected by an Australian defender.

Australia dominated the second period but were denied by a string of saves by Reg Craxton, generally held to be man of the match. With seconds left on the clock, Craxton was finally beaten again when he parried a ball which fell to Bill Maunder to slam in the winner, 2-1.

A bigger crowd of 12,000 was at the Sydney Cricket Ground for the second match won 3-2 by New Zealand. The visitors' skipper George Campbell scored just before half time, but Lennard levelled after the break. Campbell restored the lead before Jack Gilmore netted from a goalmouth scramble to make it 2-all. Campbell completed a swift counter attack to complete his hat trick and steal victory for New Zealand.

The series decider attracted another record crowd of 14,000 to the Newcastle Showground. Most local opinion preceding the clash was that Australia would have the upper hand this time. New Zealand's form against regional sides had been patchy, although many believed this just showed they were saving themselves for the big games and treating the others as picnic matches.

The Kiwis dominated the early phases but went in at half time a goal down. Australia had more of the ball as the first half rolled on and local boy Maunder blasted in the opening goal off the post. In the second half, the Australians were swept away by a tour de force performance by the New Zealand captain George Campbell.

The right sided attack of the first half had not found a way past the Australian skipper Alex Gibb and full back Cliff Gedge. Campbell directed the team to concentrate on the left where he believed they could outpace Peter Doyle and Ern Owen. Campbell, Charlie Ballard and winger Harold Balk constantly outflanked Australian defenders drawn out of position.

Within seconds of the restart, centre half Joe Kissock swung the ball to Ballard on the left who played in Campbell, who unleashed a dipping 25-metre shot in to the top corner. New Zealand moved into the lead when a mix up between Owen and keeper Rob Austin saw neither of them claim the ball, allowing Campbell to poke it over the line.

Another Ballard pass found Campbell at the edge of the penalty area able to crash home a low drive. Australia seemed to have run out of steam but held the score at 3-1 until shortly before full time when Bob Innes tore through on the right, centred from the by-line and yet again found Campbell on hand to net a fourth.

At the end of the match, Campbell was carried from the pitch on the shoulders of his team mates. Australia had found no way to deal with New Zealand's attacking ace. Alec Boyd's assessment in the *Sunday Times* was emphatic. "Undoubtedly the better side won. The winners' display after the interval was masterful, but the match will always be remembered as a triumph for Campbell."

After twelve games in six weeks, New Zealand had taken the unusual step of training without the ball in the days leading up to the deciding Test. Campbell told the press afterwards that the fitter side won the day and the Australians couldn't cope with their speed.

On his return to Wellington he was still lauding the New Zealand performance, saying on arrival "I never saw anything like it. The team played in a manner which was irresistible."

Australia's first chance to be measured on the international scene showed there was a way to go just to catch up to New Zealand. Six matches against our nearest football neighbours produced only one win and four defeats.

Opinion in the New Zealand press was that the Australians they feared would be strong in the 1922 matches were generally disappointing and held little threat in their forward line. They were satisfied that their more "scientific" football, with an emphasis on drawing opposition players before releasing passes, was clearly superior to the Australian urge to heave the ball forward.

The *New Zealand Times* story on the team's reception on return to Wellington reported Graves, the assistant manager, as saying the Australians played a spoiling game and they would be better off if they played more like New Zealand.

These weren't just the views of outsiders. The *Telegraph* was not alone in noting the deficiencies of the Australian approach. "The game demonstrated that if Australia desires to recover the Ashes they will need to change their style of play. Kick and rush tactics will have to be discarded and the long passing game played. There must be harmony in the team, a feature that appeared to be lacking, especially among the five forwards, on Saturday. Selfish play does not help a team - it retards progress and causes discontent."

Australian players and spectators had seen another team using other methods to good effect. There was now an opportunity to observe and discuss different styles of play, enough to supply the basis for argument, as the previous year's *Truth* put it. Australia's steep learning curve in the world of football had begun.

At a dinner for both teams after the Brisbane match, the New Zealand manager Harry Mayer proposed that the historic series should be marked with a memento for posterity. The two captains, Alex Gibb and George Campbell, smoked cigars with the ash gathered in a metal box supplied by the secretary of the Queensland Football Association, Bill Fisher, who had it with him when Anzac troops landed at Gallipoli.

The "Ashes" were then mounted in an elaborate trophy of fine timber from the two countries with a silver soccer ball on top and plates on the front adorned with a silver fern and a silver kangaroo. A plate on the back was inscribed with the outcomes of the two series, leaving room for the results of series to come over the next 25 years, a promise of a future filled with sporting rivalry.

This trophy was meant to symbolise the unbreakable bonds between New Zealand and Australia, on and off the sporting field. For football, it would be the bedrock of our joint development, wouldn't it?

3.
THE CHINESE CONNECTION

Australia's First Contact With Asia 1923

Australia's historic breakthrough moment of contact with Asian football was massively successful on every level that mattered. Great games, big crowds, star players, lots of publicity, high regard for Chinese and Australian players, a profit for the tour organisers and a first international series win for Australia.

The inadequacies of Australia's tour organisation were regarded as minor problems and ructions within the Chinese camp were kept away from local eyes as football won itself a cause for celebration. After the long international football drought, two well received tours in quick succession mark 1923 as a golden year.

All sorts of new thinking and sporting contacts became possible and it was no longer credible to dismiss Asian sportsmen as unworthy of Australian attention.

The link with China was hardly the result of some new understanding of the sporting landscape or cultural politics, it was the result of a naive attempt to recruit a Chinese rugby league team to make a quick profit on a tour of New Zealand. But by the time the tour plan morphed into a soccer team for Australia, there were enough people of imagination around to seize a crucial opportunity and make it work.

The original move was the brainchild of Harry Millard, an Australian born knockabout journalist who built his early career in New Zealand and was the author of the plan to hire and tour a Chinese rugby team.

Millard started on his venture with little knowledge of sport in China when he set out for Hong Kong in 1922 and soon discovered his recruitment of a team ran into the inconvenient fact that the country did not have rugby players of any variety. But he was sharp enough to see a different opportunity for sporting contact, resourceful in building from scratch a structure to deliver a tour, and persistent in driving a good idea.

It didn't hurt that he was a bit of a showman who was not averse to big noting himself. His references to his own army service, for instance, are shown to be greatly embellished when compared with the actual records of the New Zealand military.

Millard always said that he first had thoughts about sporting contact with China when he was serving in France during the First World War. He was impressed by the physique and work ethic of Chinese Labour Corps workers under his command as a New Zealand Army captain and thought they were the ideal raw material for successful athletes.

In a speech looking back on those days reported by the *Queensland Times* in 1947, Millard is quoted as saying that Chinese players impressed him in a rugby match played against New Zealand soldiers just before the Battle of Messines – a New Zealand side he said contained five All Blacks.

In post-War New Zealand, Millard went back to his job as a journalist and raised the idea of engaging Chinese sportsmen in competition. There was no real interest, and no shortage of ridicule.

When the planned English rugby league tour of 1923 was postponed until 1925, Millard finally found people interested in supplying an alternative team to fill a gap in the sporting calendar. He secured the backing of private investors and endorsement from rugby league bodies in Auckland and Sydney.

Now to find the team he had talked up. Les Cubitt, the captain of the 1920 Kangaroos rugby league team which had toured Great Britain, was recruited to train the athletes Millard was sure he would assemble. Millard spoke to Chinese consuls in New Zealand and Australia to get as much information as he could before the trip to Asia and was assured he would find good rugby players. Cubitt, Millard, and his journalist colleague Jack Shaw set out for Hong Kong in November 1922.

It quickly became apparent that there were no rugby players to be found. The footballers his Chinese contacts had told him about

Jack Shaw, Harry Millard and Les Cubitt leaving for China in 1922 to find Chinese rugby league players. Millard returns with Far East Games football champions, China.

were all *association* football players. Millard cabled home that it would not be possible to arrange a rugby tour, but perhaps soccer men might be interested in playing against some fine footballers.

Soccer organisers in Australia were indeed interested, but were also wary of potential financial liabilities. They didn't know if they could trust Millard. As a rugby man, they weren't sure he'd know a good football team from a bad one. They thought after spending quite some time in China, he may be broke and looking for somebody to pick up his tab. They were worried they might end up being liable for the money already spent by Millard's group which had been supplied by the backers of the proposed rugby league tour.

When a formal proposal for the Chinese tour finally hit the table at the Commonwealth Football Association, the board was split four all on whether to back the idea. There was a strong feeling that it was too big a risk to the limited resources of the game, and the proposal was knocked back on the casting vote of the chairman.

New South Wales Soccer Association secretary Sid Storey came up with an alternative way of finding the capital for the tour, with his association putting in £350, Queensland £250, Sydney Metropolitan Association £200 and the Granville Association £100. Football officials, including Storey, chipped in the rest to form a company called Australian Tours Limited, the entity which would guarantee the tour and hire Millard as manager. Some sections of the soccer milieu were scandalised that the game's interests had been turned over to private, profit seeking business.

While in China, Millard made the acquaintance of the chief organisers of the modern sporting scene, the Americans from the Young Mens' Christian Association who had started up the Far Eastern Games as well as a national Chinese athletics carnival and who were heavily involved in selecting the teams which participated in them.

Millard also found kinship and contacts among other newspaper journalists promoting western style sports, and the modernising Chinese nationalists who were the political champions of a sporting culture compatible with their broader ambitions in Chinese development and international affairs.

These people included the Newcastle born Walter Hanming-Chen of Shanghai's *Daily News*, a one time advisor to Dr Sun Yat Sen, the first president of the Republic of China. Chen would arrive in Sydney in 1924 as a Chinese special commissioner for trade. He was also a director of the sport focused Chinese YMCA.

Millard also spoke to Harry Ching, a journalist born in Brisbane who cut his teeth as a reporter in Mackay and Rockhampton.

Ching's mother and five younger siblings were murdered by a farmhand in a shocking incident at their Mackay family sugar cane plantation in 1911. His father, in failing health in 1915, wanted to return to China and Harry went with him.

In Hong Kong, Harry Ching found a job as a reporter at the *South China Morning Post* where he became a prominent figure and was appointed its first ethnic Chinese editor in 1922. He would hold the job for 33 years.

Ching encouraged Millard's shift to a soccer focus since, in his view, it still offered a chance to change Australian perceptions of the Chinese community and open the door to greater trade between the two countries.

In Shanghai, Millard met John H. Gray, effectively the YMCA's super sports missionary. The YMCA initiated sports tournaments, clubs, administrative bodies of all kinds in China and elsewhere in its quest to build strong Christian values, healthy minds in healthy bodies, dedicated to notions of fair play that accorded with western ideas about politics and society.

The YMCA's Elwood S. Brown had given this push an international dimension in 1913 through an Olympic-like multi sports competition, the Far Eastern Games, featuring athletes from China, Japan, Siam (Thailand), British East Indies (Malaya), Hong Kong and the Philippines, and football had featured in each of its editions. Gray invited Millard to be his guest at the 1923 Games in Osaka, Japan, giving him the chance to see China's team there.

Hong Kong's South China club, having won China's domestic regional play offs, secured the right to represent China in Osaka. They disposed of Japan and the Philippines to claim another title, their fifth in a row. South China's football impressed Millard, who was also taken with the Games set up in Osaka, an issue he would return to in later life.

Millard and Gray looked to combine good playing skills with a broad geographical representation of China when picking a touring team. They went for seven central China players, six from the south and four from the north – a total of seventeen.

Mok Hing, a player in China's first international match, pictured on his way to Australia as tour manager in 1923. Mok Hing was involved with Chinese football for half a century.

Battles on selection involved complaints from Hong Kong officials about the squad's composition and withdrawals by Beijing and Tientsin players. At the end of the squabbles, 16 players made the final list - 13 from South China, and three from Shanghai. The seventeenth spot would now be occupied by club official Mok Hing, a player and founder of the club in 1904, and a man whose career as an organiser of Chinese sport would last half a century.

These players, whose status as competitive sportsmen was held in doubt by many Australian observers, had more experience of representative football than the men they would meet in Australia. China had now been playing international football for ten years.

Any doubts about the quality of the visitors or their capacity to draw a crowd were blown away on the first date of the tour, the match billed as New South Wales versus China. The gates to the Sydney Showground were shut on the orders of the police well before kick off as fans clambered on to any vantage point they could find inside the ground, and many simply climbed over the wall. Thousands more were locked out.

The official crowd figure was variously posted as 40,000 or 47,000, but that is more likely to reflect the gate takings than the actual number of spectators in the ground. Sydney's newspapers struggled to convey images of the crush.

The Sun reported the crowd felt "more like 140,000." The *Sydney Morning Herald* noted "boys climbed up hoardings and bare poles, hung precariously on wire stays or stood on the roofs of frail looking structures abutting on to the score boards."

There was plenty of comment too on *who* had come, with Sydney's substantial Chinese population heavily represented. The *Evening News* began a story "For East is East and West is West, And never the twain shall meet wrote Kipling, never dreaming that the great Chinese nation would take to football." *The News* went on to say "over 40,000 people filled the ground to overflowing. It was a wonderful crowd - and most of it wanted to see China win."

The match was played at the Royal Agricultural Society Showground because the Sydney Cricket Ground was not available.

The Chinese team which defeated Japan 5-1 at the Far Eastern Games in Osaka in 1923. Eleven players from this squad toured Australia in August that year.

That's because the lease on the ground held by the New South Wales Rugby League effectively gave it a right of veto on whether another sport could use it.

Alec Boyd, the only journalist drawing on a personal knowledge of football in Asia due to his reporting and playing experience in pre-War Singapore, speculated in *The Referee* that had the SCG been available, the crowd might have challenged the record set in 1920 by the Australia - Great Britain rugby league test which attracted an attendance approaching 70,000.

Football's previous crowd record was the 14,000 roll up at the Newcastle Showgrounds two months earlier when goals from Kiwi captain George Campbell led New Zealand to a 4-1 victory to seal a two Tests to one series win.

Plenty of work had already gone into portraying the touring players as sophisticated gentlemen - well dressed, professional and educated - rather than the peasant figure ethnic clichés pervading Anglo Australian perceptions of their local Chinese communities. Much of the coverage of this first match found reason to compliment both groups.

The Sun had the players as "tall, arid, muscular men, quick on their feet and filled with football cunning." As for the fans, "From all the cabbage gardens, from desk and chop suey restaurants the Chinese came in excited armies to the Showground, and with them jostled all the soccer enthusiasts of Sydney, until the game itself had melted all into a common factor in sportsmanship."

The paper went on to predict that "from this day forth, the metropolis will order lettuces with a new found reverence, and look at Chinese visitors with an expression of esteem." Others praised the conduct of players and spectators alike.

The game itself was an absolute cracker, described by the *Sydney Morning Herald* as "a rapid succession of thrills." The Chinese took the initiative from the outset, their speed presenting a constant threat to the home side. New South Wales, led by Weston half back Jock Avis, fought back from two down to lead 3-2, then teen sensation Lee Wai Tong completed his hat trick to earn a 3-3 draw.

Lee tapped in a cross from Pang to open the scoring in the fifth minute, and whacked in a deflected free kick to give the visitors a 2-0 lead. Stan Bourke scored before half time, then after the break, a shorter passing home side drew level through Hancock and went ahead through Perce Lennard. Late pressure saw Hancock hit the post and Lau make a couple of spectacular saves before Lee on the break levelled the scores.

The big match repositioned football on the local sporting landscape, if only briefly. It also made a huge impression on the Chinese players. Lee, who would become the brightest star in Asian football, and whose amazing C.V. included captaining China at the 1936 Olympics and playing in five Far East Games winning sides, treasured its memory. In a 1947 Hong Kong newspaper interview looking back at his life, he nominated the Showground match as a high point of his career.

The SCG did host the lower profile second match against the Sydney Metropolis XI the following Wednesday, won by Metropolis

4-2. The Chinese were greatly hindered by a first half injury to goalkeeper Lau Hing Cheung which forced him to leave the field. Left half Lam Yuk Ying took over between the sticks.

China lined up with the Beijing based Shen Kuo Chen at left back making his sole appearance before returning to Shanghai. Shen, also known as Shen Guoquan or Shin Gook Gwon, was a Korean player and almost certainly the first Korean to play in Australia.

The big day of the first Test on the following Saturday saw a return to the Sydney Showground and a crowd of 20,000. The teams lined up as the band played *Advance Australia Fair* in honour of the Australians, and *For He's A Jolly Good Fellow* for the Chinese.

Lee Wai Tong dominated the spectacle a week earlier, but it was the Illawarra star Judy Masters who shone brighter than all others this time. The Australian captain netted four times in a powerful 5-1 victory.

Lau, injured during the week and limping on a heavily strapped ankle even before the kick off, was clearly below par. He came and failed to land a punch on Frank Mellier-Smith's cross with Masters heading in the opener.

Lee missed his chance to even the scores from the spot after Cameron's hand ball as the Chinese again showed pace and purpose in the early passages of play but fluffed their lines in the penalty area.

A blistering 20 metre drive from Andy Henderson crossed the line after crashing against the underside of the crossbar for number two, and Masters headed in another Mellier-Smith ball for the third with Lau again misjudging the cross.

A clever exchange of passes late in the first half ended with Lee Wai Tong heading in a chip from lightning fast left winger Chang Kwong.

In the second half, Masters popped up to knock in a rebound after Stoner hit the crossbar and scored from another rebound, this time from Lennard's shot against the woodwork. The emphatic winning margin was generally regarded as a little flattering to the home side with much praise flowing to a fast and creative opponent which did not take a number of chances and tired badly in the closing period of the match.

The more powerful Australians made good use of their physical strength, a plus acknowledged after the match by the Australian skipper. " We had too much weight for China and deserved to win" said Masters "but their skill and style surprised me. They play a scientific game and showed us some points." Chinese captain Leung Yuk Tong was complimentary about the home team. "Australia were too fast and far too clever for us. They gave us a football lesson for which we are grateful."

The three games in eight days had attracted around 70,000 paying fans and the gate takings had already covered the estimated cost of the original schedule of matches. Now more matches were added to the programme.

In 1923, the strong and physical New Zealanders had won two out of three internationals on Australian soil to follow up their two wins out of three record in New Zealand the previous year.

The Chinese relied on speed and short passing, the "scientific" game, which was mostly countered by Australian players trying to make the most of their bigger size to dominate their opponents. There was a contest between teams with different tactical approaches to football.

The tour schedule was relentless, with the 16 players facing a match every three or four days. Any novelty value in having an Asian football team on the field in a very white bread Australian environment quickly wore off. The Chinese side still drew good crowds, but their value now was as a competitive football team.

A midweek 2-2 draw against a Granville district selection preceded the second 'Test' in Newcastle. Newspaper reports put the crowd for the big match at between 16,000 and over 20,000, either way a record for football in the region.

Once again police intervened to remove spectators from grandstand rooftops and other precarious vantage points. Fans gave generous applause to the visitors who played their part in another red hot contest where the Australian lead was pegged back three times before the victory was secured.

Lee Wai Tong's drive just after half time to restore parity at 2-2 was the high point of the Chinese goals but was eclipsed by Judy Masters, who burst through the centre of the defence to unleash a thumping shot from outside the penalty box to re-establish the lead.

A foul by full back Ng Kam Chuen on Masters allowed Hancock to fire home the winner from the penalty spot just before full time. Lee Wai Tong's goal was his seventh of the tour, having scored in all five matches to that point.

Three days later the Chinese side was walloped 7-1 by a Newcastle selection, the first of a string of regional games which added travel stress to the physical demands of the matches.

In quick succession, they drew 1-1 with South Coast in Wollongong, 2-2 against South Maitland, 1-1 against Queensland in front of a big crowd at the Gabba and went down 4-2 to the West Moreton selection at Ipswich.

The third meeting with Australia in Brisbane drew another impressive crowd of more than 10,000. The Chinese gave as good as they got in the first half with the match report of the *Brisbane Telegraph* praising the "tricky play, superb combination, pace and pretty short passing on the part of the Chinese (which) had really predominated the situation, only to fail to be effective, because of lack of finish in front of the homesters' goal." Nevertheless, Australia went in at the break 1-0 up thanks to another strike by Judy Masters.

Right after the restart, goalkeeper Lau Hing Cheung made a hash of his attempt to punch away a cross from Wynnum left winger Jim Robertson. The ball fell conveniently at the feet of Masters to score his second. Chinese heads dropped and Masters in particular ran riot, adding guile and cleverness to an Australian side physically dominating the opposition.

Jack Gilmore added a third when Masters nodded the ball into his path, Gilmore netted a fourth goal from a Jack Bourke pass, although press reports refer to Bourke being well offside when he received the ball. Robertson's cross occasioned another howler from Lau as his attempt to punch clear saw the ball propelled into the back of the net giving Australia a thumping 5-0 triumph.

China regrouped to demolish New England 9-0 in Tamworth in a midweek canter before the fourth Test back at the Sydney Showground.

At last, Chinese skill and endeavour was rewarded with a winning scoreline. On this occasion, the Chinese forwards did not squander their chances and, but for the sterling efforts of Cartwright in the Australian goal, the margin of victory could have been bigger.

China's front three of Chang Hsi En, Wong Pak Chung and Lee Wai Tong ran rings around the Australian defenders in what Alec Boyd's match report described as "a most brilliant exposition of fast dribbling and close passing."

He was rapturous about China's undisputed star. "What can one say about Lee Wai Tong? He is the best shot I have seen in Australia, and very few professionals were ever better in this particular department. No matter how or where he gets the ball, it has got to go. He is a beautiful dribbler, and can pass perfectly. When Sydney teams field men like Chang and Lee, enormous crowds will turn up to watch them."

For a change, this match started slowly until Chang Hsi En scored with a low drive from Lee's lay off after 15 minutes. Chang and Lee were constant threats to the Australian goal, slicing through a harried Australian defence, but they could not stretch the lead before half time.

Chinese dominance continued after the restart but Australia was first to score, Hancock converting from Andy Henderson's pass midway through the second half. But China would not to be denied. Lee Wai Tong's thunderbolt 15 minutes from time flew in from the edge of the penalty area, with press reports asserting the shot burst through the net, coming to rest outside the goal. Lee's volley close to time sealed a 3-1 victory.

The Sunday Times, a paper controlled by Hugh D. McIntosh, the boss of the sports publication *The Referee*, carried a quote from the Chinese captain Leung Yuk Tong which captured his relief and satisfaction. "We are delighted with our victory. Though tired after travelling to Queensland, we never slackened up, and I think I may claim we deserved our win." Australian skipper Judy Masters had no complaints about the result. "China beat us on their merits. They have kept plugging away, and I'm glad to see them victorious. It was a fair dinkum win."

It was a great farewell to their temporary home in Sydney. A long list of matches tacked on to the original schedule sought to take the Chinese attraction to more parts of Australia, including country towns. Although this meant some less taxing opponents along the way, the volume of games for the small touring group must surely have made an impact on their performances.

An exhibition match against a Sydney Metropolis XI in the southern New South Wales town of Harden produced a 3-2 win for Sydney and a unusual experience of international football in the bush en route to a first appearance in Victoria.

An 'Australian XI' defeated the tourists 2-0 at Fitzroy Oval in front of a crowd of about 12,000. The Australian representative team featured Victorian players for the first time and one of the three chosen, Footscray Thistle inside forward John Orr, crashed a shot in off the post for the opening goal.

Adelaide's first view of an international football team at Jubilee Oval was of a Chinese side coasting to a 6-2 win over South Australia. *The Register* reported "the visiting team, both individually and collectively, played a far superior game to that of the local team."

The same venue hosted the fifth and final Test match of the tour. There were five South Australians in the starting eleven along with five New South Welshmen in front of Northumberland and Durham 'keeper Jim Robison flying the flag for Victoria. A total of 30 Australian players started in the five designated internationals, with only Cessnock forward Perce Lennard appearing in all of them.

The Advertiser account of the match drew readers attention to the differing approaches of the two teams. The Chinese "kept the ball low, and their passes were beautifully accurate and seldom rose above the turf" while the Australians "adopted lifting kicks."

The new faces undoubtedly contributed to a somewhat disjointed Australian opening against the now tightly organised and well practiced Chinese. A slowish start matured into a series of thrills with the visitors gaining the initiative.

Lee Wai Tong put China ahead just before half time, netting a low drive from Pang Kum Ying's pass. The Chinese were well on top in the second half and Pang's second assist found Chang Hsi En, who put away his chance as the Australian defenders appealed for offside.

A resurgent Australia fought back against the tiring Chinese. Denman headed against the post before Phillips, originally on the left wing before being brought inside after the second Chinese goal, scored twice in quick succession. A cross from Denman gave him the chance of a hat-trick in the final seconds but he fluffed the tap-in opportunity. Australian centre half Gilbert Storey and Chinese forward Chang Hsi En were given joint man of the match awards.

A small crowd arrived at the MCG to see China beat Victoria 3-1 before the tour rolled on to Tasmania. The tourists endured a rough crossing of Bass Strait but were sunk by the state selection 2-1 in Hobart although match reports again highlighted the skills of the Chinese, who hit the post and, in their interpretation of sporting manners, deliberately missed a penalty.

Lee Wai Tong plundered six in the 8-1 victory over Southern Tasmania and a hat-trick in the 4-1 dismissal of Tasmania in Launceston. Chang Hsi En scored three in a 5-1 stroll against Northern Tasmania.

Back on the mainland, the Chinese side eased past Victoria 2-0. The Victorians included former French international and wartime Belgian captain Maurice Vandendriessche in the line-up, perhaps making him the first European international to play against a team representing an Asian country in the unlikely setting of the Essendon Cricket Ground. The final match was a scoreless draw with an Illawarra selection at Woonona.

Despite the tensions between the Hong Kong and Shanghai factions in their group, the Chinese side wore the burdens of a strenuous tour with grace and dignity. They played good football and earned praise for their abilities, their conduct on and off the field, and for the broader Chinese community. In the young forward Lee Wai Tong, they clearly had a star who was as good as any player ever seen in Australia.

Australia too had shown lessons were already being learned about the higher standards required at the top level and newspaper reporting showed its own shifts toward an appreciation of better quality skills and tactics. There was a growing taste for greater sophistication.

Australian forward Judy Masters emerged as the best expression of a mix of the combative courage required of all Australian footballers with speed, superior technique and tactical cunning. If Lee Wai Tong was the jewel of the Chinese side, Masters was the first star of Australia's international age.

Two highly successful tours on home soil proved there were big crowds ready to see Australia battle for honours against international opponents. The appetite for this new world seemed boundless.

The games against New Zealand, home and away, had been confined to venues in New South Wales and Queensland with the home team drawing only on players from those two states. The Chinese tour was truly national in every sense.

Forty years of longing for England had so far not produced a single match with a team from the Mother Country. A fortuitous connection with China had produced a fabulous series of matches.

Australia played China before England and engaged Asia before Europe. The significance of that experience and what it told us about our place in the world would not be realised for decades.

4.
LEE WAI TONG

Asia's Greatest

Lee Wai Tong is a giant in the story of football's growth in Asia in the first half of the 20th century and is one of the greatest figures in the history of the Asian game.

He burst on to the scene as a teenage star with Hong Kong's South China club, starred in a string of Chinese teams which dominated the Far Eastern Games, captained the Chinese side at the Berlin Olympics where he was also his country's flag bearer, played for China and his Chinese clubs in 20 countries, scored hundreds of goals, coached Hong Kong and Taiwan teams to Merdeka Cup success, became secretary of the Asian Football Confederation, and vice president of FIFA.

He played club football in Hong Kong, Shanghai, and Jakarta and knocked back an offer to join Red Star Paris in the French first division. The epic world tour he led in 1936 was the first of its kind and, in China, his ancestral home proudly hosts a statue of the King of Football and a museum in his honour.

Lee Wai Tong wrote a number of books on football technique, tactics and game preparation which rated psychological values highly along with team unity and a strong sense of common purpose.

Lee also held a strong affection for Australia, a country he toured twice as a player and once as a manager. His nickname "the King of Football" was bestowed on him after he returned from the 1923 tour. As luck would have it, it fell to him as president to notify Australia that its first application to join the Asian Football Confederation in 1960 had not succeeded.

Lee Wai Tong was born in the Hong Kong village of Tai Hang in 1905 and moved to a village near Meizhou in southern China at the age of four where he began to play football. When he returned to Hong Kong as a teenager he signed up with the South China club,

The star of the 1923 Chinese tour of Australia, Lee Wai Tong, aged 17, at Sydney's Bondi Beach. Lee became the greatest figure in Chinese football.

playing in the reserve team at 16 and quickly graduating to the first team.

Still only 17, his outstanding form took him to the Far Eastern Games in Osaka, Japan in 1923 where he excelled in a championship winning side. In the final match, China defeated Japan 5-1 with Lee scoring a hat-trick in five minutes. It was at Osaka that he was seen by the Australian born journalist Harry Millard who went on to recruit the South China based squad for the historic tour of Australia.

In the first match of the tour, the Chinese drew 3-3 with New South Wales before a crowd of around 47,000 at the Sydney Showground. Lee scored a hat-trick and was recognised by all as the star of the show. He went on to outshine all others for the whole tour.

He smashed in thirty of the team's 64 goals, including five of the ten scored against Australia in five matches. His hat-trick against NSW was matched by another in a 4-1 victory over Tasmania, and he got six in an 8-1 demolition of Southern Tasmania in Hobart.

He is said to have scored more than a thousand goals in a career sprawling across three decades. Tall, strong and fast, he packed a fierce shot in both boots and loved to have a crack from distance.

Lee led South China to the Hong Kong championship, supremacy in China, and another Far Eastern Games title in Manila in 1925. In 1926, Lee moved to Shanghai when he was given the job of football coach at Fudan University. He continued to play, joining top local side Loh Hwa where the Darwin born Kwang Lim Kwong was an important figure. Professor Kwong was the tour manager for a second Chinese tour of Australia in 1927, again with Lee Wai Tong as its star player.

Lee led the Loh Hwa side to the Shanghai championship, beating teams composed of British and European players which had previously dominated the local competition. He captained a China side which was awarded the gold medal at the 1930 Far Eastern Games in Tokyo when Japan refused to play extra time after drawing with China 3-3. Both team had beaten Philippines by five goals.

Lee Wai Tong moved back to Hong Kong and rejoined South China.

Military and political conflict looked like killing off the Far Eastern Games in the early thirties, but the 1934 edition in Manila got under way in an expanded form with the addition of Dutch East Indies. Lee Wai Tong was now player/manager of the national team.

Forty thousand fans flocked to Rizal Stadium hoping for the best from the Filipino side but China's two second half goals, the second from Lee Wai Tong, secured the win in a brutal contest. China secured yet another title on the final day against Japan. Lee's goal with quarter of an hour to go wrapped up a 4-3 win. The King of Football scored the last ever goal in the Far Eastern championship.

China's progression to the 1936 Olympics under Lee Tong Wai's leadership has become legend. He pressed for the trip to Germany to take place, led a massive tour on the way there, carried his country's flag into Hitler's Olympic Stadium and captained a team which very nearly upset the British eleven.

A schedule of European tour games followed the Olympics, a first for Asian football. The tour, built around one competitive fixture in Berlin, was exactly the kind of experience proposed by ASFA Secretary Ern Lukeman in the mid 1920s to be constructed around the 1928 Amsterdam Games and which Lee would have learned about on his 1927 trip to Australia.

It was on the extended European leg of the tour that Lee caught the eye of European experts, leading to several enquiries as to whether he was interested in joining the professional leagues of Europe. By Lee's own account, Arsenal discussed the possibility with him but felt that he was, at 31, getting a bit too old for the Gunners to be taking a chance. Parisian club Red Star, having just escaped relegation from France's top flight, did make him an offer reported in Hong Kong to be worth 2,500 francs per month. He turned it down.

The Olympic trip became a Chinese football legend and made Lee an even bigger celebrity. He got offers to become a movie star - including a role in a Hollywood Charlie Chan movie - which he rejected. In Java, where he was a big hero for the local Chinese community, his number nine and an accompanying photograph became the label on a brand of wine. Promoters of South China's many trips to Java would insist on Lee's presence before signing a tour contract. Even this century, a hugely successful stage musical based on the Olympic tour, Field of Dreams, has had several seasons on the Hong Kong stage.

In 1933, Lee had a spell with Jakarta club side U.M.S., which also saw him selected for the Batavia team to contest the East Indies championship. In the crucial match against Surabaya, Lee faced Dutch star forward Bep Bakhuys. Both players scored but Batavia won 4-3 and went on to clinch the title. The next year saw Lee lead China to another win at the Far Eastern Championship while Bakhuys was installed as centre forward for the Dutch team at the World Cup.

Lee's South China went on to ever more domestic success winning championships in 1939, 1940 and 1941 before war closed down Hong Kong football. When Hong Kong fell under Japanese control he was asked to continue but he refused to be part of football under occupation and instead opted to leave and play in exhibition matches to raise money for the war effort, a move which further enhanced his standing as a Chinese hero.

After the war, he played a couple more seasons for South China before becoming the coach of the side and of the national team of China. Just as in 1936, ethnic Chinese players from mainland China, Hong Kong, Singapore and Malaya embarked on another massive four month tour which was due to begin in Brisbane leading to just one guaranteed competitive match at the Olympics in early August. The Brisbane date fell through and against Turkey at the Green Pond Road home ground of north London amateur side Walthamstow, China lost 4-0.

The Chinese set out from Hong Kong at the back end of April

playing their first match against a Manila Chinese selection on May Day, the first of five games in the Philippines. Then there were games in Thailand, Vietnam, Singapore, Indonesia, more in Singapore, India and couple of matches against the USA Olympic team before the Turkey clash. For good measure, there were five more matches in Thailand on the way home.

When the Chinese revolution ended with victory to the communists and the establishment of the People's Republic, Lee Wai Tong restricted his life and career to Hong Kong and Taiwan.

His Republic of China side - usually referred to at the time as Taiwan - twice won gold at the Asian Games. In 1954, in the week his efforts to create the Asian Football Confederation came to fruition, Taiwan beat South Korea 5-2 in the final at one of his old happy hunting grounds, Rizal Stadium in Manila. Taiwan won again with Lee in charge at the 1958 Games in Tokyo , again defeating South Korea in the final, 3-2 in extra time.

His last national team assignment was with Taiwan's campaign at the 1960 Olympics in Italy where his side went down 4-1 to a Gianni Rivera led Italian side, lost 5-0 to a Brazilian team for whom Gerson scored a hat-trick, then finally, back to where his Olympic trail began 24 years earlier - a match against Great Britain. Despite two goals from a modern South China favourite, Yiu Cheuk Yin, the Chinese lost 3-2.

Lee Wai Tong was the inaugural secretary of the Asian Football Confederation when it was formed in Manila in 1954 and went on to be a vice president of FIFA in 1965. As a representative of football in the Republic of China/Taiwan/Formosa/ Chinese Taipei - the territory has been referred to by FIFA in many ways - Lee was at the forefront of a struggle against being isolated or displaced by the People's Republic of China which asserted that it was the only entity which could legitimately be called China.

As AFC secretary, Lee announced in August 1960 that Australia's application for membership had been rejected. Members felt that as the rules of the confederation confined membership to Asian countries only, Australia's application could not be considered.

He was a champion in Hong Kong, Shanghai and Java, led Asia on to the world stage, and chose to play in Asia rather than Europe. He dominated Asia's first championships and did more than any other to establish an Asian football confederation. He was tireless in a lifetime of promoting football firstly in China, then all over Asia, then acting for Asian football around the world.

He was open to new ideas about how to promote the status of the Asian game and was a supporter of the late 1960s Asian All-Stars initiative, a concept which sought to bring into one team the likes of Israeli great Mordechai Spiegler and Japanese legend Kunishige Kamamoto.

Lee Wai Tong was a giant of the times and a man who embodied a football link between Asia and Australia for nearly 40 years. There are a few inconspicuous photographs of him on the wall of the Museum of Chinese Australian History in Melbourne, but in the grand narrative of Australia's football history, he still rarely scores a mention.

His name should be recognised and cherished in any centenary celebration of Australia's relationship with Asia.

5.
EMPIRE COUSINS

The Canadian Tour 1924

The buzz from international football had players, fans and officials alike dreaming of new adventures.

In 1924, Australia applied for membership of FIFA and started to talk seriously about going to the Olympics. Relations with the Football Association in London intensified with the firming of a commitment of an English touring team to Australia and the allocation of an F.A. trophy as a prize for a yet to be determined Australian championship.

Canada's tour of Australia was meant to promote better contact with another of the 'British' football nations and help prepare the way for the ultimate battles to come against England. The deft and speedy Chinese had provided great entertainment and no small amount of education in the game's finer points, but the more rough and tumble nature of a team a bit more like us would bring a different character altogether.

Canada's football had a decidedly Scottish accent rooted in immigrant communities of miners and industrial workers, as did many Australian football centres. The series would be a comparison of how these two outposts of the British diaspora had developed after more than 40 years of football evolution.

Australia won the Test series which stretched to six official internationals and did indeed produce some good football and exciting matches, but it also had a dark side. Beneath the public pronouncements of friendly relations and the kinship of Empire brothers across the oceans, the 1924 tour by the Canadian national team was filled with over-physical clashes notable for their toll of broken bones, send-offs and ill will.

The Canadian touring party of 16 players was headed by manager Jimmy Adam and trainer Don Morrison. Canadian opinion was that it was a good squad which reflected the state of the nation's game.

Publicity for the tour had Harry Mosher as among the best of the world's goalkeepers, and lauded forward Bill Linning as a man who had knocked back an offer to join English side Chelsea. Linning had played as a guest for Chelsea when he was in Britain during the First World War with Canadian armed forces.

Inside forward George Forrest had played for Hearts in Scotland and Armstrong had turned out in Northern Ireland's top division. Captain Bob Harley was in the Glasgow Rangers youth team before his family emigrated to Canada. More than half the squad were born in Britain, similar to many of the teams they would play in Australia.

George Anderson played in all six of the matches against Australia and made a lasting impression on Canada's international ambitions. In 1957, he played a major role in organising Canada's first foray into World Cup qualifiers.

In the Australia of 1924, the strongly British heritage of the Canadian team was seen as a significant boost to their credibility as a team, and their experience in playing against British opponents was another plus. In Sydney, *The Sun* reported, "It is fortunate that Australians should have the opportunity of acquiring greater proficiency and thereby improving their general knowledge from exponents who have added to their prowess by contact with the dons of Great Britain."

Canadian soccer had an early if haphazard involvement in international life. In 1885 and 1886, Canada sent teams to play against the United States in Newark, New Jersey. Their validity as full internationals is open to doubt but they can be seen as the first international matches in the world not involving the countries of the British Isles.

A Canadian side toured Scotland in 1888 and repeated the venture in 1891, this time also taking in fixtures in England and Wales. In 1904, Ontario's Galt F.C. went to the Olympics in St Louis and twice defeated a team from the USA in exhibition matches.

Four years before the Australian trip, Scottish side Third Lanark made a 25-match coast to coast tour of North America with 19 of the games in Canada. It was a strong side which included five players who had played for Scotland and finished in eighth place in the 22-team Scottish Football League. Third Lanark won all 19 matches but had to battle for a 1-0 outcome in the final game of the Canadian leg of the tour against a Canada XI in Montreal.

Toronto born Edward Parry captained a losing Oxford University team in the F.A. Cup final of 1879, the year he also made his debut for England against Wales. He won the Cup with Old Carthusians two years later.

Robert "Whitey" McDonald was born in Ireland, grew up in Canada and was taken back to Scotland by an impressed Glasgow Rangers touring side in 1928. He ended up winning four Scottish championships and four Scottish F.A. Cups at Ibrox and was selected to play for Northern Ireland in 1930.

The Canadians' first matches in Australia were all bruising encounters which left players injured, a trend which dogged them for the whole of the tour. By the end of their 26 matches in 81 days, they could scarcely put a team on the field.

After a scoreless draw tour opener against a Sydney Metropolis XI, Canada defeated a NSW South Coast selection 2-0, but the match was regularly stopped as treatment was given to seven injured players.

A big crowd of around 20,000 rolled up for the first major match against New South Wales. Canada played well but faded badly in the second half. Right winger Stan Bourke, married that morning, supplied crosses for four of the home side's goals in a 5-2 victory.

The New South Wales approach was rooted in physical domination. *The Daily Mail* reported the visitors "showed wonderful footwork but their players failed to mix it with the home team who were very aggressive."

Maintaining enthusiasm on the long trip was also an issue. Alec Boyd, reviewing the tour in *The Referee*, described the scene on the train back from Newcastle after the scoreless draw against Australia when he was travelling with the Canadian players.

He wrote that Harry Mosher told him "I'm through with football. I'm tired of seeing the ball." On the seat opposite, star left half Dickie Stobbart is having a stud wound filed with cotton wool and iodine. Bill Linning was "scarred and resembled the wreck of the Hesperus." There were still nine games to go.

Mosher's tour was nearly over. Three days later in Melbourne, Canada went down 2-1 to Victoria. Mosher, rushing out of the penalty area to clear a through ball, collided with an advancing Australian forward and broke his leg. In the absence of a second string keeper, full back Hank Noseworthy went between the sticks for the rest of the tour. Mosher had to have his leg broken and reset in a Vancouver hospital upon his return home.

Noseworthy did so well between the sticks that he turned to keeping goal full time for club sides Verdun City and Montreal Carsteel and was picked as a goalkeeper on Canada's 1927 tour of New Zealand.

The Canadians were criticised for a lack of pace and a killer instinct in front of goal, but they were generally praised for their midfield combination. The half back trio of Fred Dierden, Bob Harley and Dickie Stobbart won plaudits for their resolute defending and ability to pass their way out of trouble and in to advanced positions. Gold medals were awarded to the best players in the international series - Stobbart for Canada and goalkeeper George Cartwright for Australia.

In the run up to the first match, Judy Masters predicted Australia's speed would be too much for Canada and Canadian manager Jimmy Adam thought Canada's powerful half back line would make the difference.

Australia won that first match in Brisbane 3-2 after Lanning gave Canada the lead, while Stobbart's goal was enough for Canada to edge Australia 1-0 a week later on a wet and slippery pitch in Sydney. Judy Masters was outstanding in the third match, scoring two and setting up Podge Maunder for the other two in a 4-1 victory which saw Australian full back Gil Storey sent off.

More heavy rain made play difficult in a scoreless draw in

Newcastle but Canada burst back to life in the fifth Test at the Jubilee Ground in Adelaide, winning 4-1 in another knock 'em down, drag 'em out clash. Storey was this time crunched early in the game and left the field midway through the first half. No substitutions were allowed.

Canada were two up in the first half through Wilson and Linning, Wilson added another after the break and Stobbart's free kick stretched the lead to four before Orr fired one back for Australia.

Noseworthy, deputising in the unfamiliar role of goalkeeper, was involved in an ugly clash reminiscent of the one which laid Mosher low. The makeshift gloveman ran out of the box to clear and collided with Masters, leaving both on the ground knocked out cold. Both eventually got up and played on.

There was again comment on the physical battle. Adelaide's *The Register* reported the game was "fast and vigorous throughout and heavy but legitimate charging was the order of the day with the result that Australia was deprived of the services of Storey after the first 20 minutes and several other players on either side received injuries."

Now that the series was tied, a sixth international was arranged. A goal from Judy Masters settled the result in yet another brutal showdown.

Masters was given rough treatment from the outset but it was Canada who limped to the final whistle with just nine men on the field. Full back Mitch McLean was sent off. Noseworthy again clashed with Masters and had to leave the field in the dying minutes with concussion and a broken rib.

There was most likely an element of popular taste in favour of the belligerent nature of much of the football played. After all, a common line of general complaint from adherents of Australian Rules and the rugby codes was that soccer was not rugged enough to earn their favour. There wasn't enough contact, it didn't measure up to their code of masculine contest.

But there was also an increasing stream of criticism during the tour that the physical side of the game was getting too much leeway at the expense of more 'scientific' aspects. There were stinging attacks on refereeing standards, that officials were clearly letting far too much go. The final Australia - Canada match was cited as an example of what was wrong.

Parramatta's *Cumberland Argus*, a paper with strong football coverage, called for refs to show a much firmer hand. The *Soccer Gossip* column observed that "these exhibitions of rough and dirty play, if allowed to continue, will seriously impede the progress of the code."

After excoriating referees, it delivered this backhander. "Whatever other virtues some of our referees may lack, they are certainly impartial, inasmuch as they allow both teams to offend with immunity."

Incensed by the round of criticism, the match referee in the showdown at the Showground, J. Nicholson, took the unusual step of writing a letter on the matter to the *Newcastle Morning Herald* setting out the "true facts" journalists had ignored.

Nicholson drew attention to the offensive nature of the language reporters couldn't hear rather than the offensive conduct they could see for themselves. He said he cautioned Linning for foul language and told the captain (Fred Harley) to take his players in hand, but that Harley made no effort to do so.

He says he cautioned McLean about dirty play and when he then kicked an opponent he had no choice other than to enforce the Laws of the Game. Anderson had used an expression to him which was punishable by law.

Nicholson finished with this. "Never in all my career have I refereed a game of football where such contemptible and nauseous expressions have been used as that used on the field of play by the Canadians."

For all that, the Canadians observed the standard public protocols, professing themselves to have enjoyed the tour and thanking the public and officials alike for the warm reception they had received. The Canadian Soccer Hall of Fame, established in 1997, has a category honouring significant teams of the past. In 2008, it recognised the 1924 touring side as a "Team of Distinction" for its accomplishments in Australia.

On the way home, Canada drew 1-1 with an Auckland XI at Carlaw Park. In Vancouver, they were lined up to face the visiting English evangelists of amateur football, Corinthians, the day after their arrival home.

Playing at Con Jones Stadium, the football ground of Sydney born sports promoter Con Jones, Corinthians had drawn 1-1 with Vancouver the previous day. At the same venue, George Forrest scored for Canada but Corinthians won 2-1.

The stopover in Auckland opened the door for a full scale 22-match tour of New Zealand in 1927, with Jim Adam again the man in charge of the team.

China's legacy in 1923 had been a respect for the ability of Asian athletes and a general appreciation of their technical skills but biff and barge football remained a staple on the menu for football fans, and many of them preferred the rough stuff.

Critics demanded higher standards after the Chinese lifted expectations, but there was still no resolution to the implicit question of which direction football in Australia would take.

6.
THE GODS THEMSELVES

England and Australia 1925

And so it finally came to pass. Nearly 43 years after the first request for an English tour was delivered to the Football Association offices in London, a squad of 18 players finally left for Australia. The team, in the words of F.A. Secretary Fred Wall, would "not only satisfy our Australian friends, but will uphold the prestige of our game, and of the Mother Country."

The ineradicable belief in Australia had always been that only top class players from England could show the way to better football, fill stadiums with admiring fans, top up the bank account, and leave a legacy of a lasting upturn in the status of the game. This was the big chance to make it happen.

The 1925 tour was not just the point of first contact between the revered English professionals and Australian players, it was the first direct Australian contact with the highest level of the Football Association, the organisation seen to be at the very pinnacle of all authority on the game.

At last there was a chance to make Australian views and needs known to the F.A., and tour leader John Lewis, a top level decision maker, was someone who could be a crucial contact able to act with sympathy to Australia's interests. It would quickly become apparent that Lewis was not interested in discussion, he was interested in laying down the law. He was not impressed by any Australian views and found much to complain about.

While the tour was a success - big crowds, good box office, higher class football - there was also a considerable amount of friction between Australian and English officials. They clashed over match payments, the use of substitutes and general administration.

By the end of the tour, there was plenty of evidence that the case for unassailable English authority on all matters football was far from compelling. It became apparent that English ways and views did not always produce the best solutions for Australian problems. Perhaps Australia needed to start setting its own course.

News of the tour was a very big deal in Australia but was not well received by England's clubs which had long since passed the stage of being able to wave goodbye to players for months at a time. The F.A., conflicted as the only body in world football with both a national and an international mission, still saw a role for itself as a kind of football evangelist in the Empire, a view which simply irritated the professional teams of the Football League.

Tour manager John Lewis appealed to English players to make themselves available and for clubs to support them. There was so little response that Lewis resorted to a further exhortation to tour as a kind of imperial duty.

In his weekly newspaper column, Lewis beseeched the clubs to support the venture. "On sterner fields than football our colonies have proved their loyalty, and now the clubs are presented with the opportunity of showing not only their loyalty to the association, but of demonstrating to our kith and kin over the seas that we thoroughly appreciate their fealty to the Motherland."

Journalist Ivan Sharpe, a gold medal winner in the Great Britain football team at the 1912 Olympics and the first F.A. Cup Final live broadcast commentator, referred to the tour as "the greatest missionary enterprise the F.A. have undertaken".

The British press routinely spoke of the tour in terms of charity work, doing good among the Colonials, and both sides referred to duty, sacrifice and Empire. The other side of that coin - the unwavering acceptance of England's central authority, fealty to the Motherland - was not up for discussion.

At the farewell function for the team at St Pancras railway station, John Lewis spoke of the progress the game had made in Australia, although he observed that for the British public, Australia was "a soccer terra incognita." Australasia's F.A. Council representative Arthur Gibbs was among the listening crowd.

Lewis went on to speak of upholding the dignity of the game and providing colonial brothers with grand exhibitions. This general air of self regard and condescension was no doubt well meant, but it indicated an attitude which made an exchange of views impossible. The power relationship at play showed Australia was not likely to be taken seriously.

The English squad was an eclectic mix of top level players, journeyman professionals from the second and third divisions and two from non-league clubs. Eight players were from the first division, five from the second, four from the third division (South) and one amateur, Dulwich Hamlet centre forward Bill Caesar.

Only four players had taken the field in a full A international - Newcastle half back Charlie Spencer had two caps, while Stockport County forward Ernie Simms, his goalkeeping team mate Harry Hardy and another keeper, Teddy Davison of Sheffield Wednesday, had one apiece. Simms had been the first third division player to be picked for England when he started against Northern Ireland four years earlier. Bill Caesar had played in amateur internationals. Games against Australia would not be regarded as full internationals.

Two more, Jack Elkes and Len Graham, were on duty in Glasgow for the Scotland versus England match at the time of the St Pancras farewell and joined the rest of the group later at Toulon after travelling by train through France.

Fred Wall anticipated criticism of the starless nature of the group featuring players who "may not be familiar by name to enthusiasts in your country" saying they would make an excellent side.

In an interview with English football journalism doyen J.A.H. Catton, conducted for an Australian audience on behalf of *The Referee*, he cautioned "Do not worry about men with established reputations since they are not necessarily the best for a long tour". He went on to rationalise that "It is better to have good players who are young and ambitious, for they are less likely to spare themselves and rest on their oars."

Football League clubs were reticent to release players for a tour which would take up the better part of six months. There had already been criticism of the playing level of players on return from the "long" tour to South Africa under Lewis's leadership in 1920, and that took only half the time the trip to Australia would occupy. Simple availability and the absence of obstruction from club officials were important selection criteria.

As it turned out, the squad was still much too strong for its Australian opponents. England won all 25 matches on the Australian tour, scoring 139 goals and conceding just 13. They beat South Australia 10-0 and Queensland 11-0. Bert Batten alone scored 47 goals in 20 appearances, a record which caught the attention of clubs in England and helped earn him a transfer from third division Plymouth Argyle to first division Everton.

Second top scorer with 33 goals was Ernie Simms, whose career reads like a Boys Own Annual story. Simms left Luton Town to join the Football Batallion in the First World War where he suffered a serious leg injury on military service which left him with a pronounced limp. He was discharged in 1918.

He trained every night at Luton's Kenilworth Road ground in a bid to recover his fitness. When the ground was closed towards the end of the war, he took to breaking in and doing his training anyway. He was eventually caught by police but when the public learned of his story they demanded his courage should be rewarded. Luton gave him another contract and in 1921-22 he was the club's top scorer with 28 goals.

The English faced serious challenges in only two or three of their matches. Their first appearance in Sydney drew a crowd of around 45,000 for the clash with a New South Wales side which fancied that its pace might unsettle the visitors as much as it had rattled the Canadians the year before.

In the very first attack of the match, left winger Len McNaughton supplied a cross which Judy Masters headed home. One-nil in the first minute! Ernie Simms equalised for England, but Masters again finished off a neat passing sequence to restore the lead with just a quarter of an hour gone.

Bert Batten levelled again before half time and supplied the winner after the break. England won, but crucially for the tour, local players had shown the tourists might not have everything their own way. There was also a bit of swagger about their match at the Showground outdrawing the NSW versus Queensland rugby league match at the Sydney Cricket Ground next door. The NSW Rugby League had again used its lease to steadfastly deny the Soccer Association the use of the SCG, just as they had done in 1923.

In the second clash with Australia's strongest state, another big crowd showed up to see Stan Bourke put NSW in front before England recovered to overrun the hosts 4-1. However, goalkeeper George Cartwright was injured early and replaced by winger Tom Thompson as no substitutes were allowed. Things got worse. Full back Charlie Leabeater went off injured when the score was 2-1. NSW finished with nine men.

Ernie Simms scored a hat-trick in the first Test at the Exhibition Ground in Brisbane where Australia only started having any impact in the second half, but by that time were already three down. Perce Lennard knocked in McNaughton's cross to pull back to 4-1 but England went on to win 5-1.

In Sydney a week later, England won a hard fought battle 2-1 in a match where both sides missed penalties. Cartwright saved an effort from Jack Elkes and Len McNaughton blazed over the crossbar for Australia. England's second goal came after Sheringham went off injured and couldn't be replaced.

The remaining internationals were a cakewalk for England. They beat Australia 8-2 in Maitland and 5-0 in Sydney. Man of the Match medals in Sydney were presented by Jack Kerr, a veteran of the seminal NSW - Victoria clashes of the 1880s when the first invitations to England were made.

By the end of the tour, the English players were tired and just wanted to go home. Maybe their lack of focus contributed to a minor shock in the last game of the trip. Perth forward Andy Gordon beat goalkeeper Davison at the second attempt to place Western Australia ahead 1-0 at half time at Subiaco Oval. Bert

Batten plundered four second half goals to restore order in a 5-1 romp.

The tour had proven to be highly successful at the box office although some of the organisation around the games was shambolic. At Newcastle, the crowd spilled on to the touchlines and even on to the playing area. Some of the surfaces the matches were played on were rough, or boggy, or both.

Nevertheless, around 100,000 people in total saw the matches played in Sydney - about a tenth of the city's population. Another 100,000 watched tour games around the country.

The cost of the tour, at around £18,000, was a big gamble for the resource poor football scene, and although the fans poured in, the venture made only a miniscule profit of a couple of hundred pounds. Even then, England felt there were payments which had not been met. Haggling only stopped when the F.A. Council decided in 1928 to write off the debt.

Australian football's impoverished state couldn't meet the pre-tour financial guarantee required by the English F.A. Sports entrepreneur and publisher of *The Referee*, J.D. McIntosh, tipped in over £2,000 to get the wheels turning.

Like the Chinese tour of 1923, the big crowds again proved that if the product was right, there was definitely a mass audience for football, especially in the heartlands of Sydney, Brisbane, Newcastle and the Hunter Valley.

The size of the crowds encouraged some clubs, associations and players in the belief that they could move towards professional football. In New South Wales, the Hunter and Illawarra regions, already resentful of what they saw as conservative and high handed administration from Sydney, began to advocate moves to professionalism.

The South Maitland Association floated the idea of a state league encompassing teams from all three centres. In Wollongong, the players selected to represent Illawarra against England met in the dressing room on match day and demanded to be paid before they went on to the field. Their demands were met. Each player got his allotted 15 shillings ahead of kick off.

The England tour leader John Lewis was not at all impressed by Australia's attitude to player payments. The Football Association's puritanical view of amateurism led it to withdraw from both FIFA and Olympic competition in the 1920s as European nations embraced the concept of "broken time" payments.

The F.A. did not regard its own view on amateurism as just one among many in the world, but rather as something close to holy writ, the word held by football's founders and guardians. In the manner of religious fundamentalists, it was not a view open to amendment.

Broken time meant that players would be compensated for the time they spent away from their regular jobs to play football. The English view was that this amounted to professionalism, Australia was inclined to the European view. Players selected to play against England were paid a £1 per day allowance with a £5 bonus for the match.

This issue ultimately crippled any lingering chance for Australia's ambition to send a team to the Olympics in 1928 and was the first serious break in the faith Australia held in England's role as the ultimate arbiter of what was right and wrong in football. England's view - backed by British and Australian Olympic officials - clearly did not fit Australia's circumstances. On the contrary, it was a significant barrier to progress.

Lewis gave a speech at the University of Sydney sharply critical of Australia's approach to match payments and made it clear they had not heard the last of his objections. "The Australian Football Association is affiliated with the Football Association, England, and therefore must subscribe to its rules." He would be reporting this to head office.

In a letter two years later in the *Athletic News*, a W.D. De Lacey of Bondi recalled Lewis "told the authorities that he would see to it no man who played against England in one Test ever took part in the Olympic Games". This at a time when Australia was hatching a plan to go to Amsterdam in 1928, a plan Lewis must have known about and most likely discussed with local officialdom.

His Australian counterpart, Sid Storey, argued that bonuses were paid to Australian cricketers in much the same way as footballers without compromising their status as amateurs. He was right. The major difference here was a political one. The MCC did not impose its view of player payments on Australia but the F.A. did.

A wider analysis was growing that maintaining distinctions between amateur and professional ranks was all very well in England but was nothing more than a nuisance in Australia, dividing a much smaller football community struggling to support itself.

The slim attention given to the issue in England did produce a voice sympathetic to Australia. Journalist Fred Milnes was right back for England in a 15-0 humbling of France at Parc Des Princes in Paris in 1906, England's first official amateur international. He noted that Australia shared a similarity with the United States in the vastness of their countries. A team member might lose two or three days pay just to travel to the venue of a match much less play in it, a fact which may justify a more liberal consideration.

The Telegraph in Brisbane summed up an emerging Australian view on the question of payments for international players. " The consensus of opinion in Australia is that this is not an interference with the amateur status of the player... Australia must work out its own destiny in this matter. The conditions here and England are altogether different and must be appreciated in a different spirit."

Lewis's weekly column during the mid twenties in the *Lancashire Evening Post* was generally a chatty collection of observations on football and answers to queries on the Laws of the Game, but in the months after his return from Australia, the column is peppered with anecdotes from his Australian experiences, almost all of them negative.

The quality of footballs was poor, badly blown up and with at least one instance of the wrong bladder inside the casing. The travel arrangements were unsatisfactory. He was not consulted on the selection of match officials in any of the 25 matches.

The officials were anyway often not up to scratch and had strange ideas about charging which had no relationship with the Laws of the Game. Australian refs penalised an offence they called 'shepherding', an offence not referred to at all in the Laws. He apparently never discovered they were talking about obstruction.

But the chief sin in Australia was paying players in a way which compromised any claim they may have to be regarded as amateurs. He would not allow the matter to rest.

Lewis's overweening sanctimony was not reserved exclusively for footballers, he was able to offend cricketers too. A non-smoking teatotaller, Lewis told a gathering in Bradford in late 1925 that "If our cricketers in Australia had been teetotallers they might have returned with better results than they did."

Linking the losing Ashes cricket team to the consumption of alcohol brought him a storm of condemnation. England captain Arthur Gilligan described the view as "nonsense" and "an insult" while former captain Johnny Douglas said it was "a wicked shame that such an imputation should be levelled." Australia's Ashes series manager Syd Smith described the Lewis comment as "absurd in every way."

Seventy year old John Lewis was already a legendary figure in the English game. He was one of the founders of Blackburn Rovers and was in the line up for the club's first ever match. He became the vice president of both the Football Association and the Football League.

He was also known as Prince of Referees, taking charge of three F.A. Cup finals before the turn of the century and two Olympic finals, including the infamous decider in Antwerp in 1920. Lewis, already 65 years old, was appointed to referee the gold medal match between Belgium and Czechoslovakia. His relatively youthful friend, 54-year old Charles Wreford-Brown, was one of the linesmen.

It remains the only major international final to have been

abandoned. The Czechoslovakians walked off the field before half time protesting against Lewis's performance after he sent off defender Karel Steiner. In a written complaint, the Czechoslovak delegation claimed that Wreford-Brown's presence was against the rules of the competition, that "the majority of the refereeing decisions of Mr Lewis were wrong", and that "both Belgian goals were the result of incorrect decisions of the referee."

Their protests went nowhere. John Lewis had a resolute faith in his own authority and expected to be backed by football administrators. J.A.H Catton wrote in the *Athletic News* that Lewis as a referee "was known as a man who insisted on being obeyed. He was not likely to stand for any nonsense for anyone."

In Australia he was regarded as a man who went through life as if he had the rule book and held a whistle and that he would tell you when you were wrong. One commentator said he had views "as immovable as the pyramids."

Lewis was equally insistent on the issue of using substitutes for injured players, a common practice in Australia as it was in many countries. Australia's Sid Storey approached Lewis at Fremantle before the first match to request the use of substitutes, noting that this can be done under F.A. rules with mutual consent of both teams.

Lewis asked why the request had not been made before the team left London. He said Storey told him he knew the F.A. would say no. So why was he being asked to overturn a known view of the F.A.?

The *Athletic News* reported that the frustrated Storey then tried to go over Lewis's head with a cable to London reading "Australian public strongly resents action of your representatives, declining allow substitutes for injured players in first half only. We must insist that this be allowed. Tour prejudiced. Kindly cable Lewis accordingly."

That bid was firmly rejected, but *Athletic News* noted Australia's position on substitutions had been "a constant source of irritation in the course of this tour." The bad blood started on day one.

On or off the field, one thing Lewis would never accept was the questioning of his authority.

The tour may have been the fruit of the longest begging campaign in Australian sport but the blunt and belligerent Lewis made it perfectly clear that this was not likely to be the beginning of any continuing relationship. In an interview with Alec Boyd reviewing the whole venture, Lewis is reported as being "not optimistic regarding the prospects of the Football Association inviting a representative Australian team to embark on an English tour for some time to come."

Given that he had not had the chance to discuss the matter with London, this is presumably the case that he intended to argue. The prospect of professional players in the ever more demanding English scene again being released for a six month trip to Australia was pretty well zero. Now Lewis was telling Australians there was no real prospect of an away tour either.

Lewis pointed to clubs playing 42 league matches, with Cup ties and international contests also crowding the calendar. In these circumstances what chance had they of finding time to play exhibition games against overseas combinations?

There has to be some doubt about whether this was a fair reflection of English sentiment or just Lewis blowing off the disliked Australians. After all, less than twelve months earlier, the South African team went on a 26-match tour of Britain, Ireland and the Netherlands where 18 of the games were played in England.

It is true that the likes of Liverpool, Everton and Chelsea put out well below strength teams to face South Africa, but so what? They were still prepared to play. Amateur sides, including the England amateur team, were happy to play, and those dates also made it possible to add fixtures in Scotland, Wales, Ireland and the Netherlands.

Gordon Hodgson starred for South Africa, especially in a 5-2 victory over Liverpool. The Reds were impressed enough to sign him. He went on to star for Liverpool too, becoming one of the club's greatest scorers with 233 goals over ten years. At least one professional club was clearly interested in checking out the talent of the New World. Hodgson also made three appearances for England.

Lewis himself was the manager of the English tour to South Africa in 1920, a trip he believed would prove as Empire building as any propaganda which England might undertake. He was quoted in the British press as ranking South African football as not quite up to the level of second division but that there were four or five players good enough for league teams.

He noted that in South Africa towns are so far apart that teams of equal ability cannot meet each other except very occasionally, but as in Australia, did not connect the dots to see that rigid applications of his view of amateurism for players in those teams making long trips just to play were hopelessly misplaced. You weren't professional just because you lived and worked a lot further away from the football ground than your English cousins and that you were compensated for travel time.

He remarked that "travelling over the country is uninteresting. You go miles and miles without seeing a living thing." True to form, unable to comprehend a new environment, his leaden imagination merely saw the absence of the familiar.

He said Australia might be the most populous country in the Commonwealth one day but needed people who would "make great sacrifices by cutting themselves adrift practically from civilisation". People like himself perhaps since, as he told his readers prior to departure for the uncivilised world, he felt almost regret that he had promised to go as he would miss the F.A. Cup Final and the England - Scotland match. Still, duty called and he would spare no effort to make the trip a success.

He did provide some constructive advice and analysis of Australia's football situation. He saw an urgent need for good coaches, he deplored kick and rush football and praised cleverer players, he could see the pressing requirement to acquire suitable football grounds. On the hard part, how to do it, he had less to say.

At the time of the tour, Lewis was the most experienced football official in the world. Fifty years of steadfast continuous service to his beloved football had followed his efforts to invent Blackburn Rovers. Australia knew that his view carried considerable weight and, wary of the picture he might paint in London, asked the F.A. for a copy of his tour report. The reply relayed via Arthur Gibbs was that a list of matches was the only document that had been supplied. All other information was delivered by Lewis verbally. He left no paper trail.

His work in Australia would be his last major task. The team returned to England in late August and Lewis died in January of 1926. There were many heartfelt tributes from all over the country lauding his lifelong devotion to the game.

His achievements were many, but in Australia, he had proven to be a wholly inappropriate figure to lead the tour. If this was the face of the English F.A., it was surely time to look elsewhere to pursue international football.

7.
EAST INDIES AND THE PHILIPPINES
Asia, Europe and Colonial Football

The Dutch East Indies and the Philippines were two territories which became major players in the early Asian football picture but developed with much different relationships with their European roots, and both were different again to Australia's role in the British family.

While a handful of Australians went to Britain and played football, the traffic in players was largely one way in the other direction. Many players with a Filipino background prospered in Spain and many Dutch players had spells in Java in their playing history.

Scores of Dutch players moved freely between the Netherlands and the East indies. The absence of professional football at either end of the sea voyage meant payment was not formally part of the attraction, although illicit boot money could be a sweetener. Among the players bound for Java were many internationals, including big stars of the calibre of Bep Bakhuys and Felix Smeets.

A steady stream of Filipino players made their way to Spain, infusing the lineups of several top teams. Barcelona signed a string of Filipino players, most notably one of their all time greats, Paulino Alcántara. His scoring feats stood for 80 years until they were finally surpassed by Lionel Messi.

Alcántara, was without doubt the most startling success to come out of Asia in the first half of the 20th century and was the only Asian international player to become a star in Europe. He was a sensational talent and possessed the skills to be a star anywhere, anytime.

He went on to score 357 goals in 357 games for Barcelona and played in three national teams - Philippines, Catalonia and Spain. His Barcelona goals tally stood as a club record for 90 years before finally being eclipsed by Lionel Messi in 2017. He was born in the

Philippines in 1897, the son of a Spanish military man, Eduardo, and a local woman, Victoriana Riestra. The family moved to Spain when Paulino was a young boy and the Philippines was embroiled in fighting between local nationalists and the Americans who had displaced Spain as the colonial power.

He joined the amateur club F.C. Galeano where his remarkable ability immediately attracted attention. Barcelona's President and founder, the Swiss Juan Gamper, signed him for the club's youth team, but he was promoted to the first team before his 16th birthday. He is to this day the youngest ever to play for Barcelona.

His debut was in the Catalonian Championship match against Catala in 1912, when he netted a hat-trick in a 9-0 win. He was already a regular in the team when Barcelona won the Catalonian title in 1913 and was in the side to win another in 1916.

Alcántara's family decided to move back to the Philippines at this time. Paulino, who had begun to study medicine, would continue his studies in Manila. Barcelona went into something of a trophy drought in his absence. Paulino Alcantara continued to play football, turning out for the Bohemian Sporting Club who went on to win the Philippines championship in 1917 and 1918.

Alcántara sparkled for the Philippines in the Far East Games being held in Manila in 1917. His superior class was the reason the home side obliterated Japan 15-2, but his presence could not stop China from winning the tournament. Their clash was abandoned with China leading 4-0 when the Filipino keeper punched a Chinese player, an incident which led to an all-in brawl.

Barcelona implored him to come back, and he did. Legend has it that Alcántara pressured his parents to go back to Spain by refusing to take his medication for malaria unless they agreed to return.

In 1918, his former team mate, Englishman Jack Greenwell, had become coach. To the dismay of Barcelona fans, Greenwell experimented with Alcántara at the centre of a three man defence, believing a ball playing defender would allow the team to bring the ball from the back to goal scoring positions with a short passing game.

The experiment led to calls for Greenwell to be sacked. The fans wanted to see their hero thumping the ball into the back of the net. The trial ended and Alcántara returned to the forward line. This particular episode did not work out, but Greenwell is today acknowledged at Barcelona as a tactical innovator, with some seeing him as the originator of the possession based football for which the club is renowned the world over.

Less than three years after his lightning bolt showing for the Philippines at the Far East Games in Manila, he was picked in Spain's squad for the country's first ever internationals, the 1920 Olympic football tournament in Antwerp. However, he declined the invitation because it clashed with the final exams for his degree in medicine. A Spanish squad containing four of his Barcelona team mates returned with the silver medal.

The 1920s proved to be the first golden era for Barcelona, with trophies galore for a team featuring club legends Emili Sagi-Barba, Ricardo Zamora and Josep Samitier. Argentine born left winger Sagi-Barba formed a devastating partnership with Alcántara, Samitier piled in goals from a deeper midfield position, while Ricardo Zamora, the 60-cigarettes a day goalkeeper, was acknowledged as the finest in his craft. La Liga's goalkeeper of the year prize is still the Ricardo Zamora Trophy.

Even in this company, Alcántara was a stand out. His astonishing career goal scoring rate of a goal a game would catch the eye of any fan, but he also had the kind of profile which would mark him as a cult figure.

Barcelona's official website describes him as the club's first real star player. He cut a dashing figure, he was not very tall, but he had speed and a rocket shot in both feet, always noticeable playing with his trademark white hand towel dangling from the top of his shorts.

Alcántara finally made his debut for Spain against Belgium at the San Mames stadium in Bilbao in 1922, a match Spain won 2-0 with Alcántara scoring both goals. His next match, against France, earned him his nickname *El Romper Redes*, the net buster. His

30-metre piledriver is said to have ripped past the French keeper and tore through the net.

His brief, five match career for Spain yielded six goals. He played twice for the Philippines and four times for Catalonia.

Alcántara retired in 1927, two years before the start of La Liga, to concentrate on his medical career, which saw him become a respected doctor specialising in urology. His football C.V. shows he won the Copa del Rey five times, the Campionat Catalunya ten times, and the Philippines championship twice.

A friendly was played between Barcelona and a Spain XI to mark his retirement.

He continued as a club director from 1931 to 1934, but it is after this that his relationship with Barcelona becomes trickier. He is acknowledged as an all time great in the city and the club, but his support for Francoist forces in the Spanish Civil War is something many Catalans will not forgive or forget.

Alcántara was committed to the Fascist cause. He was a member of the Falange Espanola, who threw in their lot with Franco, the sworn enemy of a separate Catalan identity. He volunteered for Franco's medical service and was involved in several battle fronts.

Barcelona's involvement with Catalan identity has been with the club from the start. Its statutes are written in Catalan, it supported a petition for Catalan autonomy, and lists Catalanism as one of its four defining traits.

Barcelona's "martyr president" Josep Suñol, leader of the left wing Esquerra Republicana, was summarily executed by Franco's men during Spain's civil war in 1936. Franco's regime ordered the Catalan stripes to be removed from the club badge.

These are the kind of events which are fundamental to Barcelona's position in Catalan life and underpin the club's modern era motto of *Més que un club* - more than a club.

Alcántara's appointment as the national coach of Spain for three matches in 1951 was seen as a form of reward for his loyalty. He died in 1964 at the age of 67. His coffin was carried through Barcelona streets in front of respectful crowds. His pall bearers included team mates from his 1920s heyday, Josep Samitier and Ricardo Zamora, the goalkeeper once taken prisoner by Republicans who accused him of supporting fascists.

It is his extraordinary football talents which are remembered now. The Barcelona club honours his name, has his memorabilia in its museum, and recognises his fabulous contribution to the progress of the club. The Philippines Football Association erected a statue of the country's greatest ever player outside its headquarters in Manila in 2007.

The Philippines was one of the great centres of football development in early 20th century Asia, but the status of the game declined as Spanish influence waned. As American political presence grew, so did its sporting culture. Baseball, basketball and boxing became the dominant sports by the end of the 1930s.

In its football heyday, the Philippines provided a steady supply of players to Spain and the Philippines can be said to be the first Asian country to have exerted an influence on European football. For all his fabulous success, Paulino Alcántara wasn't a trailblazer for Filipinos in Spain. He wasn't even the first to play in the starting eleven for Barca.

Manuel Amechazurra was on the books of Barcelona for ten years between 1905 and 1915 and was most likely the first player from Asia to become a professional. Spanish football did not allow professionalism until 1924, and although Barcelona was an amateur club at this time, ace defender Amechazurra wanted to be paid.

The device found to satisfy the appearance of compliance with the rules was to hire him as a teacher of English for club officials. Club president and founder Joan Gamper, the man who would hire Alcántara, was said to be against the arrangement.

For a short time in 1915, Barcelona had three players with Filipiono ties in their squad - Alcántara, Amechazurra and Juan Garchitorena, born in Manila of Argentine heritage. Garchitorena achieved a level of notoriety in presenting false documents showing himself as a Spanish citizen, a status required of players who wanted to play in the Copa Del Rey.

His fraud was exposed when his papers were challenged by officials of an opposing team. The 'Garchitorena Scandal" cost his team a shot at a trophy when Barcelona were expelled from the Copa for fielding an ineligible player. Given the severity of the penalty and the fury of the fans, it is not surprising that none of the other Spanish Filipinos did much to attract attention to their mixed identities.

Garchitorena left Catalunya after four seasons to seek fame as a movie star in California. Under the name Juan Torena, he took supporting roles in movies produced by Fox's Spanish language stable starting with the film "*Sombras de Gloria*" released in 1929.

He was romantically linked with the Hollywood star Myrna Loy, and married actress Natalie Moorhead. He acted alongside the likes of Alan Ladd, Tyrone Power, Ricardo Montalban, Barbara Stanwyck and many other stars of the day. His movie directors included German film legend Fritz Lang.

Eduardo Teus played in goal for Real Madrid from 1913 to 1916 and played in the team which won the Copa Del Rey in 1917. He also played in an epic four match semi final against Barcelona the previous year when Alcantara scored a hat trick in a 6-6 draw. Teus went on to coach the Spanish national team in 1941-42.

Manila born Marcelino Gálatas played four years for Real Sociedad in the mid twenties and earned a cap for Spain. Julio Garcia played four years for Real Zaragoza starting in 1939, and Ignacio Larrauri led the forward line for Athletic Bilbao in the early 1940s.

The first football clubs to take the field in the Dutch East Indies, the territory we now know as Indonesia, were formed by men of Armenian background in the east Java city of Surabaya. Those Armenian connections would be part of the Indies' relationship with Australia in the 1920s and 1930s.

The football culture of the East Indies up to the 1920s was arguably the most cosmopolitan in Asia, and about to enter its most colourful flowering. It had local city based competitions, like Australia, and inter-regional contests for a national championship, also like Australia, but on an annual basis.

One feature of Dutch Indies football which did not apply in Australia was the level of exchange of football talent with their respective home territories, Britain and the Netherlands. Certainly, there were British players with good experience who came to Australia and continued to play, but there was nothing like the two-way stream of Dutch players with an international pedigree who took to the fields of Java.

The first edition of the East Indies' *Stedenwedstrijden*, effectively a national championship contested by the representative selections of Java's local competitions, took place in 1914. Batavia defeated the host Semarang 3-0 in the final. Surabaya and Bandung were beaten in the semi finals.

Even at this seminal moment in Indies football, the match included three Dutch internationals, all of whom had played in the Netherlands' first ever match against Belgium in 1905. Batavia lined up with Reinier Beeuwkes in goal, a bronze medal winner at the 1908 London Olympics who went on to earn 19 Dutch caps. Batavia's captain Ben "Jos" Stom was a full back with nine caps for his country.

Semarang inside forward Guus Lutjens played 14 times for the Netherlands, scoring five goals. His last appearance was in a 3-1 victory over Belgium just three years earlier.

That first clash between the Dutch and Belgian sides was goalless until the 80th minute when Java born Eddy De Neve put the Dutch in front. An own goal from Peet Stol drew the sides level with three minutes to go. The match went to extra time. De Neve fired himself into history by adding three more goals in a 4-1 victory.

He scored two more in a return match in Rotterdam, won 4-0. De Neve didn't get to bask in the glory for long, he was off to the East Indies with his army unit. Injury and army service spelt the end of his international career which yielded six goals in three matches.

He didn't play competitively again, although he did regularly comment on football issues and take part in football debates, publishing his memoirs to coincide with the East Indies appearance at the 1938 World Cup. He died in a concentration camp during the Japanese occupation in 1943.

This kind of living link to the Dutch football heartland continued throughout the life of the Dutch Indies scene. It brought with it a familiarity with European football and a different narrative to the British worldview which so completely dominated the Australian imagination. The infusion of top level Dutch talent was high at the time of the Australian tours, with big stars like Felix Smeets and all time great Bep Bakhuys gracing the fields of Batavia and Surabaya.

It wasn't a one way street. The pre-World War Dutch side was a European leader in FIFA's first decade, winning bronze at the Olympics not only in London in 1908 but also Stockholm in 1912. Captain Emil Mundt was born in the East Indies, as were Lo La Chapelle, Frans de Bruijn Kops, Karel Heijting, Jan Kok, Vic Gonsalves, Edu Snethlage and Ed Sol - fully half the squad.

Six of the 1912 squad were also from the east - Joop Boutmy, Nico Bouvy, Just Gobel, Caesar Ten Cate, Jan van Breda Kolff and David Wijnfeldt. This doesn't mean that they saw themselves as anything other than Dutch, but it does suggest that their Dutch and Indies sporting worlds were much closer than those of their counterparts in the Anglo-Australian sphere.

The formative years of the Dutch Indies football world were infused with Dutch internationals and through them a familiarity with top level European football. Their contact with "home", and with world football, was a lived experience, not merely an article of faith with a confirmation certificate from the F.A.

England tour manager John Lewis at the send off for the English professionals in 1925 described Australia as a football terra incognita. This level of alienation did not exist between two Dutch football cultures.

The absence of professional football in Holland meant there was no financial lure for players to stay there. Many men of playing age went to the East Indies on a tour of duty in the military, in commerce, or in the civil service

Charles van Baar van Slangenburg played six times for the Oranje and was a Dutch champion with HBS in 1925. He went to Java the next year and continued playing with SVBB in Batavia. Jan Akkersdijk played twice for Holland in 1908, the same year he signed on with Oliveo, also in Batavia.

Piet Knape, Louis Otten, Karel Kamperdijk, Joop Reeman, Frans de Bruijn Kops and other highly regarded international players all moved their talent and experience to the East Indies. Joop Boutmy won ten Dutch caps between 1912 and 1914, then spent the next ten years flitting between playing spells with HBS in Holland and Langkat and BVC in the East Indies.

Without doubt the biggest star of this Dutch world in Asia was Bep Bakhuys, easily the most significant European figure to go to Asia and play football in the pre-World War II era. His dazzling Asian career began in 1929.

Elisa Hendrik Bakhuys burst into the first team at HBS Craeyenhout in The Hague at the age of 16, scoring six goals in nine games at the end of the 1925-26 season. He was picked up by Zwolle and was still only 19 when he made his debut for Holland in a 3-2 loss to Italy in Milan.

He scored in his next match, a 3-2 win over Switzerland in Amsterdam, and found the net again in a 3-1 loss to Belgium in Antwerp in May 1929. Still just 20, he made a move to his birthplace of Java and took up a job with Bataafsche Petroleum in Surabaya.

He continued to play football with his company's team, with THOR Surabaya, and with the Surabaya regional selection at the *Stedenwedstrijden* for four years. Bakhuys starred along with his friend and Dutch national team mate Felix Smeets in the championship winning team in 1930 and 1932.

In 1933, Bakhuys scored ten goals in three finals matches leading up to the clash with Batavia. He got another two in a 4-3 loss to Batavia, a result which left Surabaya in second place. It would be his last big stage in the Indies before returning to the Netherlands.

He went back to Zwolle and straight back into the national team. In his first four matches back in an orange shirt he scored twice in two matches against Belgium, as well as doubles against Ireland and France.

A popular song, *We gaan naar Rome* (We're Going To Rome), geed up the expectations of Dutch fans with lyrics highlighting the forward line leadership of Bakhuys. Unfortunately for the Dutch, he did not find the net in the first round World Cup knockout match against Switzerland in Milan, a 3-2 loss.

In 15 further internationals, Bakhuys scored 18 times, including hat tricks in successive matches against France and Belgium. An acrimonious controversy over his move to professionalism with French side Metz ended his role in the national team. His record of 28 goals in 23 matches marks him as one of the great figures of Dutch football.

When the Australian side arrived in 1928, 24-year old Felix Smeets was still smashing in goals for the Dutch national team. He didn't play in the Netherlands' 2-0 loss to eventual winners Uruguay at the Amsterdam Olympics that year, but did play in matches against Belgium and Chile in the unofficial consolation tournament which followed. He scored in both.

He got seven goals in 14 internationals between 1927 and 1929 before his move to Java. The partnership of Bakhuys and Smeets was key to Surabaya's victory in the Indies championship in Semarang in 1930. In one match in the finals group, Surabaya hammered Semarang 12-3 with Bakhuys scoring six and Smeets 4.

Bakhuys twice played against Australia in 1931. In the first, he turned out for the Soerabaijsche Voetbal Bond (SVB), the Surabaya city selection. Australia took the lead through Lewis mid way through the first half, but Bakhuys equalised in the second half. Playing for his club THOR two days later, Bakhuys pulled a goal back when the Australians led 2-0 but was unable to stop the tourists going on to win 6-2. Two games, two goals in Australia's unacknowledged first meeting with a top line European forward.

The strength of professional football meant there was little or no financial incentive for British players to play in other countries, and the early absence of professionalism removed barriers to entry for players moving to Spain and the Netherlands from East Asia.

At least circumstances allowed players of the cailbre of Alcántara and Bakhuys to be seen in Asia.

8.
THE BOOM GOES BUST

Australian Soccer Stretched to Breaking Point 1927

The domestic tour boom which transformed the Australian soccer scene sputtered to a close in the tropical twilight of North Queensland when a Chinese side organised by Professor Kwang Lim Kwong defeated a Cairns selection 4-2. Hardly anybody witnessed the event.

The Cairns Association only learned that the Chinese would be in town by reading in the Friday edition of the *Townsville Daily Bulletin* they had defeated a local selection 7-3 in a match ending in semi darkness as the night closed in. Professor Kwong's brother Harry, a Townsville local, lined up the match.

The Association published a list of players in the *Cairns Post* the next morning with instructions to turn up at Norman Park just in case a game could be arranged. Officials boarded the *St Albans* as soon as it tied up at four o'clock on a Saturday afternoon and persuaded the Chinese to come and play. They were on the field less than an hour later. There was no possibility of publicising the match.

With a plan to go to the Olympics and visits by teams from China and Czechoslovakia on the 1927 agenda, few imagined this lowest of low key fixtures would be the last appearance of a touring team on Australian soil for almost six years.

Within three weeks of the January meeting of the national association that decided to declare its bid for a spot at the Amsterdam Olympiad, a Darwin born Chinese man arrived with a few football ideas of his own. Professor Kwang Lim Kwong came to Brisbane as a representative of the Shanghai Football Association and met the Queensland secretary Dick Tainton before going to Sydney for talks with ASFA chairman Sid Storey and secretary Ern Lukeman to discuss his offer to bring a Chinese football squad to Australia later in the year. ASFA, not having to risk its own resources and with positive memories of the 1923 tour, agreed to the proposal.

Kwong went back to China and in May returned with a team of 15 players drawn from three clubs. The star and captain, Lee Wai Tong, was now playing in Shanghai and was one of four men from the Loh Hwa side. All the others were from Hong Kong, four from South China, and seven from the Chinese Athletic Association.

The charismatic Kwang Lim Kwong was born in Darwin in 1897 to Yuen Shi, third of the four wives of Kwong Sue Duk, herbalist, real estate speculator, merchant and gold prospector.

Kwang Lim Kwong moved to China with his mother when he was twelve, and then went on to study at Wooster College in the United States when he was 17. His entry in the Wooster College yearbook of 1917 lists his ambition as to "have his home town named after him." He transferred to Columbia University later that year where he organised the New York Chinese Students Soccer Club.

Just before the end of the First World War, Kwong joined the British forces in France as a YMCA official with the Chinese Labor Corps, the support units which had so impressed Harry Millard, the instigator of the 1923 Chinese football tour. If only they had met on the western front. After the war he spent two years at Harvard Business School, graduating with an MBA.

He married in Boston in 1921 and traveled to Australia on his honeymoon where his son Robert was born, then returned to China and a life of politics, academia, business and, of course, football. He was the secretary of the Loh Hwa football club, a team which became the great touring representative of Shanghai on the Asian stage in the way that South China did for the football life of Hong Kong.

The publicity fed to Australian journalists when the team arrived highlighted the academic standing of both players and officials, as the Chinese again sought avenues to present themselves as social equals to their white European hosts. The blurb also drew attention to the claim that would be much repeated that Kwong himself, while studying at Harvard, had ranked seventh out of 200,000 American students in a survey trying find the most physically fit man.

Perhaps his ability to spin a story contributed to his subsequent appointments as English Editor at the Commercial Press and as the head of the Foreign Affairs ministry's publicity and intelligence office in Shanghai. He went on to be Chinese Consul-General in Manila, then worked in the same role in San Francisco. He was part of the Chinese diplomatic service in Geneva in the 1930s and after the war, took up permanent residency in San Francisco as the president of the Bank of Canton.

There was no way to spin out of the reality that this tour failed. It had its high points but it ended with acrimony among the players and heavy losses Kwong himself said totalled £2,300. The venture dissolved with the final matches of the tour schedule in Queensland cancelled after some players went home and the remainder effectively went on strike over their heavy workload.

In 1927, Australia's ambition outstripped its capability. Two foreign teams in the country at the same time - the Chinese and the Czechoslovakian side which came to be known as Bohemians - meant neither got enough attention in publicity or supervision. The national association, an organisation without any permanent staff, was well out of its depth. Dealing with the Olympic bid and two tours while trying to ease the festering dispute over professionalism in New South Wales and other major organisational disputes in Queensland and Victoria proved to be beyond its reach.

On paper, the Chinese squad seemed strong although clearly too small in number. They proved to be much less competitive than their countrymen of four years earlier, losing 14 of their 28 official matches, including two of the three clashes with Australia.

The first match against New South Wales drew a decent crowd of around 12,000 to see a powerful local selection face a Chinese side which had only stepped off the *Aki Maru* the day before after a three week voyage.

Lee Wai Tong opened the scoring with a trademark 20-metre drive but NSW fought back to lead 3-1 before Lee's penalty sent the teams in 3-2 at half time. NSW captain Judy Masters then ran the show with a second half hat trick in a 6-3 victory for the home team.

The Chinese suffered defeats at the hands of Sydney Metropolis (0-2) and Newcastle (2-7) but revived with a succession of wins over the relatively weaker state sides of Victoria (4-3), South Australia (4-2) and Western Australia (4-1, then 2-1), although WA won their third encounter 4-0.

Heading east again, the Chinese beat South Australia 7-1, an Australian XI which was South Australia bolstered by two Victorian forwards 3-0, and Melbourne's Metropolitan Association 5-0. Then the wheels really started to fall off.

A last minute goal gave Victoria a 4-3 triumph followed by a more emphatic victory four days later. Victoria increased the margin to 6-2 in a charity match for local hospitals, then an Australian XI looking very much like that same Victorian state selection repeated the 6-2 hiding.

The Chinese had conceded 16 goals in three matches over eight days in Melbourne. There was debate over whether this was a much weaker squad than the 1923 party or whether Australians, having been exposed to the forceful Canadians, the professionals of England and now the continental masters from Czechoslovakia, had learned a thing or two through their blossoming international football life.

In Sydney, and after a rare break of five days, China beat the Sydney Metropolis selection 4-0, restoring some confidence ahead of the first Test match. The same starting eleven took the field to face an Australian line-up comprising only NSW players except for Queensland half back Andy Park.

Masters shimmied past two defenders to set up Alex Cameron for the only goal of a competitive first half, and Chinese winger Chan Kwong Yiu equalised early in the second. But as the game wore on, the locals overpowered the tiring visitors to run up a 6-1 scoreline. Only eight thousand spectators attended the Showground for the only Test set down for Sydney.

A 3-1 win over a good quality Gladesville-Ryde district eleven in Sydney's north preceded a 4-1 loss to a stronger Newcastle selection the following day, then more train travel to Brisbane for the second Test at the Exhibition Ground, the tourists' fourth match in eight days.

Australia made eight changes for the second match, retaining only Andy Park, Alex Cameron and Bert Robertson. There were eight Queenslanders in the starting eleven. China fielded the same eleven as in Sydney

Ten thousand fans certainly got plenty of drama for their money. China began well but were knocked back by goals in quick succession, a Johnny Steele header and a Les Clark effort shortly afterwards. The Chinese fought back with two goals from Fung King Cheung and a penalty from Lee Wai Tong to go in at the break 3-2 up.

Chan Kwong Yiu increased the lead to 4-2 within five minutes of the restart before an Australia playing more long balls gained the ascendancy. Two goals from Bert Robertson levelled the scores, Cameron put Australia in front, an own goal increased the lead, and Clark completed the scoring with a minute left for a 7-4 result.

The Chinese squad was affected by injuries and a battle about returning to China to join up with the team to go to the Far Eastern Games. Southern China, having beaten Eastern China 4-1 in the regional Interport series in February, would represent China at the Games. Four touring players, all from the Chinese Athletic Association side, were selected to join the squad to take on Japan and the Philippines.

Two days after the second Test, the Chinese again put out the same eleven players to face Brisbane in a match reported as the first ever played under floodlights in Australia. The visitors won 6-3. This Queensland leg finished with a 2-0 loss to an Ipswich and West Moreton side.

The third Test in Newcastle provided further evidence of the sliding credibility of the Australia - China contests. "Australia" was the Hunter Valley bolstered by two players from Sydney, an entirely changed team from the one that defeated the Chinese in Brisbane. China's standard eleven ran out for the fifth time in a fortnight.

Inside forward Dinny O'Brien put Australia one up in the first half but Lee Wai Tong evened the score in the second. The match ended 1-1 although reports indicate the Chinese were unlucky not to secure their first Test victory.

Around five thousand fans saw the scoreless draw with the South Maitland district at Cessnock, the last Chinese match before the team fell apart.

Full back Lai Yuk-Tat, half back Wong Shui-Wah and the two wingers, teenage flyer Tso Kwai-Shing and Chan Kwong-Yiu were all about to leave the tour to return Hong Kong and join preparations for the Far Eastern Games in Shanghai. Wong Shui-Wah played in the next match, a 3-3 draw with South Maitland but after that, there were just eleven players left to complete the remaining matches on the schedule.

Frustration in the playing group finally boiled over into the public domain when it became known that the players were demanding an "indemnity" of £9 each to continue the tour. ASFA agreed to put up the cash.

Illawarra raced to a 5-0 half time lead over the reduced Chinese before being pegged back to a 6-3 win, and Gladesville-Ryde were untroubled in a 3-0 win.

The indemnity arrangement did not quell the uproar in the Chinese dressing room. Seven players demanded further payments to continue, but nobody was keen to meet this new position. Yet another match against South Maitland at Weston went ahead and was won 4-2 by the locals who were 1-0 down at half time.

With no more money available, the dissenting Chinese players went on strike. To the immense embarrassment of ASFA and the tour leader Professor Kwong, the rest of the scheduled games to be played were cancelled, although a couple of unscheduled matches in north Queensland, arranged with the help of the Cairns based part of Kwong's family, went ahead.

Professor Kwong issued an invitation for an Australian team to visit China and said he intended to return to Australia for another tour within a couple of years. Newspaper reports show he had some 1930s correspondence with Australian official Dick Tainton, and in the 1950s wrote from San Francisco to the family home of Ern Lukeman, not knowing the Australian had died.

The year's other tour also failed to produce a profit but was generally held to be successful, not least by the tourists themselves.

The short passing game of the touring Bohemians team of 1927 was a revelation to Australian fans with eyes and minds open to a new way of playing. They had seen the different approach of the Chinese, but nothing of the superior technical level shown by the Prague side.

Their three matches against Australia produced a win for the Czechs and two draws in three high scoring matches hailed at the time as some of the most thrilling matches ever seen in this country. They left Australia with two wallabies for the Prague zoo and adopting the nickname and emblem of the Kangaroos which they proudly hold to the present day.

AFK Vršovice had finished third on the Czechoslovakian table behind Sparta and Slavia, the two Prague teams which had dominated the first three seasons of the country's professional national league. The top two went on to play in the Mitropa Cup, the central European club championship also contested by the elite teams of Yugoslavia, Austria and Hungary. Sparta beat Rapid Vienna 7-4 in the two leg 1927 final.

Vršovice's consolation prize was the offer of a tour of Australia. The Czechoslovakian Consul-General Dr Svetlik had read of Australia's difficulties in signing up a touring team from France and wondered whether a team from Czechoslovakia might be welcomed. In a previous diplomatic posting, Dr Svetlik had helped organise football contacts with Turkey.

The team was billed locally as Czechoslovakia, sometimes referred to in the press as Olympic football champions, or at least as a team which had beaten Olympic gold medalists Uruguay. None of these claims were true.

Only three of the Vrsovice squad had played for their country. Defender František Krejčí's sole international appearance was against Yugoslavia in 1922 when Czechoslovakia led 3-0 in the first half but lost 4-3. Jan Knížek played in two internationals in 1926, and fellow forward Jan Wimmer played in three matches for Czechoslovakia, scoring in two of them, in victories over Yugoslavia in 1925 and 1926. The two goalkeepers, Antonín Kulda and Josef Šejbl, were guest players.

The team arrived in Fremantle at the beginning of May for a two month tour of 19 matches. The first outing was an easy romp of 11-3 against Western Australia followed by a 6-4 win two days later. South Australia was humbled 11-1 but an Australian XI put up a better showing, going down 2-1 in Adelaide.

In Melbourne, the Czechs beat Victoria 1-0 and an Australian XI 4-1 before a 9-0 canter over Southern Districts in Wagga Wagga. In Sydney, the tourists lost for the first time, 5-4 against New South Wales, in a match described by Ern Lukeman under his pen name of *Throstle* as "the most exhilirating and cleverest all round exposition of Soccer ever seen in Sydney."

He wasn't alone in his praise. The *Sydney Morning Herald's* account described "an exceptional match" and "a game which teemed with thrilling incidents and clever play." Victories over South Coast (2-1) in Wollongong and Northern Districts (4-3) in Newcastle preceded the first "Test" in Sydney.

A crowd of over 20,000 saw Australia peg back the Czechs' lead three times but eventually lose 6-4 in another thriller. Knižek's early strike was cancelled out by Stan Bourke's dipping equaliser. Havelín's effort was inadvertently directed home off the head of Crum to put the Czechs in front, but Cameron's penalty evened the score. Havelín's drive just before the break put the away side ahead again.

Arthur Veigel made it 3-3 shortly after half time, but goals from Oldřich Havelín and František Špic stretched the lead to 5-3. Judy Masters scored from Roy McNaughton's cross for 5-4 but Havelín completed a second half hat trick in the final moments for a 6-4 final score.

In the lead up to the second Test, the Czechs went down 3-1 to South Maitland and 3-2 to Queensland before recovering their winning ways 5-3 against West Moreton at Ipswich.

Another cracker of a game had the crowd of 14,000 on its feet roaring their approval at the end of a 5-5 draw. Early goals from Alex Cameron had Australia 2-0 up, Jan Eisner scored from a goalmouth scramble, winger Bert Robertson thumped into the roof of the net after Šejbl fumbled Robertson's shot, then Eisner's speed put him ahead of the defence to squeeze a shot between keeper Les Halls and the post. Australia led 3-2 at half time.

A dipping Knižek shot drew the Czechs level and a 25-metre drive from Jaroslav Hybš made it 4-3. Robertson scored from close range for 4-4, but Knižek's blast from outside the penalty area built a 5-4 lead with five minutes left. But two minutes later, Bob Kyle's curling shot from outside box brought the house down for 5-5. *The Sporting Globe* declared it to be "the best game of soccer ever played and witnessed in Queensland."

The *Globe*'s match report, under a headline "Australian Aggression Foils Slavonic Science", extolled the Czechs as having "demonstrated the true art of soccer with the science of skilled exponents." The Australians "once again proved that in the matter of speed and stamina, we rank second to no other country, and when we can add to a rapidly growing measure of skill, or polish what we already have, we will fear no football foe."

Great heights, but just three days later, the Czechs' 5-2 loss to Newcastle was derided in *The Sun* as "woeful" and "an object lesson on how not to play soccer."

After 24 hours on the train from Brisbane, the team arrived hours before the Hobart Park kick off tired and cranky to face a side always among the more physically willing opponents. The *Sun*'s reporter wrote that a penalty incident should have seen two Czech players sent off. The captain, Václav Pinc, for condescendingly patting and rubbing the hair of the referee for awarding the spot kick, and a second unnamed player for trying to trip the official after the penalty had been scored.

He described a second half which, at 4-2, became an "absolute all in" where "players of both sides did everything but play the ball." He reported that the worst incident involved a Czech forward setting up the ball which he blasted directly at the referee. The ref ordered the player off, but he refused to go. He was allowed to stay on as the confrontations continued. He concluded "As a burlesque it was a success, but it was advertised as a soccer match, not a vaudeville or butchering show."

A more orthodox 5-3 win over a Sydney Metropolis selection was the last lead in to the third and final Test. This time Australia fought back from a two goal deficit to draw this crowd pleaser 4-4. Captain Andy Park dribbled past a string of defenders to score the opener, with a reply from the Czechs variously attributed to Havelín and Knižek. Another Knižek effort from a narrow angle found the net via a deflection off Eddie Hodge with Antonín Mašata knocking in a rebound for 3-1.

A kangaroo watches over all who enter the Dolínec, home of Prague side Bohemians. The club's Australian tour of 1927 is central to its history, emblem and nickname, Klokani, the Kangaroos.

In the second half, Les Clark's header narrowed the margin but Knižek soon restored the two goal buffer. Robertson kept Australian hopes alive and Cameron scored from a Bourke corner to earn a draw. The touring squad caught a train across the Nullarbor to board the ship home and played a last match against Western Australia, a 3-2 win, at Fremantle Oval.

The largely forgotten Bohemians tour can be said to have left the most visible Australian imprint on international football. AFK Vršovice not only adopted Bohemians as the name of their team due to their newly achieved representative status of their home land, they proudly embraced an Australian identity which treasures their experience in this country almost a century ago.

This club fought for its identity against Nazi occupiers and a Communist dictatorship. The Germans in 1939 ordered that English sounding names must be changed. The club managed to argue that a latinised "Bohemia" should be accepted instead of the "English sounding" Bohemians. They reclaimed their identity as Bohemians in 1945.

In 1948, the new Communist rulers banned western names and the club became CKD Vrsovice until the more liberal era of Alexander Dubcek's government in 1968 allowed the return of Bohemians and their beloved nickname, *Klokani*, the Kangaroos. Their kangaroo club emblem is the only one in world football to proudly lay claim to an Australian identity. They should be every neutral Australian's favourite European team.

All the modern day fans who casually refer to a *Panenka* penalty, the ice cold cheeky chip down the middle of the goal in anticipation of the goalkeeper diving out of the way, should take some vicarious pride that Antonín Panenka is a Bohemians man through and through. A 14 season veteran from the '60s to the '80s who became Bohemians club president, the man pledged to advance the cause of *klokani*. What Australian could possibly argue with that?

The Czech visit provided Australians with a window to the world of central European football, one of the world's great regional football cultures. In the coming years it would give us Hugo Meisl's

Austrian wunderteam, whose play would be characterised by his journalist brother Willy Meisl as "the whirl." It would also bring forward the magical Magyars of the 1950s, the revolutionary team of Puskás and Hidegkuti.

Bohemians were not in that class, but were of that culture in its early form. They treasured the ball. They had a degree of rotation between half backs and inside forwards which offered combinations Australian players and fans had not previously seen. They played short passes to create attacking positions and exploited spaces, often big spaces, between players in more traditional 2-3-5 setups.

There was comment on the goalkeeper's tendency to throw the ball rather than kick it, even when they were trying to reach team mates as far away as the half way line. Plenty of press appraisals recognised that there was something different and perhaps superior on display.

The Czechs were perplexed by some interpretations of the laws of the game by Australian referees. Team manager Zdislav Práger, ever the diplomat in dealing with local officials and media, firmly expressed the view that some on field methods used in Australia would not be countenanced in central Europe.

In particular, there was distaste for the Australian practice of charging goalkeepers, seen as legitimate when the goalkeeper was in possession of the ball. Josef Šejbl was injured in the match against South Australia when he was brought down while clearing the ball.

On departure, the Czech party were keen to dispel the view that their players were hostile to referees and were forever arguing with them. This was not so, they asserted. What spectators saw was players who did not speak English trying to communicate by gesticulation and using their hands.

It was how they used their heads and their feet which contributed a lesson for the education of the Australian football community. A genuine affection for Australia was taken back to Prague. Michael Cigler, a Czech who arrived in Australia as a young man in 1949, published the book, *The Czechs in Australia* in 1983, which gives an eye opening account of what would now be seen as the "soft power" potential of this kind of sporting contact.

The tour got prominent coverage in Czechoslovakia and when the team returned home, an advert was placed in the local press addressed to the citizens of Prague. It read, "After a four month tour on the fifth continent, our football club Bohemians has just returned from rich and booming Australia. This now famous club has just completed the most famous tour of all time in the history of Czech soccer, winning 14 games, losing 4, and drawing the score in 2. In the history of world soccer they are placed among the elite of continental soccer teams."

Cigler notes that "Australomania" continued for some time in Czechoslovakia. A confectionary maker brought out a sweet and highly popular lolly in the shape of a kangaroo which was flavoured with eucalyptus. The sweet only disappeared at the start of World War II when it became impossible to get eucalyptus oil.

Bohemians met their obligation of offering to host the Australians on their planned European tour of 1928, indeed Ern Lukeman maintained that Bohemians had already promised to line up seven matches. Of course, the tour never happened and a connection with central European football lapsed.

Australia relied on speed, swinging the ball from wing to wing, getting to the byline and crossing, and physical power in defence and attack. It remained the dominant form in the years ahead, but they knew from their broadening experience about other methods.

There had now been seven international football tours in six years, all but one of them played in Australia. All of them had drawn good crowds for key matches but it was still a struggle to make them pay their way. What lessons could be learned?

Matches in Sydney, Newcastle and Brisbane would draw crowds and make money. Ipswich and Wollongong were also decent bets. But all other centres were likely to be loss makers. Perhaps matches should be limited to those centres that were going to produce revenue, just like the rugby codes did with their tours?

ASFA officials could see that the smaller states were unlikely to support a system which reduced or ended their access to foreign visitors. Their allies in NSW were also arguing against changes giving more power to those at club level who generated the most revenue.

The clubs push led by Bill Beaney and his Hunter Valley supporters charged that too much attention was going to the international cause and not enough was being done to make the most of the domestic scene.

There were tensions all around the country over football organisation, with divisions mainly arising from differences over association versus club competition models. Tensions in the biggest state of New South Wales were not resolved. In 1928, eleven teams split from the establishment to form the NSW State League, Australia's first semi professional league.

The move would have dramatic consequences for the national team.

Badges worn on the blazers of men on the East Indies tours of 1928 and 1931.

9.
SET SAIL FOR ASIA

The East Indies and Singapore Tour 1928

At dawn on 2 July 1928, the S.S. *Houtman* pulled in to Macassar harbour on the west coast of Celebes, modern Sulawesi, delivering Australia's national football team to the first destination of its first ever trip to Asia.

The players were keen observers of the hive of activity on the wharf and around the harbour. Hundreds of sarong clad labourers loaded and unloaded boats along a foreshore teeming with cargo transports. The players had breakfast on board before being taken on a tour of the town in cars supplied by tour promoters.

They visited the ordered, wealthy neighbourhoods of Dutch settlers and observed the relative poverty of the indigenous Macassans. They visited the Chinese cemetery. Their introductory thumbnail sketch of East Indies society took place in the course of a single morning before they returned to the *Houtman* for lunch and preparations for the match against the Macassar selection kicking off at half past four.

Macassar lined up in orange shirts, the Australians in dark green with gold markings. Two bands played the Dutch national anthem and *God Save The King*. A crowd of at least 13,000 packed the new stadium up the hill from the harbour at Mattoangin.

After two weeks at sea, the Australians struggled to assert themselves in the opening period of the game but went in at half time 2-1 ahead. They dominated in the second half, peppering a goal defended brilliantly by the Macassar goalkeeper, but could not find the net though their opponents efforts also fell short.

They had opened with a win. They returned to the *Houtman* and departed for Java with the setting sun. Australia's Asian football journey was under way.

The move to form a club based semi professional state league in New South Wales which had failed to materialise in 1927 was now on a more solid footing. Eleven teams - five from Sydney, five from Newcastle and the Hunter coalfields, and Wollongong entrant Woonona - were ready to roll. There was already even a suggestion of a regionalised second division a little way down the track with a northern division of eight sides from Newcastle and Maitland and a southern league of eight teams from Sydney and the Illawarra.

The State League made it clear it would not allow players in its teams to take part in the East Indies tour and threatened action against any man who accepted an invitation to go to Java. The national association did not select any players from the breakaway league.

Winger Harry Robertson stayed inside the official fold in order to be available for the tour and was picked. The association required the touring players to sign a form pledging their loyalty and which imposed a penalty of £200 on anybody who, having made the trip

Flying the flag on tour in Java in 1928. From left, Australian manager Ern Lukeman, captain Tom Traynor, promoter C.W. Weskin, and Australian assistant manager Bill Belliss.

to Java, subsequently joined the state league.

States were asked to nominate players for the tour with a final squad in the hands of selectors. Queensland goalkeeper Les Halls was unable to get a release from his work commitments and was omitted in favour of Balgownie shot stopper Frank Smith. A spot was held open for a Tasmanian forward but selectors felt the Apple Isle was unable to supply anybody good enough. The last spot went to Les Cook from Sydney side Canterbury.

None of the players who represented Australia in New Zealand in 1922 went on this second trip, although Bill Maunder, the first ever scorer for the national team, was reported to have turned down an invitation.

Some players born in Britain had playing experience in another country on their c.v. but only the Prahran pair Charlie O'Connor and Joe Grieves had ever travelled from Australia to play club football overseas. In the mid 1920s, both had spent a season in South Africa, O'Connor returning to the land of his birth.

The final 16 comprised eight from New South Wales, three each from Victoria and Queensland, and one apiece from South Australia and Western Australia.

The *Sydney Sportsman*, an avid backer of the state league push, lampooned the squad of "Java Jaunters" as a sub-par selection which was a fraud on the East Indies hosts and which might embarrass their home country.

When the touring team lost 2-1 on a Newcastle mudheap to a NSW eleven shortly before departure, the *Sportsman* found proof of the side's weakness and wondered whether this was a portent of disaster, a failing team unable to attract spectators becoming beggars in a foreign land. 'We may yet have the spectacle of our players having to cable home to mama, papa, wifey or even the boss for the loan of the necessary to land them back home."

Despite its difficult birth, the 1928 Australian tour of the Dutch East Indies was one of the great pivotal events in the evolution of Australian football's international identity. Although it is routinely ignored or belittled today, this was Australia's first ever trip to Asia, the modern home of all of Australia's club and country international aspirations.

Australia's first statement of intent in Asia was not in World Cup qualifiers in Cambodia in 1965, nor in joining the Asian Football Confederation in 2005. Australia's real Asian pioneers were the men who toured Singapore and what we now know as Indonesia a full 37 years before Les Scheinflug led his team on to the pitch in Phnom Penh to face North Korea.

It was the moment Australia for the first time stepped out of a British domain and into a regional environment that was humming with activity, investment and a spirit of internationalism.

Much of the criticism of the tour at the time was about the level of opposition the Australians would face, and about a presumed lack of sophistication in the football environment they were engaging. What they found was a cosmopolitan sporting culture which was already emerging as a hotbed of Asian football.

The Australians did not yet have a frame of reference to make sense of the world they had discovered. There was no light bulb moment when old certainties were tossed overboard in favour of a new ideology, a new picture of themselves and the world, but after this point, there was no way to credibly deny that Australia's neighbours offered alternative paths to football progress.

As early as 1921, the Javanese colonial capital Batavia hosted a visit by the Singapore Cricket Club, the Singapore champions, in four matches played over a week. Singapore went down 3-0 to a Surabaya selection and 1-0 to an all-Java eleven before defeating a Batavia side 2-0 and drawing 0-0 with the formal Batavia regional team.

In 1924, the booming Kolkata football league in India produced a representative touring team to go to Java to play against club sides and regional selections. The Calcutta Indians, the forerunners of the Bengal squad which would visit Australia in 1937, won five and drew two of their ten matches.

On the way to Batavia, they won three matches played in Burma and Singapore. It was the invitation from the host city which had made this other international connection possible. The Indians came to Java four years in a row.

Twelve months before the Australians arrived, a team billed as Manila also played matches in Batavia, Bandung and Surabaya, winning five times in a nine match program. "Manila" was mostly composed of players who had represented the Philippines at the 1927 Far East Games.

This team was offered as a touring team to Australia by the American sports and showbiz promoter Stewart Tait. His letter, published in the *Sportsman*, spells out the plan and gently alludes to the suspensions imposed on players embroiled in another dispute about whether were professionals or amateurs.

Football in the Indonesian archipelago was controlled by Dutch officials and colonial organisations and was enlivened by a steady stream of Dutch players spending time in Java as businessmen, professionals, tradesmen, civil servants and soldiers. Many of these players were of good pedigree, playing at the top levels of Dutch football, including in the Dutch national team.

The Dutch domination did not exclude players and teams of ethnic Chinese extraction, or indeed of indigenous Indonesian players, although there were clearly serious political issues between these camps throughout the 1920s. The growing disaffection of Javanese players, and an increasingly militant nationalist sentiment, led to the establishment of Persatuan Sepakbola Seluruh Indonesia (PSSI) in 1930, between the two Australian tours. PSSI ultimately won a struggle of nearly 20 years to assert its authority over the country and is to this day the ruling football body in Indonesia.

Australia's tour came just after the completion of the 1928 Olympic football tournament in the Netherlands. Australia's hopes of taking part in the Olympiad crashed in the political turmoil of 1927-28, but the Indies Dutch community was thrilled that its homeland had hosted the world's biggest tournament.

Prince Hendrick opened the gala but the Olympic Oath was

sworn by a footballer, the Dutch captain Henri Denis, playing at his third Olympiad. Football was embedded in Dutch Olympic culture. There had even been the vicarious feeling of being there by having an East Indies referee, Max Foltynski, officiating at the Games. There was no struggle to justify international football in Java. Internationalism was the mood of the time.

The commercial football touring circuit was already well established but there were still battles and misunderstandings about financial guarantees, the division of profits, travel arrangements, accommodation and relations between teams, associations and promoters.

Australia's first Asian tour had matches cancelled, new matches arranged, a fight between promoters over profits and liabilities and a well publicised stoush in Singapore following manager Ern Lukeman's awkward criticism of the team's treatment by local officials. On and off the field, the tour was not the beer and skittles Java holiday jaunt its critics lampooned at home.

Against Macassar, Australia went behind to a long range shot by Nit de Boach, badly misjudged by keeper Frank Smith. Johnny Johnstone engineered the reply, dribbling through the Macassar defence to have his his shot saved by Van Overheem before Charlie Deacon pounced on the rebound to score. A Johnstone pass put Deacon through to score a second. Lukeman described Macassar's play as rugged and not of a high order but thought Van Overheem's performance was brilliant.

The Australian party was flattered to find their arrival in Surabaya was the occasion for a crowd Lukeman estimated at four thousand strong waiting dockside to greet them. Anthems were played, and the players marched away from the wharf led by Lukeman carrying an Australian flag. A reception at the well appointed Concordia Club included speeches from the mayor and the British Vice Consul.

Pioneering Australian film maker Joseph Perry, at that time a resident of Surabaya as the representative of Australasian Films, was also in attendance along with Australian vaudeville stars Leeds and Lamar. Perry shot film of the Australians playing football.

Fireworks greeted the teams for the second match against the Surabaya district champions HBS, and the Australians stood with arms around each other's shoulders to perform their war cry to much cheering from a good sized crowd.

"War cries" had been in vogue in Australia and seem to have taken root after the haka of the New Zealand rugby team was performed in Australia in 1903. The folksy Australian chant can't claim any status other than a curiosity invented for this tour.

Dutch language newspapers report the song went as follows:

Ego Yah, Ego Yah!, The Emu, The Wallaby, The Kangaroo, The Wombat; Who are, who are, who are we? We are the boys from the Southern Sea, Bonza cobber, dinki di, Best of luck to you and I, We'll not fail her, young Australia, Ego Yah ... Boska!!

The war cry attracted plenty of attention, so at least it achieved its publicity objective.

Two goals from Balgownie winger Titch Thompson put the Australians well ahead, but HBS centre forward de Raadt scored before the break. After half time HBS scored twice to lead 3-2 but a late Thompson penalty completed his hat-trick and levelled the score. With a silver cup to play for, extra time was added but the sides could not be split. The local goalkeeper was again the player to catch the attention of the Australians.

The next day the SVB XI, the Surabaya representative selection, featured three HBS players including star goalkeeper Hermanus, with Australia having eight players backing up for another match. West Wallsend half back Frank Coolahan played in goal.

Australia's superiority was never in doubt. Harry Coates got the only goal of the first half, Titch Thompson and Alec Cameron added more. SVB secured a consolation goal ten minutes from time. Another routine win followed, this time 4-1 over club side Excelsior.

In Semarang, Go Ahead provided tricky opposition but were eventually despatched 5-3. The home side scored first and held the visitors to 1-1 at half time then led 2-1 early in the second half. The Semarang representative side the next day went behind to a first half penalty and were finished off 3-0. The Semarang trip ended with a 6-1 hammering of a Java Chinese XI.

Australia was made to fight by a Bandung XI which led 2-1 at half time but recovered to win 4-3 thanks to another Thompson hat trick. Despite his goals, Thompson told readers of the *Illawarra Mercury* that it was a very rough game in which he got a lot of knocking about. A goal in either half ensured Australia defeated UNI 2-0.

The first phase of Java matches yielded a draw followed by seven wins. Reports in the *Indische Courant* and *Bataviaasch Nieuwsblad* portray the Australians as fit and fast, solid at the back and with good individuals, but perhaps lacking in technique. The Australians were full of praise for the goalkeepers they played against but thought most players were not really fit enough, and the referees were not good enough.

Other match day issues surprised the touring group. For one, matches were usually played as half an hour each way rather than 45 minutes, and the positioning of referees caused some bemusement. Most refs moved up and down the touchline rather than around the pitch, so were often well away from incidents they had had to rule on.

Although the Australians over the course of the tour would play against men of Dutch, Javanese, Ambonese, Chinese, Macassan and other origins, it is worth noting that they also touched the region's important Armenian community, and its long link to football in Indonesia.

Football's Indonesian lineage is generally traced back to the Armenian Edgar brothers, John and Freddy, who are said to have brought their love of a game they learned in England when they arrived in Java in the 1890s. The brothers formed a football club, F.C. Victoria, and taught others how to play. Yet another Armenian, Eugene Mesrope, formed a second club, F.C. Sparta, in 1896.

More Armenians arrived in Surabaya over the next thirty years and as they played many different games, they established the Armenian Sports Club. The tour diary of Arch Harris records that the players were well entertained at the club while in Surabaya.

After their evening entertainment they would retire to their rooms at the Sarkies Hotel, one of a number of south east Asian hotels operated by four Armenian Sarkies brothers, the most famous of which was Raffles Hotel in Singapore. The Australians enjoyed the privilege of staying at Raffles, the luxurious hotel whose bar invented the Singapore Sling, when they arrived in Singapore. These connections were laid on by the all Armenian businessmen who were the promoters and managers of the tour.

Lukeman and assistant manager Bill Belliss seem never to have lost faith in the promoters despite the fact that tour matches had to be significantly rescheduled when political wrangles prevented any games from being played in Batavia. Lukeman and Bellis blamed the national association NIVB for the tour's problems, not the promoters, led by C.W. Weskin.

After the first phase of matches in Java, the Australians moved on to the new terrain of Singapore. Four matches in six days brought surprising results, a clumsy cultural controversy and important dates not only in the history of Australian football but also in the evolution of the game in Singapore and Malaya.

The first fixture on the list was a Singapore XI drawing on ethnic Chinese and Malay players, a line-up which can be seen as the first, albeit unofficial, team to represent Singapore. Around seven thousand fans crammed in to the Anson Road Stadium, a crush which pushed over a wall putting many in danger.

The Australians were heavily favoured to win but found themselves behind after just three minutes thanks to a goal by Dolfattah. Titch Thompson equalised shortly afterwards, rounding the 'keeper to score. A dribble by left winger Mun Fun set up Mat Noor to put Singapore ahead, Harry Robertson hit the crossbar in reply, but Singapore stood firm to lead 2-1 at the end of a 35 minute half.

Some of the Australian tour group in Singapore in 1928. Ern Lukeman is behind the girl on the stool with captain Tom Traynor to his right.

Early in the second half a header from centre forward Yong Liang stretched the lead to 3-1, a Thompson drive brought Australia back to 3-2 but a thumping Dolfattah shot restored the two goal lead. Australia piled forward, goalkeeper Melan pulled off a string of saves from the stream of shots and Australia racked up a 7-0 corner count. There was no breakthrough. To the raucous acclaim of the local crowd, Singapore recorded a famous win, 4-2.

Seven of the Australians and three of the Singapore side backed up the next day for the Malay XI vs Australia clash, with a crowd at least as big as the day before in attendance. The Malay side drew on players from Singapore and Selangor, the two sides who would contest that year's final of the Malaya Cup. This is the first Malay representative side to play against a national team..

Full back Chiang Shiang left the field with a knee injury after twelve minutes leaving the team to play the rest of the match a man down. *The Straits Times* describes an exciting match with poor finishing. The only goal came early in the second half when Thompson headed in Charlie O'Connor's cross.

A Thompson hat-trick was the centrepiece of a comfortable 6-0 thrashing of a Singapore European XI, leaving only a clash with the Singapore's top club, the British Army side the Duke of Wellington regiment, which had not lost a match in the previous two championship winning seasons.

It was a tough tackling encounter which ended in a 2-2 draw. Thompson fired in Cameron's cross for the first goal, Sansom equalised for the Dukes, Thompson netted again from a Deacon pass, then the tiring Australians were put under heavy pressure for the final 20 minutes. With just a minute left, the referee blew for handball and a penalty, converted by the Dukes' full back Hall.

The soldiers resolved that the silver cup up for grabs should be awarded to the visitors. The trophy was donated by the Alsagoff family, the prominent Arabic traders and landowners, representing another part of the new multicultural experience of the tourists. The Alsagoffs, originally from Yemen and still prominent in Singapore, owned the land leased to the Sarkies brothers who operated the Raffles Hotel.

It was the familiar rather than the new which seems to have appealed on the night of the final match. The Duke of Wellington players invited the Australians to the sergeants mess for dinner. The Arch Harris diary notes they got "a real good meal, something like what we get at home. We had mashed potatoes, cabbage and corned beef, with a very fine steamed pudding to follow."

Lukeman and at least some of the players were irked by what they saw as disrespectful treatment by their hosts in Singapore. The team had been treated well in Java and Lukeman expected the same generosity to be extended to his travelling party in Singapore.

He later told the *Malayan Saturday Post* that an international touring team would have received honours from the mayors of any Australian city they visited, but in Singapore the arrival of the Australians appeared to be a matter of no concern to anybody outside football circles. The civic receptions of Java were not part of the Singapore experience.

After leaving the British colony, he wrote a letter to the *Straits Times* which included the line "Summing up the whole position we feel that the reception at Singapore was conservative, chilling and not what we expected from fellow Britishers."

He made a point of praising the football knowledge and level of appreciation shown to the team by "Asiatic" fans, and compared it favourably to the muted approval of their "fellow Britishers." *The Straits Times* observed "Lukeman's tribute to the sportsmanship of the Asiatics is so well merited that it is a great pity it should be made the vehicle for an implied insult to the British spectators." It described Lukeman's letter as "childish, insulting and misleading."

The paper pointed out that two clubs had extended honorary memberships to the visiting players and the Singapore Football Association presented them with a special cup. Lukeman's comments were "sheer fatuous nonsense." *The Straits Times* offered its sincerest sympathies to Australian readers "lest anyone is sufficiently misguided to regard the tone of Mr Lukeman's letter as indicative of the general characteristics of his fellow countrymen."

As for another trip to Singapore, Lukeman noted in *The Referee* that it had not been considered, but going by the feelings in the touring party, including his own, "I am certain that very few, if any, would be enthusiastic over the tour."

Lukeman also had words of criticism for the football establishment in Batavia, who had effectively banned the Australians from playing in the East Indies capital. The local association wanted a bigger slice of the proceeds of matches than that taken by other cities and could not agree terms with the tour promoters, who, now unable to schedule matches in Batavia, arranged more fixtures in Surabaya.

A frustrated Lukeman blasted local and national officials based in Batavia and praised their counterparts in Surabaya, Bandung and Semarang. His scathing open letter appeared in several newspapers. " It seems incredible that a team representing the

Australian Soccer Football Association should be allowed to be in an island famed for its hospitality for three weeks at least without having received a note of welcome from the Dutch East Indies Football Association."

He went on to describe his party as ambassadors of peace and goodwill who had been treated in a way which would compare very unfavourably with the kind of reception Australia would give international visitors.

Both the Singapore and Batavia incidents were seen by those receiving these broadsides as high handed comments by a man leading a group with an inflated sense of his own importance. Certainly the comments were less than diplomatic, and issued in public when private words might have had a better effect.

On the other hand, they can be seen as Lukeman insisting that the national football team of Australia that he led should be treated with respect. Lukeman opted for public statements which were effectively appeals to local opinion over the heads of football administrators.

The incidents also point to his insistence on the higher status of international football, a view apparent in his conduct and published commentary throughout the 1920s and early 1930s. He was a confirmed internationalist. The modern notion that Lukeman pursued the 1928 tour purely to score points in a domestic dispute is complete nonsense. Australia had on and off correspondence with Java about touring for about five years.

Back in eastern Java the football resumed with extra fixtures arranged to make up for the cancellation of the Batavia matches. This meant nine games would be played in 18 days in eastern Java, five of them over nine days in front of fans in Surabaya whose own fatigue began to show at the turnstiles.

Harry Robertson scored twice in a 3-1 win over the Bandung selection, there was a 4-0 win over Cheribon, Semarang club side M.O.T. held Australia to a 2-2 draw and provided six starters for the Semarang regional selection which went down 4-1 the next day. Club side H.B.S. played a scoreless draw against Australia in the first of the Surabaya matches, while another club, Excelsior, went down 3-1 to the visitors three days later.

Despite the acrimony between authorities in Batavia and the promoter C.W. Weskin, a match was arranged between the NIVB selection and Australia to take place in Surabaya the day after the Excelsior clash. Although never recorded as a full international, it was a match between the representative teams of two recognised national associations.

An NIVB lineup had been announced while the Australians were in Singapore, when the match still looked like it might go ahead in Batavia. Only six players of that team started against Australia on a bright Sunday afternoon, along with two originally listed as reserves and three newcomers. An injury to Frank Smith forced Australian full back Arch Harris to play in goal.

Australia scored first through Alex Cameron, but Batavia forward Rehatta equalised just before half time. Match reports remark on a tiring and well below par Australian side struggling against an East Indies side which was stronger on the day.

The 30 minutes each way encounter finished 1-1, with two five minute periods of extra time to follow to determine the winner. Rehatta popped up again to score the winner, although all newspaper reports noted that he was clearly offside and the goal should never have stood. One of the papers later published an extensive postscript, perhaps under pressure from the referee van de Kasteele, that it did not intend to imply that the officials had been anything other than scrupulously impartial in their decisions.

The remainder of the tour matches were routine victories for Australia. A 5-1 blitz of Surabaya featured a Cameron hat trick, a 3-0 win over local club THOR, and finally, a comfortable 4-0 victory over the best of Makassar.

Australia's first ever Asian tour included 23 matches for 17 wins, four draws and two defeats.

Upon their return to Australia, the touring team was lined up to play New South Wales at Newcastle's Hobart Park, a match won by the state side 2-0. Wins for NSW at either end of the big trip enabled detractors to deride the status of the touring team, but there was also some popular admiration for this pioneering side.

Within a fortnight of their homecoming though, tour promoter Weskin was reported to be bankrupt and that the intransigent Australian position on their share of the gate takings had been a major consideration. Dutch language newspapers pointed to poor management and hefty payments allocated to Weskin and his associates as significant contributors to the tour's shaky financial result. The cancellation of the potentially lucrative Batavia dates was also a factor.

But there is doubt about whether Weskin actually was bankrupt. There does not appear to be any official documentation to back the newspaper story which may have been another piece of the endless mischief and point scoring between the Batavia and Surabaya camps and Weskin's status in Surabaya society seems to have remained intact.

For all its tribulations, the tour must be regarded as a success. It was Australia's first trip to Asia. It contributed to the development of national teams in Singapore and Malaya as well as the Dutch East Indies. It exposed Australian players to the demands of overseas touring in a way which trips to New Zealand never could. It provided different kinds of football to play against.

Here was proof that international contact did not have to rely forever and solely on a dream of playing in England. Asia offered other productive possibilities.

It also showed that the absence of capital at home need not restrict the development of the national team. Foreign investment, in the form of fees for overseas tours, was now proven to be a viable option.

10.
HAVE BALL WILL TRAVEL

Travelling Players, Australia and the Football World

The big new world of international football gave players the chance to travel around the globe not only to play in international club and country competitions, but also as part of their own personal career paths and simply because playing football was something you could do anywhere.

While tours and tournaments were the main vehicles for this mobility, individual players also got around the world, including players from Asia and the Pacific. Jimmy Jackson, Arthur Savage, John Cuffe, Charles Dacre and Alf Jennings went from Australia to England and Scotland; Paulino Alcantara was the most prominent of a posse of Filipinos in Spain; Celtic liked the look of India's Mohammad Salim, and New Caledonia's Numa Daly was on the books of Marseille.

The New South Wales excursion to New Zealand in 1904, the first overseas trip by any Australian team, had as one consequence the transfer of players to another country. Granville centre forward Waddell and Sydney inside left Medcalf were selected for the tour after impressing in inter district matches.

Frank Waddell was the first player ever to score against New Zealand, netting the only goal of the game for New South Wales at Dunedin's Caledonian Ground. Both Waddell and Medcalf joined Wellington Swifts for the 1905 season. Waddell captained the Wellington team in a 5-3 win over New Zealand in a warm up match for the trip to Australia.

Maurice Vandendriessche, French international and wartime captain of Belgium, was the most prominent link in Australia with the non-British world of football bursting into life across the globe. He was selected for regional sides - Flanders, New South Wales and Victoria - and played for clubs in France and Australia - Roubaix, St Kilda, Northern Suburbs and CASG Paris.

He wasn't the only European international in Australia. Season one of the semi-pro NSW State League in 1928 offered the skills of Austrian international Willy Stejskal, a man whose most notable contributions to the game would come later in life as a coach.

Willibald Stejskal made 60 appearances for the Viennese powerhouse Rapid over seven seasons at a time when Austria was becoming the leading light in the high skills football culture of *mitteleuropa*. The club won four Austrian titles and one Austrian Cup while Stejskal was there.

His sole international was in front of over 20,000 fans in Vienna against Hungary in 1918, a match the Austrians lost 2-0. Austria's coach was Hugo Meisl who went on to build Austria's *wunderteam* of the 1930s and is recognised as one of world football's greatest coaching innovators.

Rapid Vienna developed a relationship with Bulgaria and supplied coaches for that country's first matches in the early 1920s, starting with Leopold Nitsch, and succeeded by Willy Stejskal for a clash with Turkey in Istanbul won 2-1 by the Turks.

Stejskal had taken time out from Rapid to act as player/coach of Italian side Modena in the 1921-22 season. Soon after the end of his time with Rapid in 1923 he moved to Bulgaria to be the first coach ever appointed by Slavia Sofia before returning to Italy to coach and play with Cavese. He was the club's top scorer in a First Division South competition where Cavese just missed out on the playoff finals.

Stejskal signed with Sydney side Metters in 1928 after advertising his availability in the press. His varied background was remarked on in the local papers where it was noted that he had played in eight countries and spoke seven languages, although English was not one of them.

It seems this footballer, trained in the considered skills of the central European game, was at a loss to come to terms with some of the football he encountered in Australia. Soccer official, journalist and historian Sid Grant, writing under his pen name *Celtic* in *The Cessnock Eagle and South Maitland Recorder*, gives prominence to

Stejskal's contribution on a trip to the Hunter Valley as Metters crashed 5-1 to Kurri Kurri in front of 2,000 fans. Grant noted that Stejskal showed he was "well schooled in positional play", but "could not understand the kick and rush methods of the Kurri-ites."

Back in Europe, he was appointed coach of FC Metz in 1932 for the very first term of France's new 20 team professional league, split into two groups of ten. Metz finished ninth in its pool and was relegated. In wartime Belgium, he coached both Gent and Cercle Brugge between 1942 and 1944. After the war he was in charge of lower division side KSV Waregem in 1948-49.

A lower profile career coaching youth and amateur teams burst back into prominence in a topsy-turvy 1952-53 season for Ajax Amsterdam. Ajax started the season with former Scottish international Robert Thomson in charge, swapped him mid-season for ex-Dutch national team manager Karel Kaufman, then after two months switched again and called on Emma SC's Willy Stejskal for the remainder of the campaign.

Stejskal's star player was club legend and centre forward Rinus Michels, best known now as coach of the total football Dutch side that reached the final of the 1974 World Cup, won the Euros in 1988, and who was named FIFA's coach of the century in 1999. Not bad company for a 1920s NSW State League defender.

The Swiss player Willy Schaufelberger, who worked at his country's consulate in Melbourne, played alongside Maurice Vandendriessche for St Kilda and won a call up to an Australian XI for a match against the touring Bohemians in 1927. The later Anglicised Bill Schaufelberger went on to star at the card table as Australia's leading bridge player.

In Australia, people yearned for any international flavour in their football diet. It was common across the country to see "England" versus "Scotland" matches where the teams were made up of players from those backgrounds. England cricket sides on tour in Australia were inveigled into playing football matches against local sides too, all in good fun, but evidence that people still clung to even these matches as some kind of vestige of an international life.

Other cross cultural football contact happened at an informal social level as players embraced the opportunity to make football connections an increasingly clueless administration was unable to provide. It was common in Australia for the crews of visiting Navy ships to put out teams to play local opponents when they were in port.

British Navy vessels were likely to have a team ready to roll. In the first years of the 20th century, HMS Powerful had a team in the local Sydney competition for the duration of its Australian deployment. In 1910, a Fijian team defeated an HMS Powerful side when the ship was in Suva.

Visiting navy vessels weren't always from Britain. Local players, craving any kind of connection with new international opponents, also met teams from the navy ships of the Netherlands, Germany, Argentina, Chile and Japan. The Australian sides were of varying quality from full state selections to out of season teams cobbled together from those available.

In 1928, training squadrons from Japan and Argentina were in Australia at the same time. The *Idzumo*, *Yakumo* and *Presidente Sarmiento* were berthed together at Farm Cove while in Sydney.

The Japanese had arranged to start their Australian visit with a match against the state team of Western Australia but cancelled when it became clear their crew did not include their more capable players. Men from the ships still turned up to watch the replacement match at Cottesloe Oval, a clash between East and West Perth.

The handsome three masted sailing ship *Presidente Sarmiento* is now a tourist attraction in Buenos Aires. As a training ship, it made thirty nine circumnavigations and its crew of trainee midshipmen eagerly sought contests for their football team when visiting the ports of the world.

Their matches in Australia included a 7-1 defeat of a Perth side and a narrow 2-1 victory over an Australian navy team in Sydney. The reputation of this pioneering international football ship is remembered at the Estadio Fragata Presidente Sarmiento in

Buenos Aires, the 20,000 capacity home ground of lower division side Almirante Brown.

Men from the Chilean training ship *Generale Baquedano* played matches in 1931 including a clash with Metters, who after a slow start won the NSW premiership that year; the sailors of the German vessel *Köln* beat Western Australia but lost to South Australia in 1933, another German ship, *Karlsruhe*, played in Brisbane in 1934, and players from a three ship Dutch squadron led by the *Sumatra* and based in Surabaya played a series of matches around the country in 1930.

Personnel from Japanese navy ships may have been reluctant to be tested in 1928 but sailors from the *Iwate* and *Asama* played in Western Australia and South Australia in 1932, while *Asama* and *Yakuno* footballers played full state teams in 1935, losing 10-3 to South Australia and 12-3 to Western Australia.

The advent of the Hakoah club in Melbourne in the 1920s provided a base for a disparate group of players the *Sporting Globe* reported came from Switzerland, Austria, Germany, Palestine and Russia. Jack (Itzhak, or Isaac) Skolnik was the chief Hakoah organiser and sometime player chiefly responsible in 1939 for the tour of a team from the British Mandate in Palestine built around the Maccabi Tel Aviv side.

In 1928, Jack's 19-year-old brother Yehuda arrived in Melbourne after a successful stint with Hapoel Tel Aviv. The younger Skolnik was waiting for word about whether he would be included in a Jewish team from Palestine being lined up for a tour of England being financed by Sir Alfred Mond, who was ennobled as the first Lord Melchett that year.

The early revival of Hakoah in Melbourne after World War II was in no small way due to the efforts of former Viennese winger Kurt Defris, a man who had early experience managing Austrian amateur teams on tours to France, Hungary and Czechoslovakia.

He ran the Jewish Recreation Club football team in wartime Shanghai in a competition which had teams drawn from the city's Russian, British, French and Portuguese communities. The competition's Tung Wah side was run by Lee Wai Tong.

Defris was prominent as a Victorian football administrator throughout the 1950s and was much involved with ice hockey and table tennis. He was awarded an Order of Australia for services to sport in 1976.

Hakoah was the most prominent of a string of clubs built primarily on religious or ethnic community foundations. Vandendriessche's pre-First World War Association Sportive France-Australie (ASFA) was essentially a French wool buyers social kickabout side in North Sydney, but the football became more earnest as the years wore on.

Most significantly, Melbourne's Savoia club, formed by players from the Italian community, established itself during the 1930s. The club was shut down during the war and its players dispersed by wartime internment, but it revived in the late 1940s.

It has been through a lot of reformations and name changes in the decades since then. As Juventus, the side became a major force in Melbourne during the 1950s and 60s. Brunswick Juventus moved into the National Soccer League in 1984 and the following year defeated Sydney City 1-0 in both legs of the grand final to become national champions.

It is true that Australia's football scene before World War II was, like just about every other aspect of Australian life, overwhelmingly British. In football, value attached itself to British contacts far more than any other experience, including intimate links to football in Europe, Africa and South America.

But this does not mean that Australia was completely outside the orbit of the new internationalism inherent in a sport the whole world now seemed to be playing. Non-British players infused the local scene, a handful like the high level Vandendriessche and Stejskal, or the youngster Skolnik, brought valuable new perspectives

Others, the pioneers of community clubs like Hakoah and Savoia, brought new flavours that would become part of the staple diet after the war. Even Australian international players of British descent - Tennant, O'Connor, Grieves - had knowledge born of playing in Africa and South America. More casual connections such as those from visiting ships introduced still more proof of the prevalence of the game around the world.

Friends in Asia had links to European colonial centres which provided interactions which were much different to those which characterised Australian relations with England. The Dutch East Indies in particular had a relationship with the Netherlands which was far more supportive than England ever was with Australia.

The Dutch enabled the development of football through an exchange of amateur players, by providing information and political support through both KNVB and FIFA, and finally by providing training facilities, coaching support, accommodation and finance for an excursion to the World Cup.

When Australia's long exile from football's First World ended with the English amateur tour of 1937, Australians were soon mentioned as transfer targets as assessments of their quality by touring players reached the ears of English clubs. Winger Roy Crowhurst and inside forward Bully Hughes were linked to Newcastle United, Bury and Bolton, and both were quoted as having received offers from Newcastle.

They and many of their team mates might well have been able to prove themselves up to the mark in Britain if a more co-operative culture had developed. After all, men in simpler pre-War times had shown themselves to meet the required standard.

There were big obstacles in the way for Australian players and fans wanting to take part in the brave new international world, but they still succeeded in making more connections than modern opinion generally recognises.

Australia's football was not quite an isolated monoculture.

11.
TOM TRAYNOR AND ERNEST LUKEMAN

Australia's First Leaders in Asia, 1928

Australia's East Indies tour in 1928 was the first move to the continent which became the home of all the country's international ambitions.

It was a bold move which challenged presumptions about the sporting value of what might be found in a place like Java. It opened the door to a new field of opportunity in Asia. The Australians found a football scene in vigorous health on a tour that cost the cash strapped local scene nothing, and the national team proved it could pull a crowd overseas.

On the field, the leader of the Australian charge was the fast, popular and highly competitive England born captain Tom Traynor. Off the field, the breakthrough was steered by another Englishman by birth, Ernie Lukeman, the team manager.

Lukeman is the unacknowledged father of the team we now know as the Socceroos. For the whole period between 1922 and 1931, an era which takes in all of Australia's first 70 matches and all nine of the country's international series, Lukeman combined worked as team selector, team manager, referee, honorary secretary of the national association, football journalist and point of contact with overseas football.

He, above all others, encouraged the men around him to be ambitious for the national team. In the 1920s, Lukeman advanced the idea of playing at the Olympics, playing in Asia, joining FIFA, and undertaking a world tour. His commitment to the team cost him the only job for which he received year round payment - his position as a staff sergeant-major with the Australian Army.

Ernest Stephen Lukeman was born at Smethwick in Birmingham in 1882 and played amateur football before emigrating to Australia in 1908. He quickly established himself as a referee in Sydney and within two years of his arrival in Australia became an official of both the Referees Association and the NSW Football Association. He enlisted in the Army Instructional Corps in 1915 and stayed in the military for over 13 years.

Lukeman was involved in restarting the Commonwealth Football Association after the war and became Honorary Secretary in 1920. He corresponded with New Zealand over the tour across the Tasman which saw Australia play international matches for the first time. He was part of the selection committee picking the touring group.

In the return tour of 1923, Lukeman refereed New Zealand's first match against NSW, a 2-2 draw. During that year, in his capacity as the secretary of the Commonwealth Football Association, he received an invitation from FIFA for Australia to become a member, an invitation he commended to delegates of the next CFA meeting. He lodged the application to join FIFA in 1924 but the process was not completed and Australia remained as a member of the Football Association without its own affiliation to the world body.

Lukeman was an enthusiastic backer of Australia as an active force in international football and was the author of a plan to take the Australian team to the 1928 Amsterdam Olympics, paying its own way, and using that tournament as the centrepiece of a grand European tour. He procured promises of big matches in Europe through contacts such as Zdislav Práger in Prague and his friend Maurice Vandendriessche, who was well connected in France and Belgium.

The political battles in Australia, Britain and continental Europe over the amateur status of players was the chief factor in killing the plan.

Lukeman wrote about football in the sports paper *The Referee* under the pen name *Throstle*, a moniker taken from the songbird of his native Staffordshire. A throstle perched on a football crossbar was the original emblem of West Bromwich Albion, the big club in the neighbourhood of Lukeman's youth.

His columns were heavy with news of prospective international opponents for Australia, and during the domestic upheaval of the late 1920s, he urged football to maintain its international dimension. The trip to Java and beyond in 1928 was Australia's eighth major tour, home and away, in the course of seven years. Lukeman did not allow domestic struggles to derail international life.

Australia had exchanged correspondence with football officials in Batavia for about five years by the time the terms of East Indies trip were agreed. The advent of the semi-pro State League shut off access to many top players but the tour group was still a decent squad.

A day out from departure from Sydney there was an eleventh hour personal bombshell for Lukeman. Two months after submitting his leave application, the Army notified him of its refusal to let him go. He had to choose between resigning from his job or abandoning his team. He chose to go with the players.

The national body, by this time known as the Australian Soccer Football Association, lobbied for Lukeman's reinstatement. The campaign went to Defence Minister Sir William Glasgow, who rejected appeals to bring Lukeman back into the fold.

Sid Storey, in his capacity as the chairman of ASFA, wrote to the Prime Minister to ask him to intervene. He refers to the tardiness of the handling of his original request for leave, points to Lukeman's exemplary military service record, and notes that sending teams overseas "is of both commercial and educational value to the young Australians" and "helps to advertise our country."

He goes on to describe how China honoured Professor Kwong and Mok Hing for the leadership of Chinese teams in Australia in 1923 and 1927, and draws attention to the rewards accorded to the managers of the English tour of 1925 and the Bohemians in 1927.

He makes mention of Sir Frederick Toone, who was rewarded with a knighthood after managing three Ashes cricket tours to Australia in the 1920s. There was no change. In England, the card carrying member of the British Fascists, cricket manager Toone, got a knighthood. In Australia, soccer manager Lukeman effectively got the sack.

Ern Lukeman took a second team to the East Indies in 1931 but at the end of the domestic dispute and the appointment of new office bearers on the reconstituted ASFA board, Lukeman bowed out. He was now working as an agent for the AMP Society but continued to write about football. He never gave up his call for Australia to tour the world.

In October 1936, Ernest Lukeman collapsed and died while walking along the street not far from his home at Drummoyne in Sydney's inner west which, in the absence of a proper office, had also served as ASFA's official address.

His motto was said to be 'Australia First'. He was an internationalist who brought vigour and belief to the promotion of the Australian national team. His career and his writing show a man with a far broader view of international football than any other official in the pre-World War II decades.

He was proud of his English heritage but was able to conceive of an Australian sporting role which went beyond the world map's pink territories of Empire. He understood football's global reach, he was the first Australian official to do so, and he backed his judgement with action.

Ernest Lukeman chaperoned the Australian team through its first decade, dared to dream of Australia on the world stage, and was the man who took Australia to Asia.

His captain on that first Asian adventure has also slipped off the radar.

The walk from the River Tyne ferry wharf at South Shields to its main beach will likely take you down Ocean Road, a street pedestrianised to allow the easy passage of crowds that don't come as much as they used to. Its heyday as a venue for working class holiday outings has long gone but an admirable kind of determined English seaside optimism remains.

Ocean Road is also where you will find a statue of John Simpson Kirkpatrick, the young South Shields man who became an Australian First World War hero. Simpson and his donkey, bringing in injured Diggers from the beach battlegrounds of Gallipoli, is perhaps the most emblematic Australian image of the Great War. A second statue of Simpson can be found at the foot of the steps at the main entrance to the Australian War Memorial in Canberra.

Noble, fearless and dutiful in the face of endless danger, the stretcher bearer was shot dead after just three weeks on the Turkish coast. His legend grew after his death as admirers talked up the contribution of an indisputably brave man simply doing his job.

Simpson grew up in a house in South Frederick Street and went to the local Mortimer Road School. During school holidays, he worked with a donkey taking kids for rides up and down Herd Sands beach, just where Ocean Road emerges from its final stretch through the handsome Marine Park to deliver visitors to the sea shore.

Future Australian captain Tom Traynor, back row third from left, with Ebbw Vale team mates, winners of the Welsh section Southern League.

Tom Traynor was another local who would serve in the war, be mentioned in despatches for bravery, and forge a lasting connection with Australia. He lived in Orange Grove, a couple of hundred metres from South Frederick Street, went to Mortimer Road at the same time as Simpson, and became the captain of the first Australian football team ever to play in Asia.

Simpson was a couple of years older than the footballer, but at school, his younger sister Anna was in the same year as Traynor. There's a reasonable chance they may have been known to each other.

Thomas Smith Traynor is a great pioneer of Australian football. He does not have a statue anywhere and is rarely even mentioned in any review of the country's football history.

Traynor started out as a centre forward at school and as a pre-War teenager banged in 40 goals in a single season for his local side Laygate. He trialled with South Shields and Preston North End in 1914, but the arrival of war stalled any prospect of a professional career. Just 20, he joined up with the Durham Light Infantry and went off to fight in France.

His military record notes an unspecified 'act of bravery and devotion' on the Somme in March 1918 during the Germans' last push. Away from the battlefield, he is another to have taken part in the military football scene which took in so many figures who would influence the course of post-War football in Australia along with the likes of Judy Masters, Harry Millard, Maurice Vandendriessche, and Kwang Lim Kwong.

He played for South Shields in the makeshift Victory League in 1918-1919 which filled the space until the Football League was able to return in the autumn of 1919. Traynor remained with South Shields and took his place as a half back in the club's first Football League fixture, a 1-0 loss away to Fulham at Craven Cottage.

However, it would be one of only four appearances that season. The *South Shields Gazette*, in a profile published in 1921, noted that "Traynor, it will be remembered, took ill at about this time, and this took him off the team." It was a spot he never recovered and he spent the whole of the next year playing in the reserves.

A sympathetic *Gazette* painted a picture of a player whose talents didn't quite work in his favour. "There's virtue in a man's versatility; he can get into the stride of a fast moving forward and get goalwards; or fall into the happy knack of playing the 'stopper" on the intermediate line and cultivate at the same time the fine art of "feeding"; or again, act the stonewaller at full back - the player who can achieve these things is not one whose powers can be discounted."

Traynor moved on to the Welsh side Ebbw Vale in the Welsh section of the Southern League.

The north east had already earned the description 'the hotbed of football' due to its production of so many professional players. Competition for places was fierce. One of Traynor's contemporaries, fellow South Shields triallist Jimmy Seed, lived five kilometres away at Whitburn where he too had a spell working down the pit, and would have stayed there if not for the offer of a contract by Sunderland.

He went on to play sporadically for England during the 1920s and became a legendary figure as manager at Charlton Athletic. One of the stands at Charlton's home The Valley is named in his honour. In his 1958 autobiography, *The Jimmy Seed Story*, he recalls that "in Whitburn, soccer is meat and drink to all the boys, and when I was later playing in top soccer some thirty boys from our village had progressed to League football."

In his first Victory League outings for South Shields, Traynor played either side of the half back line with another local boy, Jack Grimwood. While Traynor's career didn't quite take flight, his mate went off to enjoy eight years with Manchester United, playing in their promotion winning side of 1924-25.

Traynor played South Shields schools football with full back Warneford "Warney" Cresswell and they both started in the post war opener at Fulham. When Traynor moved to Wales, Cresswell was picked for England. He is the only South Shields player to play for England while at the club. Another team mate was Harry

Higginbotham, a man always identified as Scottish, but who was born in the Sydney suburb of Ashfield.

On the brink of the Great War, Traynor worked underground at Westoe Colliery as a tracer, a man whose job was literally to use tracing paper to set out or copy maps, plans and diagrams. His move to Ebbw Vale meant a job too with the Steel and Iron works.

He was recruited by yet another South Shields born player, Jack Peart. Traynor took over as player/manager when Peart moved on to play for Port Vale in 1922. Ebbw Vale won the Welsh section of the Southern League under Traynor's leadership in 1923. In 1925, Traynor quit, bought a ticket on the S.S. *Bendigo*, and left for Australia. The ship's passenger list describes him as a clerk.

He arrived in Sydney in early 1926, played briefly with Canterbury, then moved to Brisbane where he lived for more than five years. He signed for Shafston Rovers during the 1926 season as they limped to seventh place in the eight team Brisbane competition. Traynor

The Commonwealth Football Association committee elected at the annual general meeting in Sydney in January 1924. This meeting moved to seek affiliation to FIFA with Ernest Lukeman (seated second from right) later lodging an application.

shone in a failing side, and in his first full season, Shafston rose to second place.

He was selected for Queensland for the first time in the second clash with New South Wales in August of 1926. Despite the fact that Queensland came back from 3-1 down to defeat the visitors 5-4 in the first match, selectors made several changes for the second, including the introduction of Traynor at left back.

Queensland won 2-0 with newspapers praising his cool play and leading role in organising a 'scientific' approach to defensive work.

By 1927, he was a mainstay of the Brisbane and Queensland representative sides, playing against the touring Chinese team and Bohemians of Prague. He also made his debut for Australia at left back in a 6-4 loss to Bohemians in Sydney. The Brisbane *Courier Mail* described him as "the Queensland captain, Traynor ... a left back of the cool, calculating type, a tower of strength to his side."

Amid the turmoil of 1928, the national association finally pressed ahead with an invitation to tour the Dutch East Indies. The team selected was by no means the best the country might have been able to field, but still one of good quality. Traynor was announced as captain. Australia played 23 games in a little under nine weeks, winning 17. Traynor was among the most prominent players on an arduous, trailblazing tour which flew Australian colours in Asia for the first time.

These would be his last appearances for Australia. He continued to play club football in Brisbane with Norman Park and Thistles but decided to go back to England in 1931, thus ending his football career. He may still be unrecognised in Australia, but it is his shirt which is the only Australian part of the FIFA Collection of playing kits held at England's National Football Museum in Manchester.

He was a lively character socially, popular with his team mates and respected as a smart and able defender and skipper. An avuncular character in everyday life, he was fiercely competitive where sport was concerned. He is remembered in his family as a man whose desire to succeed turned social tennis games into intense contests.

His reported views on football in Australia as he prepared to depart were an honest, if perhaps harsh, assessment of the evidence of over five years experience. "Any third class English team could defeat the best eleven that Australia could field," he said. "This is natural, this is because many men who would be outstanding on the soccer field engage in Australian Rules or rugby. Also, there are no first class coaches here.

He lived in London after his return to England working for many years at Battersea Power Station where he was active in unionising the workforce. His respectful workmates honoured his commitment to their joint cause when he retired.

He cherished his time in Australia and prized the mementoes of his contributions to the Australian game. He made one last visit as a tourist in the 1960s. He died in England in 1985 unrecognised by the football community he had served so well as Australia's first captain in Asia.

12.
NEW AMBITIONS

Growth and Big Ideas in Australia and Abroad

The 1920s football explosion produced booming Olympic competitions, new regional tournaments and the birth of the World Cup. It was a time of unprecedented numbers of international matches and big thinking about the game's future all over the world.

In Australia, the international drought had well and truly broken and big ideas about expansion were voiced for the first time. The years 1922 to 1928 saw Australia play over 60 matches, half of them against opposition from Asia. Australia proved to be a box office attraction in Singapore and the Dutch East Indies, and at home, big crowds had turned out to see touring teams from China, New Zealand, Canada, England and Czechoslovakia.

It was clear that Australia had, at least in some centres, a sizeable and commercially significant audience for football. It also had a national team that could pull a crowd overseas. The boom led to a push for a degree of professionalism at club level on the eastern seaboard and a national team dream of the Olympics, FIFA membership and world tours.

Tragically for the game, these ambitions for club and international football ended up falling either side of a divide which tore football apart in its heartlands for almost five years and seriously damaged the national team. On the world stage, the allegiance to the Football Association and failure to independently connect with FIFA gravely deepened Australia's international isolation.

While World War 1 ravaged Europe, football bounded ahead in other parts of the world, especially in South America. There were two editions of the South American championship played during the war and another in 1919 all featuring Brazil, Argentina, Chile and Uruguay. The championship was played every year during the

1920s. In 1916, the South Americans formed Conmebol, their own federation to run international affairs in their region.

In Asia, the Philippines, China and eventually Japan continued the Far Eastern Games football tournament they had begun in 1913. Other regional competitions flourished in the 20s and 30s along with the Olympics and the World Cup.

Europe's first post-war competition was the military based Inter Allied Games of June-July 1919, a celebration of the comradeship of the victorious wartime allies featuring teams from Italy, Greece, Romania, Belgium, USA, Canada, France and Czechoslovakia. Czechoslovakia beat France 3-2 in the final at Pershing Stadium in Paris.

This well run tournament was put in train by a YMCA group led by the American Elwood Brown. It represented something of an echo of Asian football since the organisers' experience with the game to this point was that they had now run four editions of the Far Eastern Games football competition.

FIFA's second president, the Englishman Daniel Burley Woolfall, died in October 1918, leaving secretary Carl Hirschmann to keep the organisation going almost single handedly from his office in Amsterdam. Hirschmann's efforts were crucial in getting 14 teams, all European except for Egypt, to take part in the 1920 Olympics in Belgium where the gold medal was awarded to Belgium after Czechoslovakia walked off the field in protest at the refereeing of John Lewis, who would later be a controversial figure in Australia as manager of the English touring team in 1925.

FIFA's attempts to reassert itself were initially hindered by the reluctance of the British associations and some others to include wartime enemies in the new football world. England, Scotland, Ireland, Wales, France, Belgium and Luxemburg did not want any contact with Germany, Austria or Hungary and discussed setting up a new Federation of National Football Associations.

During 1923, the year international football arrived in Australia via New Zealand and China, a now resurgent FIFA made a big effort to reach out to football organisations in non-affiliated countries to inform itself about conditions around the world. In his official Report from the Secretary to the FIFA Congress in Paris in 1924, Hirschmann listed nine Asia-Pacific lands among 27 territories that had been contacted - Australia, British India, China, Dutch East Indies, Indo-China, Japan, New Zealand, Palestine and Siam.

He went on say these approaches had led to membership applications from five countries - Australia, Bulgaria, Dutch East Indies, Greece and Peru. Australia's application did not progress, but all four of the other countries were full members within 18 months.

The Australian application was signed by Commonwealth Football Association secretary Ern Lukeman, who had notified delegates to the January 1924 meeting of the CFA in Sydney that they would be asked to support a resolution to join FIFA. He said Australia had been invited to affiliate and he recommended that they vote to do so.

Hirschmann received Australia's application in February 1924 and three months later notified FIFA members in the Official Communications newsletter that Australia wished to make a tour around the world "starting in October 1924 in Italy, through Europe, the United States of America and Japan." Associations interested in playing Australia should cable the CFA in Sydney.

Lukeman's communication with Hirschmann had proposed nothing less than football's first world tour.

There were newspaper reports that indicate Australia thought there might be a chance to play at the 1924 Olympics but that was never likely. The Olympics remained a target, but 1928 became the new aim as a centrepiece of a Grand Tour to Britain, Europe and elsewhere.

The Football Association's reconsideration of its international situation led it to rejoin FIFA after all in 1924, but it also moved to strengthen its position with Empire members. F.A. historian Geoffrey Green described this shift as "a tightening of bonds between the Football Association and the Dominions, achieved by the presentation of Challenge Cups to Australia, New Zealand and

Canada, and cemented subsequently by a series of comprehensive tours by F.A. teams to these great countries and also to South Africa."

Australia was delighted to receive a cup and host a tour by English professional players in 1925, and since the F.A. had rejoined FIFA, Australia became a subsidiary member of FIFA anyway. However, this position would become a serious impediment to progress when the British Associations left FIFA again in 1928. South Africa and Canada, withdrew from FIFA as independent members in 1926, a move seen inside FIFA as being orchestrated by London.

FIFA's new President Jules Rimet accepted the resignations while complaining both countries were in arrears in their subscriptions while Belgium's FIFA delegate Rodolphe Seeldrayers, who succeeded Rimet as president in 1954, was less accommodating.

Well respected in England and a journalist never shy about airing his opinions in the pages of *La Vie Sportive* and *L'Echo des Sports*, Seeldrayers told the FIFA Congress in Rome of his surprise in hearing of the withdrawals which he noted had taken place a short time after the meeting of the British Associations. He publicly challenged his English friends to offer an explanation. He didn't get one.

Like Australia, South Africa wanted closer ties with the old country and sent a touring team to Britain, Ireland and the Netherlands in 1924. The South Africans also dusted off a plan first developed nearly 20 years earlier, the formation of an Empire Football Association, which would co-ordinate Dominion tours and refashion the F.A.'s International Board which adjudicates on the laws of the game.

That would always be off limits. The *Athletic News* took the view that the South Africans were welcome but, like other dominions, they should know their place and be like Australia, that is, another face among the mini parliament of the F.A. Council. "Australia for many years has had a voice on the Council, in exactly the same way as the Elementary Schools Association is represented. These representatives have all the rights and privileges of members, save for actual voting." It is not likely the Elementary Schools Association had international ambitions.

This kind of patronising view simply did not recognise that Empire nations had any legitimate interests that needed to be accommodated by English decision makers. South Africa canvassed support for its ideas around the Empire, including Australia, who offered some guarded but favourable comments. The plan did not proceed, but Australia ended up arguing a similar case to the F.A. in the mid 1930s.

There were no football tours for Australia in 1926, although as usual, the sporting public was tantalised by newspaper stories about potential meetings with a host of countries - Scotland, South Africa, India, Canada, New Caledonia, Java and even the de facto world champions, Olympic gold medallists Uruguay.

Enquiries and invitations seemed to swirl around the globe like snowflakes, all of which fell melting to the ground. Australia needed a plan to take its team forward instead of hoping that the next foreign cable would offer a useful opportunity.

In the 1920s, all international competitions were regional, including the one England played in, the British Home Championship. The single exception was the Olympic football tournament. For Australia, this would take priority over an Empire Association of the kind envisioned by South Africa.

The Commonwealth Football Association annual meeting in Sydney in January 1927 announced an intention to play at the next year's Olympiad, a venture which would be the centrepiece of a European tour with gate revenue from tour matches expected to provide the finance. An informal meeting with the Australian Olympic Federation took place in April which discussed affiliation with the AOF and a plan for football to pay its own way to the Games.

Lukeman kept contact with former French international Maurice Vandendriessche who regularly travelled between Europe and Australia in his role as a wool buyer. Vandendriessche, asked to use his contacts to line up matches in Europe, reported that he had three ready to go in Paris, Roubaix and Brussels.

The offices of the Czechoslovakian consul Dr Svetlik were called on in dealings with football officials in Prague. A tour invitation to Czechoslovakia was issued specifically to procure an invitation for a return trip to Europe. Czech tour managers left Australia in 1927 saying they were confident they could arrange a string of matches in central and eastern Europe.

In August 1927, the International Olympic Federation announced that it would accept the principle of "broken time" payments for players in Olympic football, acknowledging a widespread practice in the European game. The move was met with howling objections in Britain, where sports officials wondered if it was possible to send a team of any kind to an Olympiad where the fundamentals of amateurism would be so rudely compromised.

Australian Olympic officials shared their concerns. National soccer officials Ern Lukeman, Sid Storey, Bill Belliss and Harry Dockerty ploughed on regardless. The October conference of the Australian Olympic Federation in Melbourne officially rejected any contact with the broken time principle, ending any hopes of progress.

In early 1927, the ever lively Australian Olympic figure Ernie Marks outlined his proposals for the development of sport around the Pacific rim. Marks was now the secretary of the Amateur Athletics Union of Australia and New Zealand and sat on the board of the International Amateur Athletics Union.

Marks, who had encouraged the football scene to engage with the Olympics in a speech in 1913, called for the establishment of a Pan Pacific Games, an Olympiad for the Pacific Rim. He had just returned from a trip to east Asia where he had been impressed by the progress of athletics, especially in Japan and the Philippines. He also cited the Chinese football tour of Australia as further evidence of a growing Asian sporting prowess.

He saw his Pan Pacific Games as operating in tandem with an 'Asians only' Far Eastern Games rather than replacing them.

He suggested good venues for these sporting festivals would be Manila, Hong Kong, Yokohama, Los Angeles and Sydney. These new Games would help Asian athletes reach world standards and would overcome cost and travel stresses faced by Pacific competitors wanting to go to the Olympics. The idea was supported in some newspaper commentary but did not take root.

Australian soccer's Olympic push took place against a backdrop of a battle over how best to divide the spoils of the new revenue producing world of top level football. The multitudes who queued to see the English team in Australia had paid nearly £20,000 at the turnstiles although the profits would be totted up in hundreds, such were the costs. Some critics thought inept administration rather than cost was the biggest problem.

Clubs in the Hunter Valley coalfields had grumbled for years about the NSW Soccer Association regime before building their case to start a new league which put gate money exclusively into the lap of the clubs themselves. They wanted an end to a centralised administration which designated playing venues, claimed a share of the gate takings, allocated teams to various leagues according to whether they represented districts, restricted players' playing options to teams in the district they lived in, and prevented elite teams from playing in one unified competition.

The Maitland Association wanted the top clubs of Newcastle, the Hunter Valley, Sydney and the Illawarra in the same league. One division, a home and away season with no playoff finals, and all gate money to stay with the home team. The Hunter sides argued that despite all the international activity, playing standards had not improved, and had even gone backwards.

They wanted the best teams - and the best players - in one league with an economy to make it happen. British background officials wanted as far as possible to replicate the structures of the best the game offered, the league set ups prevailing in Britain. They wanted professional football.

The NSW Association accused the big clubs of selfishness, of walking away from the broader interests of the game. They would take away representation from districts. They had no provisions for the development of juniors. They would effectively penalise teams and players from poorer communities. The state Association's members, the regional associations, would be deprived of the resources which made the game tick below the top level, while the proposed State League would channel the stream of money to the haves rather than the have-nots.

The push for a state league in 1927 fell short at the start of the year after the Illawarra teams got cold feet, but Weston club secretary Bill Beaney got going with a grassroots campaign to have another shot which would not be stopped in 1928. Antagonism between the Association and the State League camps continued to bubble.

The broken time dispute, and the F.A.'s lingering discomfort about FIFA's declaration that it alone was the supreme body of international football, led it to resign from FIFA in 1928. As a result, Australia too left the FIFA domain and endured a lengthy isolation from the vibrant mainstream of world football.

England led the British associations out of FIFA after a meeting in Sheffield in February 1928. FIFA's Amsterdam congress three months later took the decision to stage a World Cup open to all players, and Uruguay was confirmed in 1929 as the venue for the first tournament. Uruguay undertook to pay for the passage and accommodation of participating teams, to distribute any profits, and to solely bear the burden of any losses.

A bid to go to the Olympics had aready failed and now a link which could have seen Australia invited to the World Cup, at the expense of Uruguayan organisers, would also slip away.

Australia stayed loyal to the Football Association in London while friends in Asia embraced FIFA. Australia was now marooned in an international football organisation that didn't actually take part in international football tournaments. That the F.A.'s schism with FIFA should blow up over the issue of broken time, where a disenfranchised Australia supported the FIFA position, was a bitter irony.

While the F.A. made absolutely no effort at all to facilitate competition for its Empire members, FIFA pursued its stated aim of promoting football between countries by, among other initatives, designating councillors for regions active in the game.

William Campbell was appointed councillor for Central America and attended a tournament in Havana in 1930 where Costa Rica, Cuba, Guatemala, Honduras, Jamaica. Mexico, Panama and El Salvador competed for a championship and discussed the formation of a regional organisation, finally recognised in 1938. He was subsequently appointed commissioner for North American qualification matches for the 1934 World Cup.

A stream of leaders from the Dutch East Indies took on the role of councillor for Asia. Dick Veenman, a Batavia based figure in the Java football scene involved in the politicking which forced the cancellation of key Australian tour matches in 1928, was followed in the post by Willem van Buuren and G.L.P. Bouman.

The role of councillor gave the Dutch East Indies a direct line of communication with the FIFA secretary. Correspondence in the FIFA archives shows Carl Hirschman and his successor from 1932, Ivo Schricker, were routinely in conversation with Java and encouraged other countries in Asia to use Batavia as a point of contact in international matters.

This vital connection put the East Indies in touch with thinking at the heart of world football at the same time as Australia's failing link with London became even weaker. Arthur Gibbs, Australasia's advocate at the F.A. Council in London, resigned due to ill health in 1928 and died in 1929, the year Veenman was lined up as FIFA's man in Asia. Gibbs wasn't replaced in London until Len Pike's appointment in 1937.

The desire for international contests around the world bred a succession of new regional competitions. The Scandinavian countries started their Nordic Championship in 1924; Romania, Greece, Yugoslavia and Bulgaria got the Balkan Cup going in 1929; an unofficial Central American championship kicked off in 1930; and Egypt, Turkey, Greece and Palestine received FIFA approval for an Orient Cup. At the conclusion of Australia's tour of New Caledonia in 1933, the Sydney based French language newspaper *Le Courrier Australien* carried a story about an Asia-Pacific cup to feature New Caledonia, Australia, China and Dutch East Indies.

FIFA was well aware that the world's oldest non-British regional competition, the Far Eastern Games, was the primary vehicle for international football in east Asia. FIFA's official journal *World's Football* ran a front page story in 1930 about the most recent championship in Tokyo and a quite detailed account of the history of the Games.

FIFA opened the door for Asian participation at the 1934 World Cup by reserving a position at the finals in Italy to be contested by China, Dutch East Indies, Japan, Siam and the Philippines. However, no competition took place. Schricker then wrote to Asia's FIFA members to propose that the Far Eastern Games competition should double up as the qualifying competition for Asian countries wanting to compete at the 1938 World Cup.

While an increasingly isolated Australia spent a big chunk of the 1930s crying poor, and unsuccessfully going cap in hand time and again to the F.A. for financial assistance, Asian FIFA members were receiving letters informing them that any team reaching the World Cup finals would have their expenses covered.

Schricker wrote to the Chinese in 1932 to tell them that each national association taking part in Italy's World Cup in 1934 was entitled to receive payment of travelling and hotel expenses for a maximum of 17 people. This included railway fares second class, sleeping cars second class, and for sea travel, second class tickets on a first class steamer, or first class tickets on a second class steamer.

Hotel and food expenses would be paid at three dollars per day per person with half a dollar personal allowance to apply during the trip and for every day spent in the host country starting five days before their first match and ending two days after their last match. The same guidelines applied in 1938.

FIFA was providing financial incentives and actively promoting not only its World Cup, but also regional competition and a tacit acknowledgement of the regional organisations which could support them. In the commemorative book FIFA 1924-1929, the United States Football Association's first president, Gus Manning, foreshadows a FIFA "super body" with regional groupings sending representatives to HQ once a year.

In his 1934 memoir 50 Years of Football, F.A. Secretary Sir Frederick Wall criticises the impracticality of FIFA trying to run football around the world, that it is "an excellent organisation but too unwieldy" and that it is "a mistake to attempt to legislate for and govern the United States and South America." In practice, FIFA's actions acknowledged a degree of regional self government within a global system, although President, Jules Rimet, opposed continental confederations which he believed would undermine FIFA's central authority.

It was in fact the F.A. that was running the more centralised international administration which decided what its members could and couldn't do. In Australia's case, the F.A. not only did nothing to advance engagement in international competition, its actions with regard to the Olympics and the World Cup served to prevent that engagement taking place.

Australian domestic football politics certainly divided and weakened the local game, but the decision to pursue Australia's international cause only under the umbrella of the Football Association was calamitous.

13.
RETURN TO JAVA

The East Indies Tour 1931

The years following the historic East Indies tour of 1928 were disastrous for Australia's international football. In the seven years of 1922 to 1928, Australia hosted or took part in eight international tours featuring teams from New Zealand, Hong Kong, China, Singapore, Malaya, Canada, England, Czechoslovakia and Dutch East Indies. In 1929 and 1930, there was nothing but wishful thinking and lost opportunity.

The war for control of the game in New South Wales dragged on and on. The New South Wales Association would not cede control to the breakaway State League despite the steady movement of players, teams and fans to the semi professional competition.

No deal in New South Wales meant no prospect of tour matches in that state, and since that's where the money was, there was no action for the national team.

Preparations for the first ever World Cup gathered pace during 1929 with the momentous event itself taking place in Montevideo in 1930. One of the greatest developments in 20th century sport started the planet's biggest competition and shifted the world's football gaze away from Europe for the very first time.

In an Australia obsessed with sport, it got hardly any attention. Participation was never considered, the status of the World Cup, if mentioned at all in the press, was dismissed. How could there be a credible world championship without British teams? In any case, soccer devotees were too consumed with civil war to think about this revolutionary event.

The few mentions that were made were about crowd control and street violence amid the high excitement and gratuitous references to a Latin inability to control passions. Sharp eyed readers would see that Uruguay beat Argentina 4-2 in the final.

In early 1930, the secretary of the West Australian Soccer Football Association, Jas Gibbs, announced that after making enquiries in Batavia, he had received an invitation for his state to tour the East Indies. A letter from Java published in the West Australian press invited a group of 20 players for a 13 match schedule taking in Surabaya, Malang, Semerang, Jogjakarta, Bandung, Soekaboemi and Batavia. All travelling and hotel bills to be paid by the hosts, all players to be paid five guilders a day living expenses to cover "drinks, cigarettes, etc."

The tour did not go ahead but it did open the door for another visit by an Australian national team. The fact that a weak state like Western Australia was now freelancing a bid for international action is an indicator of the level of frustration around the country with the self obsessed obstinacy in New South Wales.

The second tour was part of the 30th anniversary celebrations of the founding of the Surabaya club side THOR, (Tot Heil Onzer Ribben). There was general recognition that Lukeman was the best qualified to be Australian manager, even among those football factions with no great affection for the Commonwealth Association. He had the experience of 1928 under his belt, and a record of doggedly pursuing the interests of the national team at home and abroad.

His joint manager on this venture was to be J. Owen Wilshaw, in charge of junior football in Victoria and also a member of the national selection committee. Wilshaw and Sid Storey tied in a vote to go as joint manager but Wilshaw's name was pulled from the hat to settle the issue.

Like Lukeman, Wilshaw was from Staffordshire in the English midlands. A profile in *Sporting Globe* reported that after playing as a youngster with the local Trentham club, he moved into administration with Stoke City, usually dealing with reserve team matters. He was a member of the Staffordshire F.A., nominated by West Bromwich Albion and Wolverhampton Wanderers. He was secretary of the Stafford Rangers club before leaving for Melbourne in 1920.

He quickly became involved with Victorian football administration but left when the state imposed a new district based system which he felt unduly restricted the freedom of players. He rejoined in 1928, managed the Victorian team at the 1929 national championships in Adelaide, and took over the reins of the junior game in 1930.

His administrative skills were respected outside the confines of the football world where he was secretary of the South Melbourne manufacturer Titan Nail and Wire, a company taken over by BHP in the 1930s.

Two months before his appointment for the Indies trip, Wilshaw was the first Australian football official to write about the likelihood of Australian participation in the new-fangled World Cup. He expressed the view that an Australian team would not be disgraced in any world series of games but thought it unlikely the country would have any part in the new competition.

Unless qualifying matches could be played in Australia, the expense would kill the idea. If there were to be some kind of pro rata reimbursement of costs for southern hemisphere countries, that could change his view, but otherwise, no deal.

What the Australians didn't know was that for the first World Cup there were no qualifiers and Uruguay had offered to cover all the costs, including travel and accommodation, of participating teams. The next World Cup in Italy offered participants exactly the kind of financial sweeteners sought by Wilshaw.

The second East Indies tour was briefer and without the fanfare of the first. This was most definitely a work trip without much in the way of touring and entertaining with a heavy schedule of 13 matches in just 27 days for a squad of 19 players.

The opener in Makassar kicked off in the late afternoon following the formalities of an introduction of the players to the Governor and the presentation of garlands, a ritual which preceded every match.

Wilshaw later reported in Melbourne's *Sporting Globe* that

the match was a fast, even contest until Brunswick's Peter Lewis scored for Australia, after which the visitors had complete control. Lewis scored again ten minutes after half time, and by Wilshaw's account, shoddy Australian finishing was chiefly responsible for the modest final margin of 2-0.

A rough sea passage to Surabaya was blamed for the Australians being in less than tip top condition to face the city's champion club HBS. A big crowd saw Uktolseja score on the quarter hour and give HBS a half time lead. Australia equalised but Uktolseja scored the winner.

The right half for HBS in this match was a promising 20-year-old student, Achmad Nawir, who would later achieve fame as the captain of the Dutch East Indies at the 1938 World Cup in France. He is rightly honoured as the first Asian team captain to appear at world football's premier event. A detail passed over is that the first national team he ever played against was Australia, in HBS colours, on this day.

The first impression of the local press was that the Australians looked like a decent side with some good individual players, but they were not of the standard of 1928.

Two days later, Australia had a comfortable 4-0 victory over Surabaya's Chinese club Tiong Hua, returning to the field the next day to face Singapore's best, the British military outfit Combined Services. The Australians later declared this to be the best match of the tour.

The Singapore side dominated the early play but Queenslander Les Clark scored first. Raybould equalised, Jim Donaldson put Australia back in front, Woodward levelled again for a 2-2 half time scoreline. News agency copy reported several Combined Services shots hit the crossbar, but goals from Lewis and Clark secured a 4-2 win. Match referee Max Foltynski had been an official in several matches at the 1928 Olympics in Amsterdam.

The pages of *Java Bode*, whose unnamed football writer had been underwhelmed by the first showing of the Australians, praised this match as one of the best ever seen in Surabaya, with honours deservedly won by the men in green and gold.

The match report remarks favourably on a game played at a great pace between two teams applying an almost identical method of play with zigzag combinations - long diagonal balls - used to undo their opponents' defences. This is contrasted to the short passing style favoured by local sides.

And so, having now played 27 matches over two tours, the Australians finally made it to the Dutch East Indies capital of Batavia. Their first opponents, the local champions Hercules, made light work of disposing of an ineffectual Australian side.

Inside forward Soemo put Hercules 1-0 up at half time and completed a hat-trick in a 3-0 victory. Like Nawir, right winger Henk Zomers went on to play in the 1938 World Cup.

Two goals from Gavin Russell set up Australia for a 3-1 victory over Batavia's ethnic Chinese club UMS, followed the next day by a date with the Batavia regional selection. Only two of the victorious Hercules line up featured in the starting eleven, defender Davies and hat trick hero Soemo. Lukeman might have recognised names from Australia's 1928 loss to the East Indies, forwards Malaihollo and the scorer of both East Indies goals in a 2-1 defeat, Rehatta.

All three goals in this clash came in the first half. Les Clark turned in Bunny Muir's cross to open the scoring, dangerman Soemo again scored to level, and heavy Australian pressure caused Batavia centre half Eddie Meeng to put though his own goal. Batavia goalkeeper Becker saved a penalty from Lewis.

Writing in the *Sporting Globe* after his return from Java, Wilshaw lamented "this game, in common with most of the others, was spoiled by the decisions of the referee, which were so obviously wrong that it is a wonder players can do anything at all. Some offside decisions were ridiculous."

The final fixture in Batavia was a routine 4-0 victory over club side SVBB.

Eddie Meeng's service in the Navy deprived him of the chance to play in the 1938 World Cup, but his younger brother Frans did make the team. A Dutch media interview Meeng senior gave on the occasion of his 99th birthday offered a fascinating insight into the East Indies football world of his youth.

He says that although football was amateur, as in the Netherlands, nice pocket money could also be picked up. Thirty or forty guilders a game could be made, the equivalent of a week's pay for many men off the field.

The Australians' brief trip to Bandung saw former Queensland boxer Max Gornik acting as a most popular host, with other Aussies roped in to provide a welcome. The playing part of the side trip did not go so well. Bandung led 2-0 at the break, then 3-0, before Frank McIvor pulled one back.

Wilshaw conceded that Bandung were the better side on the day but again complained about the refereeing, describing the decision to allow the opening goal of Laktoero to stand as "wretched." His account says the Australians were nonplussed to see a goal awarded after the ball had been out of play and the Australians were preparing to take a goal kick.

The local Dutch language newspaper report sees this incident as one of clever persistence, that the Australian left back pretended the ball had crossed the line and left it, the winger retrieved the ball and crossed for inside left Laktoero to score. The report expresses disappointment in the Australians' diminished standard and describes the 1928 side as being head and shoulders ahead of the current mediocre group.

The return to Surabaya began with a high profile match up with the Surabaya district selection. The local forward line included inside forwards Uktolseja, the player whose goals for HBS sank Australia early in the tour and had played against the tourists in 1928, and Tetalepta, who would go on to play for the East Indies at the Far East Games of 1934 in Manila.

The line was led by one of the all time great figures of Dutch football, Bep Bakhuys. A sensation as a young player in the amateur football scene of the Netherlands, Bakhuys moved to Java where he played three eventful seasons before returning to Holland, rejoining the national team, and carrying the hopes of his countrymen as the star of the Dutch side to contest the World Cup in Rome.

His astonishing Oranje scoring record of 28 goals in 23 matches says all you need to know about his international class. In this match, a Lewis goal put Australia in front in the first half, but it was Bakhuys, getting his almost inevitable goal, who deprived the Australians of victory.

A scheduled match against an all-Java Chinese XI made way for a simple rematch with a Tiong Hua side looking to turn around their 4-0 flogging of two weeks earlier. Alas, this did not go well for them. Australia led 3-0 at half time and cantered to an 8-1 drubbing. The Australian performance was hailed locally as evidence the Australians could indeed operate at a high level.

The last match in Java was another stroll, with Australia easing past club side THOR 6-2. It was the second time Bakhuys lined up against Australia but his goal this time only briefly brought THOR back in to the contest at 1-2 before the onslaught continued. The tour ended in Makassar with the exhausted Australians doing enough to get a 1-0 result against the regional selection.

The Australian team was clearly weaker and less representative than the first to visit these shores, but they had generally performed well against decent opposition. Nine wins from 13 matches was an excellent result from a highly demanding match schedule.

This was a no-frills tour compared with the first, and the Australians grumbled that they were not accorded any particular level of attention by officials, especially in Batavia. Wilshaw thought the pitches poor, the refereeing worse and that the tour had taken place too late in the year. The now more diplomatic Lukeman commented that playing standards had risen considerably in the three years since the first visit.

For all the irritations, they had nevertheless deepened and extended their football fraternity with the country which had now given more support to Australia than any other territory in Asia.

In November 1967, Australia under 'Uncle Joe' Vlasists won the eight nation Vietnam National Day tournament in Saigon. It was a significant achievement, the first tournament ever won by the national team, and in extraordinary wartime circumstances.

Three days after the tournament win, the players arrived in Jakarta and defeated Indonesia 2-0 through goals to Ray Baartz and Atti Abonyi. The return was 36 years in the making, but the Australians were back in Java.

14.
THE AUSTRALIAN CHAMPIONSHIP

Interstate Nation Building 1928 - 1936

Back in the early spring of 1924, the Australian football world was walking tall with the new found confidence of adulthood. The Canadian tour had just drawn to a close a year after the successful Chinese and New Zealand tours, all events providing living proof that Australia was a genuine part of international football.

The crowning confirmation of that status was the news from London that the Football Association had committed to send an England team to Australia in 1925. A second confirmation of maturity was the F.A.'s donation of a handsome trophy for competition between the states, another new expression of national identity through a national interstate championship.

At the September F.A. Council meeting at Russell Square in London, chairman Charles Clegg presented the trophy to Australasian representative Arthur Gibbs describing it as a token of the regard the F.A. had for the Australian associations. He went on to say that whenever and wherever it was possible for assistance to be given by the parent body it would be given with pleasure.

Gibbs in reply reflected on the long march to Australian recognition and his own role in it having captained the Victorian side in the first intercolonial contests against New South Wales 40 years earlier. He said receiving the trophy was the culminating point of his football career and told the Council the trophy was assured of a most cordial welcome in Australia.

It was indeed welcomed, but ten years later, interstate contests had already crumbled through neglect into insignificance. Another five years on, the secretary of the national association, Roy Druery, was reported to be proposing to melt the trophy down, sell it, and distribute the profit to member associations. He complained that the cup cost more than a pound in insurance and that it was littering up his home.

No decision was taken on the matter, and even if Druery's comments are regarded as a tasteless joke, it has to be noted that England's biggest symbolic contribution to the development of football in Australia disappeared from view and was never seen again

The donation of the cup was recognised as an act of generosity but the gift was not coming to Australia as a result of any campaign or development request. The cup donation was part of the Football Association's early 1920s push to draw Empire nations closer to London which also awarded cups to Canada and New Zealand.

The English F.A. Cup celebrated its 50th anniversary in 1922 with the Cup Final moving to the new Wembley Stadium in 1923. That first Wembley final attracted an official crowd figure of 125,000 but many observers estimated the crowd to be double that figure.

The F.A. Cup had been hugely influential in popularising football in England. It is not surprising that English opinion saw a national cup challenge as a proven winner in promoting and uniting football interests. Nevertheless, the cup was part of a one size fits all Empire policy of the F.A. deciding what was best for the colonies and was not the result of discussions about issues Australians themselves saw as priorities.

For all the initial fanfare, four years passed before a competition actually took place and that involved only four states. The 1927 Australian Soccer Football Association annual conference in Sydney was presented with a plan for a nine team event to be held in Sydney, but with four of the teams coming from the biggest state. They would be New South Wales, Newcastle, Illawarra and Sydney Metropolis. Bigwigs in Sydney argued there would have to be at least two teams from New South Wales in order to make the tournament financially viable.

By the time the Australian championship started in 1928, the big political splits over control of the game were under way and were boiling hot issues, greatly diminishing the status of a New South Wales selection omitting State League players and leading to the absence of Queensland.

The draw had New South Wales facing Victoria in Sydney and Tasmania hosting South Australia in Hobart with the two winners to play in the final. Only three matches, but it took nearly four months to complete the schedule.

In late May, before the Australian tour of the Dutch East Indies, New South Wales fielded a team without any Sydney players to face Victoria. Centre forward George Smith scored inside five minutes and again after half time to put the home side up 2-0, but the visitors produced a big shock with two goals from Baker and another from Thompson to win 3-2. In July, Tasmania earned a 1-1 draw with South Australia then beat them 3-1 in a replay to reach the final.

A Melbourne final in mid-September meant Victoria could include internationals O'Connor, Lewis and Johnstone who had just returned from the East Indies trip. The home side dominated on a blustery day, O'Connor was man of the match, Lewis scored twice and Johnstone once as Victoria defeated Tasmania 3-1.

The championship scheduled for 1929 consisted of one match, a 2-1 victory in Adelaide for South Australia over Victoria.

Political turmoil killed plans for further championships until 1932 when the biggest battle, control of the game in New South Wales, had been settled. The newly reconciled and reconstituted national association made a big effort to stage a meaningful competition over ten days in Sydney, Newcastle and the Hunter Valley. All states bar Western Australia took part.

The first matches were close – South Australia edged Tasmania 2-1, Victoria drew 4-4 with Queensland, then South Australia shaded Victoria 4-2. Then, at Wallsend's Crystal Palace ground, a New South Wales side stacked with northern players went a goal down before storming back to crush Queensland 9-1 with George Smith scoring five.

New South Wales belted Victoria 7-0 at Gladesville in Sydney, Queensland humbled Tasmania 9-2, then New South Wales used Alf Quill at centre forward instead of Smith in an 11-0 obliteration of Tasmania in Newcastle, Quill netting four.

South Australia disposed of a disappointing Queensland 4-0, Victoria beat Tasmania 7-0 and New South Wales again went behind before easing to a 4-1 victory over South Australia.

The grand final at the Sydney Cricket Ground attracted four thousand fans who saw a comfortable win for the home team. Smith was restored to the lineup, wore the captain's armband and bagged four in a 6-1 rout which newspapers agreed would have seen a bigger margin but for the efforts of West Torrens goalkeeper Peter McKinley, who boasted a spell with Scottish side Cowdenbeath on his resumé. Charlie O'Connor, now with Adamstown, won titles with different states, Victoria and New South Wales.

This well run tournament had produced great goals and for the first time brought leading players together from all over the country. It united the tribes after years of bickering and warfare but it did not succeed in becoming the national championship implicit in the comments of Clegg and Gibbs in London or its promoters at home.

In Sydney and the Hunter, local opinion was that the football carnival simply proved what they already knew - that New South Wales was far ahead of the other states. They had scored 37 times in five matches, the closest margin being a 4-1 when the team eased off after South Australia's centre half Watson left the field with a head injury.

The next edition was set down for Melbourne in October 1934, a football feature of celebrations marking the centenary of the city's establishment and which would see the first entry of a team from Western Australia. Selections had been made, train tickets bought, leave arranged and hotels booked only for interstate associations to be notified by telegram that the whole tournament had been cancelled due to the lack of suitable grounds.

The Victorian Association had proceeded all year on an agreement that matches would be played at Olympic Park, but Victorian Association secretary Harry Bingham called a halt claiming the ground's operators had reneged on their contract and efforts to find alternative grounds had been fruitless.

As it turned out, the contract for the use of Olympic Park was a verbal agreement that nobody had thought to get in writing. Instead of football, there would be a rodeo.

Despite the fact that football was struggling to rub two pennies together, football haters could still call up images of immense soccer wealth to frighten their own constituencies. Melbourne Australian Rules official W.J. McDonnell, secretary of the VFL second 18s, told a dinner in 1933 that the controllers of the Australian game needed to be wide awake to "the menace of soccer."

The Age reported that McDonnell claimed he had information that £250,000 was waiting to come from England for football in Australia. He went on to say England had a pool of £1,000,000 waiting to be used to foster the game. When questioned about his extraordinary assertion, McDonnell gave the Melbourne *Herald* an emphatic assurance his information came from a reliable source.

Adelaide hosted the 1936 championship as football's contribution to celebrations of the centenary of South Australia. Victoria sent an inexperienced squad of 13 and New South Wales, having originally notified the organisers that the cost of travel meant they would not defend their title, finally decided to go with a very young squad.

Organisers agreed to subsidise the cup holders by giving up a share of the gate money, knowing that if the big boys didn't come, the tournament would be cancelled. Even then, New South Wales selectors decided not to consider players from top clubs Metters, Adamstown, Weston and Goodyear, all still completing a state fixture list in late September. Star centre forward George Smith pulled out and was replaced by 18-year old St George recruit Jim Brown.

The cup consisted of three hopelessly one sided matches. New South Wales overran Victoria 10-0 with the teenage Brown scoring four, South Australia demolished Victoria 9-1 with Birkalla Rovers forward Thompson netting five, then New South Wales blew away the hosts 6-0.

There was little enthusiasm left for a competition now seen as a burden of duty, a financial impost, and a competition likely to be won at a canter by New South Wales even when they were fielding a B team. A plan to have another national carnival in 1938, relying on a guarantee against loss from organisers of Sydney's 150th birthday celebrations, did not win favour.

The F.A. originated football nation building plan envisaged by Charles Clegg and Arthur Gibbs had withered. England representatives visiting Australia in 1937 heard more Australian requests for assistance in developing the game to pile on to the routine requests made to the F.A. Council, but since the £250 trophy, described by Gibbs in 1924 as the handsomest he had ever seen, had failed to generate any lasting benefit, what was the point in listening to Australians who couldn't seem to organise anything by themselves?

For the F.A., there seemed to be little point in investing in Australian football.

15.
MAURICE VANDENDRIESSCHE
Australia's European Advocate

Although Australia was fixated on British football and hung on every word emanating from England's Football Association, the most significant European individual to act for the Australian cause was not British, he was the Franco-Belgian Maurice Vandendriessche.

Vandendriessche played representative football in France, Belgium and Australia and was the first person to advocate for Australia in continental Europe. He was connected to some of the great football personalities of the age in a career as a player and activist which spanned 30 years - half of that time spent in Australia.

When New South Wales lined up to face New Zealand in Dunedin on July 23rd 1904 it was the first match to feature an Australian side playing a national team. This was the first appearance of a team we came to know as the All Whites.

New South Wales was a de facto Australian representative side in terms of the quality of its playing personnel but not, in the manner of the times, representative of the game as a whole in Australia. New South Wales won 1-0.

In Europe, football's international expansion continued apace. On May Day 1904, France and Belgium played a 3-3 draw in Brussels in what was the debut international match for both countries. They joined Hungary, Austria and Czechoslovakia as the only European nations to have played a full international.

The year's biggest event happened off the field. On 25 May in the back office of the Union des Sociétés Francaises de Sports Athlétique (USFSA), six European nations signed on to become the founding members of the Fédération Internationale des Football Associations, FIFA. The clash in Dunedin came just nine weeks after FIFA's formation and preceded the emergence of the national teams of all bar five European countries.

The year also saw the debut of a teenage player in USFSA's Championnat du Nord who would go on to be selected for France, Belgium, Flanders, New South Wales and Victoria. He would become Australia's first lobbyist in Europe, a man who set up matches in France for Australian players during and after World War 1, arranged fixtures for Australia's aborted European tour of 1928, and become a friend and advisor to the post-war secretary of the Commonwealth Football Association, Ern Lukeman.

Maurice Vandendriessche was born in the northern French city of Lille in 1887 and came to prominence as a fast and classy teenage half back for France's leading team in the early 1900s, Roubaix. In 1902, 1903 and 1904, Roubaix won all three finals of the Championnat du France but lost 1-0 to Parisian side Gallia in the 1905 final.

Nineteen year old Vandendriessche shone in the next season's campaign and played against Cercle Athletique du Paris in the Championnat final won 4-1 by Roubaix. He was absent in the 2-3 loss to Racing in the 1907 final, but back in the lineup for the 2-1 victory over the same club in 1908.

That year, aged 20, Vandendriessche played well in what was effectively a national team trial as the league selection of Le Nord defeated Paris 1-0. He was chosen a few days later to make his international debut at right half for France against Switzerland in Geneva where France were 1-0 down at half time but recovered to win 2-1, Vandendriessche setting up the winning goal. He retained his place for the big match against the England amateur side at London's Park Royal ground, home then of Queens Park Rangers.

England, led by star forward and captain Vivian Woodward, thrashed the French 12-0 with Woodward scoring a hat-trick and William Jordan netting six. France, along with other European teams of the day, measured their progress with matches against the revered teams of England, and while they were chastened by this hiding, they saw the match as an important lesson in the development of French football.

Although two more double digit defeats followed in the next two years, better contests followed with England winning 3-0 and 4-1 in two games in Paris before the war.

The trip to England was a big event, not just for the international match, but also in relations between the two countries. FIFA had originally been shunned by an English establishment dismissive of the Europeans in 1904 but who joined in 1905 and later in 1908 would see the F.A.'s Daniel Woolfall become president.

The 1908 match was attended by the Football Association secretary Fred Wall and Chairman Charles Clegg while the French delegation was headed by André Espir. Another French official, André Billy, was a match linesman. Espir and Billy had picked the French team, so clearly knew Vandendriessche.

FIFA's historic foundation document shows the signature of André Espir as the proxy representative of Madrid F.C., and therefore, in this context, of Spain. After the resignation of FIFA's founding president Robert Guérin, also in 1908, Espir became a FIFA vice president.

Vandendriessche was again selected for France's next match to play Belgium but, just three days before kick off, withdrew from the team and announced that as a 21-year old adult, he was now declaring Belgian nationality and would no longer be available for France.

He continued to play for Roubaix and developed his off field career in the wool industry. In that capacity, he moved to Australia in 1910, settling in Melbourne. In 1911, he immediately attracted attention as a prominent new player for St Kilda.

He moved to Sydney the following year and joined Northern Suburbs where he again drew favourable notices and was selected as a reserve for New South Wales in matches against Queensland and Tasmania. Vandendriessche also established the Association Sportive France-Australie, which he affiliated to the NSW Soccer Association. ASFA was a social team of French wool buyers which played friendly matches only. Nevertheless, it is most likely the first 'ethnic' team to be formally registered in Australia.

Over three seasons, Vandendriessche became a well known and popular figure in Sydney soccer circles where he built a friendship with Lukeman and played for a Sydney representative team against an Illawarra line-up which included rising south coast star and future Australian skipper Judy Masters.

He returned to Europe when war broke out, joining the Belgian military in France but continued to play football at every opportunity, often in matches raising money for Belgian refugees. Vandendriessche turned out for the top Parisian side Club Athlétique de la Société Générale (CASG) where he was again a prominent player in a highly successful team.

CASG Paris reached the semi finals of the new national Coupe de France in 1917-18 but lost 1-0 to eventual winners Olympique. In 1919, CASG defeated Olympique 3-2 in extra time at Parc des Princes, although Vandendriessche did not play in the final.

During the war, he arranged matches for Australian and New Zealand players as early as 1915, sometimes taking part. He played as centre forward in a CASG Paris eleven bolstered by two Belgian international guests, Gaston Hubin and Fernand Wertz, against 'Anzac F.C.' in Paris in 1917. Wertz went on to play for Belgium at the 1920 Olympics, CASG centre half Albert Jourda played for France at the 1924 Games. CASG won the match 2-1.

Seven weeks later, Vandendriessche was the captain of Belgium's unofficial national team of military personnel in a 3-0 victory over France where the teams were introduced to the guest of honour, the founder of the International Olympic Committee, Baron Pierre de Coubertin.

In 1919, European football was still trying to re-establish itself after the trauma of war. The American YMCA persuaded the U.S. Army to stage a multi sports tournament, a kind of military Olympiad, for soldiers who had taken part in the fighting..

The Inter Allied Games at the American built Stade Pershing in the suburbs of Paris was a grand enterprise involving around 1,500 competitors in more than a dozen sports. It was a near enough replica of the three editions of the Far Eastern Games the YMCA had already staged in Manila, Shanghai and Tokyo starting in 1913, all of which included football tournaments. Both the Inter Allied and Far Eastern games were designed and run by the young YMCA officer Elwood Brown.

The football tournament was a serious affair involving eight teams and a long list of major European international players. Although Australia's military sports administrators trialled 70 to 80 players to recruit a rugby team, they did not enter a team in the association football section

Despite his wartime captaincy of the Belgian military team, Vandendriessche did not play in the Belgian side but did turn out in two significant representative games. While the Inter Allied Games were in progress, he took the field for the *Lions de Flandres*, the Lions of Flanders, against the Paris based Ligue de Football Association (LFA).

Few knew more of the horrors of war than the people of Flanders. The re-emergence of a team to represent them for the first time since before the war, and to play in Paris, was a source of pride and excitement in the north. *Les Lions*, put together by the Olympique Lille club president Henri Jooris, had Vandendriessche as centre half and captain in a side containing five players who were, or would become, French internationals.

The LFA line up had seven such players in its starting eleven and six who had played in a 2-2 draw with Belgium in France's only official international match in 1919. The two sides played a 4-4 draw with *L'Auto*'s match report quoting LFA skipper and long time French international Lucien Gamblin pointing to the brilliant performance of Vandendriessche.

Six of the starters in this match were in the French squad for the Olympics the following year.

In November 1919, Vandendriessche played in a match to mark the first anniversary of the Armistice, this time for northern France against a Brussels selection, another game packed with internationals. This match seems to have brought his European representative career to a close. His next representative team would be that of Victoria.

He returned to Melbourne after the war and rejoined his first Australian team, St Kilda. In 1923, he played for Victoria against New South Wales in a 5-1 loss in front of 5,000 spectators at Sydney's Wentworth Park, and against the Chinese touring team led by Lee Wai Tong. That same year Vandendriessche played in the St Kilda team which defeated Footscray Thistle 2-1 in a second replay to win the Victorian championship playoff having already won the Dockerty Cup, beating Preston 1-0 in the final.

He became the president of the St Kilda club but continued to play. His appearance for St Kilda at the age of 39 in their 4-3 loss to Navy in the 1926 Dockerty Cup final seems to have been his last big game but was not his final action in Australian football.

In the course of his work as a wool buyer, Vandendriessche travelled back to Europe for a few months every two years. Aside of his work, he kept up to date with his European football contacts.

He headed to Europe on business in 1927 and was asked by his friend Lukeman to see if he could arrange matches for a planned European tour by Australia to be built around participation in the 1928 Olympic Games in Amsterdam. Lukeman reported in his column in *The Referee* that a letter from Vandendriessche confirmed that matches "may be arranged in Roubaix, Brussels and Paris."

Vandendriessche returned to Australia in September and spoke to the *Adelaide Advertiser*, confirming the French arrangements and talking up Australia's chances of success against a couple of Europe's most illustrious teams. The *Advertiser* reported that he had "witnessed the Italian and Spanish national teams in play during his visit to his homeland and considers that Australia has a fine opportunity against these nations, and that the tour should be a great success."

Vandendriessche was among 35,000 fans in Paris who saw France score first but need a goal in the final minute to salvage a 3-3 draw with Italy. Four weeks later, France again took the lead through his former CASG Paris team mate Jean Boyer, but were overrun by Spain 4-1.

Given that seven of Italy's starters against France at Stade de Colombes were subsequently included in the squad that won the bronze medal in Amsterdam in 1928, Vandendriessche's optimism about Australia's chances was a big call. Even taking into consideration that he was keen to pump up the tour, or as Lukeman put it in *The Referee* "anxious for the tour to take place", it is an extravagant claim for Australia's football. Four players each from those French and Spanish teams also went to the Amsterdam Olympiad.

Nevertheless, Vandendriessche was a football personality of considerable standing, only a few years on himself from playing at the highest levels of French and Belgian football, and the only person in the country able to use his own on-field experience to make an informed assessment of where Australian playing standards were in comparison to Europe.

Vandendriessche was clearly a networker in his commercial life and it is likely he similarly kept up contacts from his sporting world, especially as had used football links to raise money for the care of refugees and to arrange wartime matches which gave some Australian players their first experiences of playing in Europe.

His Roubaix-Tourcoing fellow debutant for France, Gabriel Hanot, became captain of France after the war but retired after being injured in an air crash. In the 1920s, he became a journalist for *L'Auto* and *Miroir des Sports*. They had both been part of the Parisian wartime football scene in which both men represented their countries.

Hanot reminded his readers in *Miroir des Sports* in 1925 that Vandendriessche was one of the best players in France at that time and informed them that he was still playing in Australia. Hanot went on to be French national coach and is generally acknowledged as the man who came up with the idea for the Ballon d'Or award for the world's best player and for a competition for Europe's champion clubs, the European Cup, now evolved into the European Champions League.

Henri Delaunay, who refereed matches Vandendriessche played in, became FIFA secretary in the 1920s and was the person who set the wheels in motion for the establishment of the World Cup. Delaunay became the driver of a European championship for national teams, proposing a competition in 1927 which was not played until 1958. The winners' trophy was the Henri Delaunay Cup. The Euros continue.

In 1916-17, Delaunay also started the Coupe Charles Simon, now known as the Coupe de France, won by Vandendriessche's CASG Paris in its second year.

The World Cup proposal was carried to fruition by Jules Rimet, yet another internationalist from the French football world who became FIFA President in 1921 and stayed in office until 1954. The World Cup came to be known as Jules Rimet Trophy. Rimet was involved in forming FIFA and became president of the French Football Federation in 1919, the year of Vandendriessche's last appearances with Coupe de France winners CASG.

Vandendriessche captained wartime Belgium when the team was under the aegis of Baron Édouard de Laveleye, the first chairman of the Belgian Football Association, president of the Belgian Olympic Committee, the man who lodged the bid for the Olympics to go to Antwerp in 1920 and FIFA's first honorary member.

Vandendriessche's first selection for France was made by André Espir, assistant to FIFA's first president Robert Guérin, and who became FIFA vice president.

His selection for Flanders was made by Henri Jooris who became Rimet's deputy as the founding vice president of the Football Federation de France when the French game was unified in 1919.

It is not possible to say with certainty what kinds of ongoing links Vandendriessche had with these figures, the men who determined the shape of the biggest competitions in international football, but these are the people - Rimet, Delaunay, Espir, Hanot, de Laveleye, de Coubertin, Jooris and others - who populated the milieu he moved in.

As a person who arranged matches during the First World War, and on behalf of Australia in the 1920s, he must have had dealings with European national officials. It seems more likely than not that he was connected to some of the most influential figures in the history of European and world football. Vandendriessche's links to the top end of the Australian game ended with the death of Ern Lukeman in 1936.

He continued to be a well known figure in the wool industry and expanded his interests from wool buyer to wool processor, establishing a processing plant near Liverpool in Sydney's south west. Although he continued to be a regular visitor to France, he settled permanently in Australia and became a naturalised citizen. He died in 1959 after a half century involvement with his adopted country.

Maurice Vandendriessche provided a direct link to the early days of the new centre of world football and the coterie of French innovators with irresistible global ideas. He brought a unique football perspective and field of knowledge to Australia and freely gave his support for the development of Australia as a team in international football.

Alas, Australia did not find a way to make the most of his unique experience

16.
THE ASIAN CHAMPIONSHIP

The Far East Games, 1913-1934

On a warm February afternoon in 1913, local club champion side Bohemian ran on to a football pitch in Manila's southern Malate district to face Hong Kong's South China. The match was the sole football fixture of a new multi sports tournament being referred to as the Far Eastern Olympics, staged to coincide with the already established Manila Carnival.

The two teams were picked to represent their respective countries, so this was in effect Philippines versus China. The home side won 2-1. Nobody made much of the event at the time, but both countries could later take pride in being the first teams ever to play an international match in Asia.

The Far Eastern Games receive very little attention these days but they should be recognised for the ground breaking achievement that they were for Asian and world football.

The Games established the first regional championship in the world outside Britain. They provided an international stage for both of the superstar Asian players of the pre-War era, Lee Wai Tong and Paulino Alcántara. They were the tournament platforms which launched three Asian teams on to the world stage, Japan and China at the 1936 Olympics, and Dutch East Indies at the World Cup in 1938.

While Australia's efforts to play on a bigger stage foundered, our major east Asian contemporaries constructed a regional response to the challenge of building international contests. After the failure of the push to go to the 1928 Olympics, Australia's international life continued without a competitive purpose. The Olympics of 1956 was the first competition to include Australia.

China, Japan, Philippines and eventually the East Indies built their own competitive grouping, an Asian championship in the form of the Far East Games.

Over 21 turbulent years, the tournament would be dogged by internal political struggles and had its existence threatened by war, but it grew to be a major event attracting big crowds to purpose built stadia.

The International Olympic Committee's honorary secretary, Frederick England, wrote in the IOC Bulletin in 1928 that the Far Eastern Championships were "recognised throughout the athletic world as second in importance only to the world's Olympic Games."

This new field of Asian sporting identity actually owed its life to a bunch of Americans who had little interest in football. These were the dedicated Protestant missionaries of the Young Men's Christian Association, who saw the development of sport and athletic ability as central to the task of promoting a robust Christian moral code. Strong men of good conscience would create a new, modern Asia dedicated to openness, democracy and Christianity.

In 1909, Elwood Brown travelled from Chicago to the U-S ruled Philippines to become the YMCA's Physical Director in Manila and soon became president of the Philippine Athletic Association. Clarence Robertson was Brown's counterpart as YMCA Physical Director in the city of Tientsin, where he initiated the first and highly successful Chinese national athletics championships.

The two men met on holiday in the United States, discussed the Chinese event, and hatched a plan to begin an Asian Olympic Games. Brown advanced the idea in trips to China and Japan and brought their YMCAs on board to form the Far Eastern Olympic Association.

In 1912, Brown issued invitations to China, Japan, Siam (Thailand), British East Indies (Malaya), and Hong Kong for a competition to take place the following year. There was plenty of interest in a range of sports, but only the Philippines and China nominated to play football.

The second tournament in 1915 was held in Shanghai and again featured only two football teams, but this time with two matches. The first ended in a bruising, goalless draw which saw both sides have a man sent off, with China edging the Philippines 1-0 in the second.

This tournament took on the flavour of a kind of football festival, a celebration of the growing popularity of the game as much as a competition for honours. The informal carnival staged after the championship decider saw China defeat Philippines 3-1, Shanghai Britons beat Nanyang 8-0, with the Shanghai side defeating China 2-0.

The third version in Tokyo in 1917 fleshed out the competition to three teams with the addition of Japan, represented by the young men of the Tokyo Higher Normal School. This step changed the way Japanese regarded international competition although their entry proved to be shaky to say the least.

China blitzed the hosts 8-0, and the Philippines managed a goal every six minutes to finish ever so slightly ahead, 15-2. This was due largely to the influence of the man leading the Filipino forward line. The Tokyo Games was the only opportunity for a broader Asian audience to see Paulino Alcántara, the biggest Asian star of the pre-War era who was a sensation at Barcelona before and after his spell leading the line for the Philippines.

Even Alcántara's presence couldn't give Philippines the title. In the match against China, the Filipino goalkeeper punched the scorer of a penalty which gave the Chinese side a 4-0 lead. A general melee ensued, the Philippine side stormed off the pitch, and the match was abandoned. China, again represented by the South China club, beat Japan 5-0 to assert its dominance.

A chastened Japan sat out the 1919 tournament in Manila, won by China 2-1 in a play off with the Philippines after each had beaten the other in the previous three days.

In 1921, the performance of the Chinese team across a range of sports was not great and fans were not at all happy with a below par result at home in Shanghai. This made the success of the football team a matter of great pride. China extended its winning run defeating Japan 4-1 and Philippines 1-0. The Filipinos' 3-0 defeat of Japan saw them finish second.

The sixth Games in Osaka in 1923 was an altogether more sophisticated event than the last time it was staged in Japan. The new Osaka City Stadium drew a cumulative 250,000 fans with football a leading attraction. Here was the proof, after a decade of contests, that the Games had become the mass sports occasion its proponents had hoped for.

Among the spectators was the sports journalist Harry Millard, who, having seen the successful side in action, became the link which established the first Chinese tour of Australia a little over two months later with much the same squad.

Millard was deeply impressed by what he had seen in Osaka, and not just by the football tournament. He began to press the case for broader Asia-Pacific contact including Australia, arguing that it would benefit sport, trade and international peace.

He kept up his campaign for 25 years, writing to the Prime Minister's office after World War II to advocate the creation of an Asia-Pacific sports festival. His view was dismissed in Canberra.

What Millard saw on the field was a confident and athletic team comfortably brushing aside its opponents. China defeated Philippines 3-0 in the opener, with the Philippines bouncing back to beat Japan 2-1. The Chinese were untroubled by Japan in the third match, winning 5-1.

Philippines finished second to China as the Games returned to Manila in 1925. Japan didn't score in their two matches, but a 2-0 loss to the winners and a 4-0 setback against the Philippines in the tournament opener were regarded as acceptable performances.

Arguments over player payments which had plagued European and Australian football during the 1920s intruded onto the Asian scene for the eighth Games in Shanghai in August 1927. Members of the Chinese side had been hurriedly called back to Shanghai from their elongated, sometimes acrimonious and financially failing tour of Australia.

Players from the Shanghai club Loh Hwa were in any case excluded because they were deemed to have received payments which contravened their amateur status. Leading Filipino players were also banned for having taken 'illegal' payments.

The politicking did not upset the Chinese procession towards yet another title. A 5-1 victory over Japan was followed by a routine 3-1 result against the Philippines. In between, the Japanese edged the Philippines 2-1 to record their first ever victory in an international match.

This was a significant milestone for Japanese football. It was held to prove the effectiveness of the studious passing which had gained the ascendancy there.

As a marker of where Australia was in relation to Asian football, it is worth noting that in three matches played the previous month against a comparable Chinese team, the team in green and gold thrashed the Chinese 6-1 in Sydney, scored freely again in a 7-4 victory in Brisbane, but were made to settle for a 1-1 draw in Newcastle as Lee Wai Tong netted yet again to earn his side a share of the spoils.

Japan's star at the tournament, Shigemaru Takenokoshi, was a disciple of the Burmese coach Kyaw Din, whose pioneering coaching in the 1920s earned him a place in Japan's Football Hall of Fame. This was Takenokoshi's second Far East championship and he would go on to captain the side in 1930.

Takenokoshi was the coach of the Japanese team at the 1936 Berlin Olympics which fought back from 2-0 down to beat Sweden 3-2 and become the first Asian team to beat a European nation in an international match.

Takenokoshi's link to Australia came 20 years later as the manager of the Japanese team at the 1956 Melbourne Olympics. In a first round match at Olympic Park, a first half penalty from the boot of Graham McMillan and a second half effort from Frank Loughran gave Australia a 2-0 victory.

In Tokyo in 1930, Takenokoshi's men brushed aside the Philippines 7-2. China, with Lee Wai Tong still leading the line, were also untroubled in beating the Philippines 5-0. The big showdown for the championship ended in a thrilling 3-3 draw.

The Japanese were happy to settle for the status of joint winners, but the Chinese were awarded the gold medal after Japan declined to play extra time. Football had now grown to be serious box office. Over 400,000 sports fans attended the Tokyo Games with football highly prominent among the attractions.

The tenth edition of the Far Eastern Games in 1934 only just managed to get to the start line after a series of political disputes looked like it would scupper the event.

Japan wanted to introduce its puppet state Manchukuo, its territory in occupied China, but the Chinese refused to consider any action which would in any way imply recognition of Japanese sovereignty over its land and rejected the proposal out of hand.

Disputes dogged these Games and it became clear this would be the last edition. The Dutch East Indies took part for the first time with a squad featuring some players who had played against Australia in 1931 and some who went on to play at the 1938 World Cup.

The venue was the just finished Rizal Memorial Stadium, built on the site of the old Carnival Grounds where the very first match had been played way back in 1913. The new dominance of American sports was evident in the opening event of the stadium, an exhibition of baseball skills by a U-S All Stars team led by Babe Ruth.

The bad mood which had preceded the start of the tournament became even darker in a brutal opening match between the home team and China. Lee Wai Tong's goal killed the contest after Tam Kong Pak's opener for a 2-0 Chinese victory.

But the extraordinary physicality shocked spectators, which included the Japanese and Dutch Indies squads in the stands. Four Chinese players were carried off injured and two Filipino players left with broken bones, one a fractured arm, the other a broken ankle.

In the second fixture two days later, the Dutch East Indies

side led 2-0 at half time and went on to overwhelm Japan 7-1. The following day, China and the Indies both missed penalties in a goalless first half before China won 2-0, and Japan recovered from their drubbing to beat Philippines 4-3.

Philippines surprised in their last game, beating East Indies 3-2, and China held on to beat Japan 4-3 to take their ninth successive Far East championship gold medal.

Crowd trouble affected basketball, baseball and boxing and committee rooms couldn't deal with the broader political questions which killed off the Far Eastern Games and the Far Eastern Athletic Association which organised it.

At the FEAA Congress, Japan insisted on the inclusion of Manchukuo but the Chinese would not yield. The FEAA collapsed and the scheduled 1938 Shanghai Games never took place.

Japan, without the old regional championship to play in, and with their scheduled Olympic tournament cancelled, started its own version in wartime Osaka in 1940 grandiosely described as a celebration of the 2,600th anniversary of the Japanese empire. Japan won, ahead of a Chinese side lacking in representative credibility, Philippines and Manchukuo.

The Far Eastern Games played a crucial role in maintaining and developing Asian international football in a competitive environment. Now that the Far Eastern Games were over, international ambitions in east Asia turned to bigger stages.

At last, Asian national teams stepped forward to meet the world at the Olympic Games and the World Cup. The Far Eastern Games had provided a springboard to reach greater heights.

17.
CRUISING THE PACIFIC
New Zealand and New Caledonia, 1933-1936

The new regime in charge of the Australian game from the early 1930s endorsed a degree of professionalism never before seen in club football. In tough times, players could earn a handy bit of cash playing against other men who were also motivated to be at the top level and good enough to be there, who trained at least twice a week and were much fitter than in days gone by. Spectators were drawn to their matches in New South Wales and Queensland.

But as for showing the public Australia was part of the biggest sporting movement in the world, forget it. Times were undoubtedly tougher, but it is also true that the new regime was utterly ineffective in advancing the national team. It was no longer the priority among the most powerful interests in the most powerful states which ranked it below the demands of their semi-professional clubs.

Since NSW and Queensland ran the national show, the rest of the country would just have to put up with it. What else could they do?

In the seasons from 1923 to 1927, Australia had played 25 times on home soil against foreign opposition, with another eight matches played by an 'Australian XI', a side we would see now as a national B team.

After 33 games in five years, the next five years passed without a solitary home fixture. The internationalists at ASFA kept the flag flying with two tours to the Dutch East Indies but domestic politics made home games the remotest of chances.

A full six years after the shambolic end to the tour of Professor Kwong's Chinese side, Australia's national team at last ran out on home soil in an international match. This was the first series under the new national regime dominated by the State Leaguers of New South Wales, which in turn was run by power brokers in the Hunter

Valley.

For all the expansive talk of world tours, Olympic participation and hobnobbing with the great powers of Britain and the emerging powers of Europe and South America, the opponents were our cousins across the Tasman, the even more isolated New Zealand. Neighbours, but ten years estranged from Australian contact.

New Zealand's international diet in the intervening decade had been a series of matches against another Chinese touring team of players largely from Shanghai in 1924, and a tour by Canada in 1927. This tour looked like a breakthrough for both countries.

It did the job of reuniting the two, but lost money at the gate and was seen as an on field disappointment. The three international matches were all won by Australia against a side whose early tour results signalled that they would not be very competitive. In the mud in Sydney, New Zealand were dismissed 5-0 by New South Wales and clobbered 7-1 by Northern Districts in Newcastle.

Only 5,000 came to Brisbane's Exhibition Grounds for the first Test, evidence of the diminished expectations of local fans. New Zealand were better than their early form suggested but they were definitely second best.

Burly centre forward George Smith drove in Roy Crowhurst's cross for the only goal of the first half, although the Kiwis almost scored first, Bill Chapman's effort cleared off the goal line by Charlie O'Connor.

There was a flurry of goals after the break - James Kershaw turned in Barton's cross to equalise, Smith put away Gorring's pass for Australia's second, Gorring himself got the third but Chapman kept New Zealand in the game. Bill Zuill palmed away Smith's header with ten minutes to go and Gorring was on hand to kill off the contest.

The verdict of the local press was that the tourists had done reasonably well but were not as good as the class of 1923.

Another sparse crowd attended the topsy-turvy second Test at the Sydney Cricket Ground, where Australia's superiority looked set to bury New Zealand. Two goals to Smith, one apiece for Bully Hughes and Alec Cameron and a Roy Crowhurst effort which went in off Alex Stenhouse put Australia 5-0 ahead at half time.

In a classic game of two halves, New Zealand's fightback brought them within a whisker of glory at 5-4 with goals from Chapman, Murray Kay, a penalty from Jim Kershaw, and a Charlie Ives goal which benefitted from a Jock Parkes deflection. Bully Hughes knocked in Crowhurst's cross to end the resistance at 6-4.

New Zealand looked more like the talented side that beat Queensland 5-1 before the first Test, but the second consecutive defeat meant the series was lost.

In the third clash, yet another sluggish start saw New Zealand go two goals down before they began to play. Bill Edwards finished off a neat move for Australia's first and Cameron fed Crowhurst for the second. Kershaw knocked in a rebound to get New Zealand on the board, then scored from the penalty spot after being upended by Evans. A George Smith header put Australia in front and his solo effort ended the scoring.

There was no doubt the Australians were the better side. Local commentators concluded that Australia's standards had risen when measured against New Zealand sides ten years apart, with some taking the view that Australia's greater exposure to international opposition, particularly to the English players of 1925, had enhanced their education.

In tough economic times the loss of £550 on the tour was a significant setback. As public interest waned, ground admission prices dropped, but evidently without much response from the sporting public.

Australian officials asked the New Zealanders to cough up money to help meet the shortfall since, they argued, this was brought about by the Kiwis' poor performances. There were also complaints that team manager and sole selector Harry Godber, in his desire to give young talent a chance, had not picked the best players available.

In his tour report, Godber conceded that the squad had "passengers", but attributed the weakness of the tour to economic conditions, playing tough games early in the schedule and inadequate publicity. It was a sour note to end a series which had at least been friendly and sporting. In any case, plans lapsed for a reciprocal tour to New Zealand in 1934.

During the year, the usual grand names were dropped by officials said to be pursuing an ambitious international agenda. France, Italy, Spain and others were said to be engaged in correspondence with ASFA Secretary Roy Druery who said these options were being investigated not because they warranted attention on their merits, but because of the apparent reluctance of English, Scottish and Welsh associations in responding to Australian requests.

The president of the NSW State League, Tom Crawford, was invited to speak at the opening of a new grandstand at Clyde Oval when New Zealand played Granville. His comments, reported in the *Cumberland Argus*, present a good snapshot of the international football thinking of the times.

On the obsession with England, he observed that there was a public desire to beat England at cricket and rugby league. "It doesn't matter what the scores are, the people turn up and cheer. But I am sorry to say that, outside those two spheres of sport, if the visitors are not better than the home team, the people stay away."

Certainly there was a balance to be struck between cost and competitiveness, but Crawford's comments were surely in any case at odds with the facts. A look at attendance figures for international matches in the 1920s shows they were invariably the best drawing events of the season. Crowds may not have always been as big as organisers wanted, but the notion that "people stay away" was at best dubious.

The first away tour following the conclusion of the political battles which had torn the game apart was to New Caledonia. Some of the State Leaguers who had denounced football tourists to the Dutch East Indies as "Java Jaunters", vacationing players in a place where we could surely learn nothing, were now portraying a trip to Noumea as a step forward.

The formula for the 13-man squad was seven players from New South Wales and two each from Victoria, Queensland and South Australia. The squad was strong and captained by St George's bullocking centre forward George Smith.

There was little knowledge in Australia about how good the opposition might be but, whatever the challenge, the Australians were confident they would be superior. Star half back Jim Osborne told me in an interview in 1997 that the players approached the trip as an end of season holiday rather than a genuine sporting battle.

There were three matches arranged against a New Caledonia selection although a fourth benefit match also took place. The Australians led 1-0 at half time in the first clash but had to rely on a late header by skipper Bert Murray from Hec Gorring's corner for a 2-1 win.

The other matches were much easier, yielding victories of 4-2, 7-3 and 5-0. Smith netted hat-tricks in the last two internationals, goalkeeper Jimmy McNabb was praised by the locals, and the midfield combinations of Alec Cameron, Jim Osborne and Roy Crowhurst also drew favourable reviews.

New Caledonia's first football was played in 1910 and the first football clubs started the following year. A handful of the early pioneers in French Polynesia had some experience in the football of France. The founder in 1930 of the club Olympique, Numa Daly, was on the books of Olympique Marseille in the 1920s. The current national stadium of New Caledonia is the Stade Numa Daly.

Bert Murray and Charlie O'Connor both had letters published in the Australian press giving accounts of the tour. They remark on the impressive hospitality of their hosts and the enthusiastic response of crowds attending the matches.

Murray wrote in the *Brisbane Telegraph* that the big roll up for the first match against New Caledonia meant organisers ran out of tickets but fans were allowed entry so long as they had paid. He claimed the secretary of the New Caledonian Association told him more than one third of the population of Nouméa had paid for admission.

He described the New Caledonians as "very speedy and exceptionally fast on the ball". He went on "They don't do very much dribbling but take the ball first time from any angle and swing it about quite a lot, sometimes right from one wing to another. They also play very hard but clean football , and as a result quite a few of our chaps have been knocked about a bit. Their two wingers and goalkeeper were very good players, and their left back if he had a little more pace would hold his own in any team in Australia."

Murray thought their general standard was about the same as the New Zealanders they had played earlier in the season, although they played a much different style. In three matches against the Kiwis in Sydney and Brisbane, Australia won by scores of 4-2, 6-4 and 4-2 with a similar team line-up to the New Caledonian games, Smith blasting home seven goals.

O'Connor wasn't impressed by the first Nouméa club players they encountered, an amalgam of two teams the tourists hammered 8-1. He thought they had "very little knowledge of the finer points of the game, a kick and rush was their only means of attack."

He was also less complimentary of the fairness of the opposing players and the standard of officiating, at least in the first and closely fought match against the New Caledonian selection which he described as "a rough 'un", in which the bumping of players not in possession of the ball was a common occurrence passed over by the referee.

The second last match of the tour was against the club side Impassible, who were awarded the trophy as the first New Caledonia champions just before the kick off. George Smith scored inside two minutes but Henri Payan, one of the two wingers to have made an impression on Bert Murray, equalised shortly afterwards. Smith got a second just before half time and the tourists cantered to a 6-1 victory after the break.

Nobody in Australia read any particular significance into the South Pacific sojourn, but there was some speculation in the

Sydney based French language newspaper *Le Courrier Australien* about what kind of football may lie ahead. The paper ran a story by its Nouméa correspondent Raymond Legran about a *Championnat du Pacifique* to be contested by Australia, New Caledonia, China and Dutch East Indies with games likely to be played in Sydney.

Alas, the Oceania Nations Cup was still forty years away.

If 1933 showed that Australia had moved ahead of New Zealand in playing standards, the 1936 tour left no doubt that a chasm now separated the two countries. Australia won all 12 matches on their New Zealand tour, including three full internationals, frequently by huge scores.

The magnitude of the Australian triumphs prompted manager Sid Storey, unembarrassed by his own isolation from world developments, to opine that Australia could compete with any non-British country while New Zealanders wondered what they would have to do to catch up.

In the early tour matches, Australia had not been troubled by provincial opposition, beating Auckland 5-2, Wellington 9-1, Canterbury 7-1 and Otago 5-2. In the starting eleven for the first international at Dunedin's Logan Park, only Bill Chapman remained in the New Zealand side from the clashes of 1933, while Australia had five still in the squad.

New Zealand scored first through a John Skinner penalty, but after that had little in the way of goal opportunities. Within a few minutes, Billy Price knocked in Alec Forrest's corner and Alec Cameron netted from close range. George Smith finished off a move which brought the ball the length of the field and the Australians went to the break 3-1 up.

To be fair, New Zealand were considerably hampered by injuries. John Hatchard left the field with a leg problem while centre forward Andrew Leslie was carried off with a damaged ankle. Leslie returned for the second half but was obviously restricted. Price got a second and Smith completed a second half hat-trick to finish with four in a final score of 7-1 in favour of Australia.

A training run 9-0 outing against Westland in Graymouth led to the Basin Reserve Wellington and the second Test.

Australia were unchanged except for left winger Donaldson replacing Forrest, while New Zealand brought in nine new faces in a bid to stop the rot. It didn't work and the Kiwis went down 10-0, a debacle which was New Zealand's heaviest defeat in a full international match.

Once again, the home side were unlucky with injuries. Half back Archie McQuarrie went off with an eye problem, while Ossie Cleal and Stan Cawtheray continued though limited by their knocks. Nevertheless, as the NZ Press Agency reported, the team was "never happy against the speed and brilliance of the Australian attack."

A couple from Smith and one each to Price, Cameron and Donaldson had Australia five goals to the good by half time. Another from Cameron and a 25-metre blast from Smith stretched the lead to seven within eight minutes of the restart.

Australia took to showboating to entertain the crowd, or, as the *Evening News* had it, "they employed their remarkable dexterity of ball control to great advantage which they did not appear to be trying to cap with scores." It was that bad.

In the final minutes, Smith got two more to bring his personal tally to five, and Price picked his way past a couple of defenders to bring up double figures.

Australia knocked in another hatful in a 9-3 demolition of Taranaki before the final Test at Blandford Park in Auckland. New Zealand's eight changes included the recall of two players from the first clash, whose result now didn't seem so bad after all.

Rain made the pitch heavy and further discouraged demoralised local fans with only around two thousand prepared to show up. Those who braved the constant rain saw a much improved New Zealand side, still in the contest 1-1 at half time, drift away to lose 4-1 to a fitter and better organised Australia. Outclassed, certainly, but at least this time Australia had to overcome some genuine Kiwi pride and fighting defiance.

Cameron scored first when he latched on to keeper Alf Smith's parry of a cross, and New Zealand equalised when full back Reg Haggett blasted a ball from the half way line which dipped under Jimmy McNabb's crossbar.

Donaldson crossed for Price to score, Cameron emerged from a goalmouth scramble to get another, and Price converted a left wing cross to bring up the 4-1 final score.

Later matches saw the defeats of South Auckland 13-1 and Wanganui 9-1. The Australians amused themselves in the final match pursuing the 13 goals required to bring up a tally of 100 for the tour. They made it, beating Wairarapa in Masterton 13-2. New Zealand's utter humiliation was complete.

The *Evening Post* noted "their visit has again demonstrated that the standard of play on this side of the Tasman has a long leeway to make up before our players can hope even to stretch the Australians. The display of the tourists has revealed the naked truth in regard to our soccer, and that is that the finer points of the game are entirely lacking from the code in New Zealand."

The writer went on to lament the absence of basic skills of positional play and passing. "Two distinct and often debated styles of soccer were seen. New Zealand played a kick and rush game from back to front. Australia played a dashing game which was as outstandingly cohesive and smooth working as their opponents' was rugged and vigorous. There is no gainsaying which of the two has the greater appeal and will achieve the greatest following for the game."

The New Zealanders were probably the first to praise the sophistication of Australian football. George Campbell, star and captain of the early 1920s New Zealand teams which had been so successful against Australia, told Australia's manager Sid Storey the Australians had developed amazingly and that their style now reminded him of the Scottish game. That is, a style built on speed and passing.

In an interview with the *New Zealand Herald*, Storey was diplomatic about the skills of the hosts but advised that "kick and rush" must be eradicated. "The greatest weakness was in passing the ball, the players not taking sufficient care that their passes reached their objective."

He attributed Australia's higher level to two factors - fitness and international experience. He explained that Australian teams trained twice a week and that it was a point of personal honour to come on to the field fit and prepared for ninety minutes of the hardest play. We even played with three available match balls so that there was no respite from action even when the ball went out for a throw in.

Australia's playing style required men of a high level of fitness so that "if he tackled and failed he could whip around and try again, and if he failed then come back a third time. Inside forwards had to come back and help to bring the ball upfield ... the wing halves had to go after the ball on all occasions as if they were facing an opponent. This style of play required every man should be in perfect condition."

The lack of this kind of mobility and preparedness to cover team mates, especially in defence, was pinpointed by England tour manager John Lewis as a major deficiency of the Australian game in 1925. Here was as a specific example of tactical improvement born of exposure to a higher level touring team.

Storey was adamant that exposure to international football had been crucial to Australia's growth. "... our game in Australia has been vastly improved in recent years by matches with overseas teams ... Since 1922 we have played eight foreign countries ... The English team gave Australia a great lesson in the game, but our standard has also been improved by contact with the other teams. Australia feels now that we could pit our strength against any soccer playing country in the world outside the British Isles. "

"Even against an English team we would not be disgraced for in 1925 we played good football against the English professional side, and since then our standard has improved out of recognition."

Storey knew international experience was the key to Australia's top level development and had played his part in arranging tours in the 1920s. But he was now part of an administration more effective in beating its chest about how good it was rather than actually delivering fixtures to test that view on the field.

While Storey's confidence and optimism were admirable, he appears to have had little idea about how much the rest of the world had also improved in the past decade. His comments were on the newsstands two weeks before the start of the Olympic football tournament in Berlin, a real test of standards for the football countries of the world which proved to be an eye opener for the Great Britain delegation.

Australia was not there and would not be part of the World Cup to follow. Australia may well have been competitive with at least second tier nations at this time. Lack of affiliation with Australia's Olympic administration, as well as the unresolved questions over amateurism, made participation in an Olympiad impossible. Cultural loyalty to the Football Association over FIFA took away any chance of going to the World Cup.

Some international lessons had yet to be learned.

18.
ASIA IN BERLIN

China and Japan at the 1936 Olympics

The Olympic Games of 1936 was the first global football tournament with an Asian presence. Japan and China, at war with each other at home, provided the double bill of Asian players to be measured against the mighty powers of the world game.

Both emerged proud of their achievements.

Japan recorded the first victory of an Asian national team over one from Europe when they defeated Sweden, and China gave the Great Britain side a terrible fright before succumbing 2-0. China's real achievement was completing football's first world tour either side of that match, a sprawling 40 match odyssey across Asia and Europe.

Political enmity between China and Japan had brought to an end 20 years of contests at the Far Eastern Games, the last of them taking place in May 1934, a tournament held at the same time as the World Cup in Italy. The Far Eastern Games expressed a regional football culture. Berlin was the step up to a global consciousness. There would be no looking back.

The status of football at the Olympics had been under pressure since the 1920s over rules on amateurism and the rapid growth of professionalism. The arrival of the World Cup in 1930 meant there was now a new pinnacle for football.

The Los Angeles Games of 1932 did not include a football tournament at all, mainly reflecting the amateurism disputes, but German Olympic organisers were very keen to bring football back. The game may not have been regarded as a necessary drawcard for sports fans in California, but the committee in Berlin knew a good competition would generate plenty of revenue at the turnstiles. Football accounted for a third of the Olympic gate money at Amsterdam.

There was confidence too that Germany would be competitive. In ten years under coach Otto Nerz, Germany progressed from a European also ran to up and coming star with medal ambitions. Nerz was also a dyed in the wool Nazi who talked up the team's chances with his Party associates.

In 1936, the founder of the modern Olympics, Baron Pierre de Coubertin, was being considered for the Nobel Peace Prize yet Adolf Hitler got to declare the Games open. Such was the optimism of the German football elite that they invited Hitler to Germany's first round clash with Norway, along with Hermann Göring and Heinrich Himmler. The Norwegians rose to the challenge and beat a disappointing Germany 2-0. Hitler left before full time and never went to another match in his life.

It was the end for Nerz who was replaced by Sepp Herberger, a hero of post-war German football as coach of the side which went on to win the 1954 World Cup in the "miracle of Bern."

Japanese football was very bookish, with new imported coaching manuals attracting the attention of clubs in the absence of much direct evidence of new trends on the pitch. Nerz's book "*Fussball*" was translated by Yukichi Yamada in the late 1920s and used as a guiding light for his Keio Soccer Club.

German passing football ideas, themselves with roots in the Scottish game, were much in vogue in Japan at this time and were deployed by the University of Tokyo and Waseda University sides which supplied most of the players in the Japanese squad. Nerz's philosophy also emphasised intensive physical preparation. This also became part of the Japanese approach.

It took the Japanese team two weeks to travel to Berlin on the Trans-Siberian railway, but the squad arrived well before the competition was due to begin. Finding the money for the trip was a serious issue, with fund raising activities going as far as selling commemorative tea towels. Pharmaceuticals magnate Gohei Tanabe, already a benefactor of Japanese football, made a substantial donation to get the team on the road.

Japan's first opponent was Sweden, a team which believed itself to be in the running for a medal. The plan of Waseda Uni based coach Shigeyoshi Suzuki was to stack the midfield with as many as six players, with only one full time defender sweeping up behind them.

At Hertha Berlin's inner city Stadion am Gesundbrunnen, the Swedes were comfortable in moving to a 2-0 half time lead, AIK Stockholm centre forward Erik Persson netting both goals. Suzuki's response after the break was to commit more men forward.

Shogo Kamo pulled a goal back four minutes into the second half and Tokutaro Ukon equalised in the 62nd minute. The Swedes flagged and the physically strong Japanese surged. With five minutes to go, Tokyo University forward Akira Matsunaga torpedoed Swedish hopes with a third goal.

Sven Jerring, who became a legendary figure in Swedish broadcasting in a career spanning over fifty years as a sports journalist, called the match live on Swedish radio. His disbelieving voice delivered a famous commentary to his audience at home. *Japaner!, Japaner!, Japaner!* (Japanese, Japanese, Japanese) was all he could get out at one stage to describe the still running, still swarming opponents.

The energetic Japanese were brought back down to earth in the second round. Vittorio Pozzo, coach of the Italian side which had won the World Cup, put out a vastly more experienced selection which demolished Japan 8-0.

They were held to a 2-0 half time lead but Japan's resistance collapsed to concede five goals in the last quarter of an hour of the match. Pisa forward Carlo Biagi scored four and L'Aquila front man Annibale Frossi got a hat trick before Giulio Cappelli finished the scoring in the final minute.

The Italians went on to win the gold medal. It was steep learning curve for Japan, but this pioneering team had won many admirers. The Japanese announced an intention to compete in the 1938 World Cup and at the 1940 Olympics which were scheduled for Tokyo. Surely the Japanese would do even better there? War, of course, ended those dreams along with millions of others. Match winning goalscorer Matsunaga died in military action at the Battle of Guadalcanal in 1943.

The Chinese team was allocated only a modest budget for the Olympics but they reached their goal with a radical plan to raise money and popular support for their campaign. Asia's best team, the country which had done more than any other to promote the cause of football across the continent, adopted a typically adventurous plan to make their dream a reality.

China considered any player of Chinese origin to be a candidate for Berlin, not just residents of the Republic. Among the 22 to make the final cut were four players who had played representative football in other countries.

Chua Boon Lay was regarded as Singapore's finest player and had played for Singapore in the Malaya Cup. The first national team he ever faced was Australia when he took his place in the Singapore side which defeated the tourists 4-2 in front of ecstatic fans jam packed into the Anson Road Stadium in 1928.

Tay Kwee Liang, another Singaporean playing as a forward for Hong Kong's South China club, was also in the squad. Chan Chen Wo, born in Java and also playing club football in Hong Kong, made the team too.

Tio Han Goan was another notable selection who had never played club football outside the Dutch East Indies. A forward with the ethnic Chinese club Tionghoa of Surabaya, he scored a hat trick for the Indies in a 7-1 thumping of Japan at the 1934 Far Eastern Games in Manila and had even played against China at the same tournament.

Forward Yik Yeung was also in the squad as one of 13 South China players. He came to Australia in 1941 as a winger with the Eastern club of Hong Kong and stayed, settling in Sydney. He joined a Leichhardt-Annandale side at Lambert Park which included international full back Jack Evans and the future Australian goalkeeper Norman Conquest.

After eight matches in China, the Chinese group left for a tour which took in 27 matches over two months in Vietnam, Singapore, Java, Sumatra, Malaya, Burma and India. They won 23 and drew four. There were de facto internationals with Vietnam, Burma and India.

The Chinese aimed to rouse the Chinese diaspora of south east Asia, earn money through a share of gate takings, and hone the skills of the team on its long trip to Germany. This worked well until they reached Europe when the matches ground to a halt in the weeks before the big game at Mommsenstadion.

The tour became a legend in China. In 2004, theatre director and writer Anthony Chan's fictionalised drama *Field of Dreams*, a musical based on the tour, had its highly successful debut season on the Hong Kong stage. It has since enjoyed several revivals and has itself been on tour to Beijing.

Japan's defeat of Sweden the day before was the hot football news when China took the field against Great Britain, who were making their first appearance at the Olympics since 1920. Though there was a world of difference between professional and amateur players in 1930s Britain, the squad was still believed to be competitive and was skippered by Bernard Joy, who had played in a full international alongside ten professionals earlier in the year.

Perfunctory preparation is usually cited in British accounts to explain why the team struggled to overcome China but the vigorous Chinese held their own in the opening stanza and went to the dressing room still confident and 0-0 at half time.

The British pulled ahead through Scotsman Mac Dodds ten minutes into the second half, and Lester Finch got a second ten minutes later. The Chinese, themselves without recent match practice, and used to the half hour each way form of much Asian football, could not find the resources for a late fightback. Their Olympic dream was over.

The Chinese tour crammed as much experience as possible into the space around the Olympics. It was the kind of tour Australian dreamers like Ern Lukeman had imagined they could build if they were able to secure a berth at the Olympics in 1928. Perhaps Lee

Wai Tong discussed the Australian plan while on tour in 1927.

Over the course of just 19 days, China played a further nine matches in six countries. They beat mid table Swiss side Servette 3-2 in Geneva and drew 2-2 with the French top flight's Red Star in Paris. All other games were lost, the biggest, an 11-0 drubbing by Austrian champions Admira playing a pass and move brand of football Lee marvelled at when interviewed by the Hong Kong press on his return home.

The *China Mail* reported that Lee himself was offered a contract by Red Star Paris and quoted him on a link to Arsenal after playing at Highbury. "George Allison, the Arsenal manager, told me after our game against the Casuals that he would have signed me on as a professional had I been 22 years of age, but at 32, I was a veteran."

The standard of play at Berlin was still held to be pretty high despite the fact that after 1930 the Olympics was no longer the top table for international football. For those enjoying a rare excursion to the delights of world football, whether Japanese, Chinese, or for that matter, British, the forum was a skills and tactics eye opener.

The British delegation was led by Stanley Rous and Charles Wreford-Brown. Rous would in time become the head of FIFA and would try to reconcile Australia with world game rules when the transfer dispute which led to Australia's exclusion from international contact reached its high point in the late 1950s. Wreford-Brown was a classic Victorian sporting gentleman who would lead the second English tour to Australia in 1937.

They could see with their own eyes that British methods had fallen behind, and said so in a report back to London. "It was the view of all, or at any rate the majority of members of the official party that our style of play in some respects does not compare favourably with that adopted by some of the other national teams - Austria, Norway, Poland etc. The W-formation meets with scant favour by the majority of national teams, and generally speaking the old methods which have for their object attack more than defence proved more effective and certainly much more interesting to watch. "

"There is some reason to believe that our own professional teams will this season be reverting to the type of football which obtained for so long a period and was only changed because it was thought to meet the situation created by the alteration in the offside rule. If this is so, an improvement in the results of our international games may follow."

They saw that the prevailing English football ideas had become rather old fashioned and that the rest of the world was developing its own ways, not only in tactics, but also in training, and indeed in creating sporting relationships with each other through FIFA and through tournaments.

For the Chinese, the W-M "third back" system had never been adopted and was regarded by them as still being new. Lee Wai Tong did not think it suitable for his squad, and would not become suitable until the players were a lot fitter. On his return home, he told the *Hong Kong Telegraph* that they would need to develop stamina in order to be able to adopt any of the new British and European ideas they had encountered.

"If for example we wanted to play the third back game it means we must have a half back line so physically powerful that our wing halves can stand the pace of playing both in the attack and defence."

The great "whirl" of Willy Meisl was the epitome of the high technique middle European style which made Austria's football so sophisticated. It was the football which had taken Austria to the Olympic final and which pervaded not only the Admira team which overwhelmed China, but also Mitropa Cup holders Rapid Vienna who also defeated China 4-2.

Admira and Austria Vienna supplied nine of the eleven players for their national team when Austria defeated England's Arsenal dominated side 2-1 just two months before they met China.

As the Australian scene lost its way down blind alleys and became increasingly isolated, its contemporaries in Asia had found ways to navigate a course to international significance and a genuine engagement with football's higher levels. Their European trips had been a thrilling education.

Over five years in the mid 1930s, the top end of Asian football progressed from the regional platform of the Far Eastern Games in Manila, stepped up to the Olympic stage in Berlin, and now contemplated the World Cup in Paris.

Elite Asian football had joined the world mainstream and left Australia in its wake.

19.
JAPANESE GLORY, KOREAN SHADOWS

The Tangled Emergence of Japan and Korea

Japan's epic victory over Sweden at the 1936 Olympics in Berlin was one of the great high points of Asia's football development.

Sweden led 2-0 before being run over by a relentless, super-fit Japanese team whose determination earned a famous victory which ended any illusion that European sides were somehow inherently superior.

This first Japanese team to step into the limelight contained a Korean star in the person of Kim Young-Sik, a player unable to represent his own country because of its colonial domination by Japan. When Korea finally emerged in its own right after World War II, it would become Asia's most successful 20th century power.

Six years before the Berlin moment, the Japanese made a serious push for success at the Far East Games in Tokyo, a tournament which had only delivered one win to the Japanese, a 2-1 victory over the Philippines in Shanghai. They united behind a kind of mission statement by manager Shigeyoshi Suzuki and captain Shigemaru Takenokoshi.

The statement began "First surpass our opponents in terms of work rate and then beat them with organised play". Japan managed only a draw with China in Shanghai, not bad given China's routine successes at the Games, but the team's effort in putting meat on the bones of its declaration overwhelmed the Swedes.

From the start, Japan placed a high premium on ideas and learning. Japan's football development drew strongly on its education system where football took root in a handful of schools and universities in the first years of the 20th century. Chief among them was the Tokyo Normal High School, which started contact with other schools.

When Japan finally ventured onto the international stage at the

1917 Far East Games, the country was represented by the school. They were hammered 5-0 by China and a whopping 15-2 by a Filipino side dominated by Barcelona goalscoring phenomenon Paulino Alcántara.

The big losses were a reality check for the Japanese but they were setbacks which boosted Japanese ambitions to improve and take their place at the forefront of Asian football, just as they aspired to be the region's pre-eminent developed nation.

Japan didn't take part in the next edition of the Games in Manila in 1919 but it was still an important year. The F.A. in London gave the Japanese a silver cup to be awarded to "the winning team of the Japanese championship." Trouble was, there was no real national championship nor a national football body to organise one.

The gift of the cup stimulated moves to establish what we now know as the Japanese Football Association in 1921. The trophy came to be known as the Emperor's Cup, and the competition to win it is to this day a high prestige part of Japan's sporting calendar.

The link to the F.A. came through the football fan British diplomat William Haigh, who had not only seen competitions between Tokyo and Yokohama teams, he had seen a chance to enhance relations between two countries about to exchange visits from each other's royal families, Crown Prince Hirohito and the Prince of Wales.

Australia had been making cap in hand submissions to London for almost forty years by this time but had not achieved this kind of encouragement.

The end of the First World War and the continuing Russian civil war following the Bolshevik revolution led to other brushes with European football. German prisoners of war, in Japan after the seizure of German territories on the Chinese coast and the northern Pacific, played in Hiroshima.

Czech soldiers who were prisoners of war in Russia or isolated by military action went home by travelling through Siberia to Japan and then the United States. The Japanese were interested to see the methods of the central Europeans, different to most of the English football they had been taught. One of these soldiers was Zdislav Práger, who, a few years later, would be the manager of the Vršovice team which came to be known as Bohemians Prague on their 1927 tour of Australia.

With higher education playing such an important role in the life of football, it's not surprising that learning from books played such an unusually prominent role in taking the game forward. The Burmese student Kyaw Din, who had been brought up on a playing diet of Scottish short passing, arrived to study in Tokyo in 1922. He wrote a text book on football tactics which was in high demand after he assumed coaching duties at Waseda High School.

In May 1923, Japan hosted the Far East Games in Osaka, where journalist Harry Millard saw an athletic festival which greatly influenced his future thinking, and where the Chinese side again dominated its opponents at football.

Four months later, the Great Kanto Earthquake devastated eastern Honshu, including Tokyo. The quake killed William Haigh and forced Kyaw Din to leave for Kobe where his authority rose as the city's team rose to new heights under his direction. The team that won Japan's first match, the 2-1 victory over the Philippines, was mostly drawn from the pool of players brought on under Kyaw Din's direction. Both Haigh and Kyaw Din were later inducted into Japanese football's Hall of Fame.

Inter-collegiate games, high school contests and the Emperor's Cup drove the domestic game during the 1920s with the Far East Games offering a chance to measure performance levels against China and the Philippines. But as the decade drew to a close, the Japanese started to think more ambitiously.

The Japanese contingent at the 1928 Amsterdam Olympics did not include a football team, but the head of the delegation, Yozuru Noza, was asked to contact FIFA to apply for membership. Japan felt confident enough to have a go at the Olympic stage. The absence of football on the Los Angeles sporting program for 1932 meant 1936 would be the date of their debut.

Japan's domestic scene increasingly incorporated players and teams from territories occupied or claimed by Japan, such as Taiwan, Shandong and Kwantung on the Chinese coast, the Manchukuo puppet state in Manchuria, and Korea, annexed by Japan in 1910. Trial matches for the Olympics included players from all the territories of the Empire.

Most prominent of those were the Koreans, who were making an ever bigger impact on Japanese football. In 1935, Seoul Shukyu-dan beat Tokyo Bunri University 6-1 to win the Emperor's Cup, and become champions of Japan.

The following year, another Seoul based team, Poseung College, went down 3-2 to Keio University in the final, and in 1937 reached the semi finals only to be edged out by Kobe University. 1938 saw a third Seoul side, Yonhi College, reach the semi finals and draw 2-2 with Waseda University. The drawing of lots saw Waseda advance to the final and beat Keio 4-1.

Korean football fans believed their players would feature strongly in the Japanese squad for the Berlin Olympics, but in the end only Kim Yong-Sik made the cut. After Berlin, and with ambitions to make a serious impact at the Olympiad of 1940 due to take place in Tokyo, more Korean players were taken in to the national squad.

Japan confected "international" competitions between 1939 and 1942 featuring its colonial client states in China, Philippines, Manchuria, Mongolia and Korea. Japan won all these matches except one, the very last match of a Japanese state about to change forever. In August 1942, Japan played a Korean selection in Busan and was comprehensively thumped 5-0.

In the broad sweep of international football since World War II, we can now see that Korea was Asia's most successful nation. But to track the development of Korean football in the first half of the twentieth century, it is necessary to disentangle the Korean story from that of Japan..

South Korea qualified for the World Cup in 1954, then every tournament from 1986 onwards. They finished fourth in the World

Cup they co-hosted with Japan in 2002. They got through to the Olympics, winning the bronze medal in 2012. They have won the Asian Cup twice and been losing finalists four times, including a 2-1 extra time loss to Australia in a heart stopping final in front of a packed Olympic Stadium in Sydney in 2015.

Then, of course, there is North Korea. Two appearances at the World Cup finals and always remembered for the first, in England in 1966, when they beat Italy 1-0 and had Portugal on the ropes 3-0 before Eusebio led a classic fightback to win their quarter final clash 5-3.

In a qualifying tournament boycotted by almost all of Asia and Africa, North Korea had to beat Australia to get to the finals. This task they achieved with ease, brushing aside the Australians 6-1 and 3-1 in two matches at Cambodia's National Stadium in Phnom Penh. Seven of Korea's starters in the famous Goodison Park clash with Portugal played against Australia.

In the next two World Cups, the long trail of colonial era Korea's football culture also touched Australia.

Football was only played by a handful of schools in Korea in the early part of the century but became a much bigger affair from the 1920s. Intercity clashes between Pyongyang and Seoul were fiercely contested and seen by ever bigger crowds. Regional rivalries built, there was substantial support from media companies, and national championships began.

But Japan's annexation of Korea in 1910 meant the development of football was ultimately under Japanese control, and Korean football talent was also annexed by Japan. Nevertheless, Korean teams always found ways to set up contests with Japanese teams, and wins over the Japanese were celebrated like no other. In the 1930s, Korea based teams did increasingly well in Japanese competitions.

In 1935, Gyungsung F.C. won Japan's top trophy, the Emperor's Cup, hammering Nagoya Commercial College 6-0 in the semi final and Tokyo Bunri University 6-1 in the final. They went on to win the All Korea championship in 1936 and 1937.

Half back Kim Yong-sik was the star of Gyungsung's show. His domination of the Emperor's Cup led to a call up for the Japanese squad for the 1936 Olympic Games in Berlin. This was the start of a seven year spell representing not the country of his birth, but the country which was preventing him from doing so.

Korean fans were at the same time proud to see their countrymen reaching new heights and resentful of their suppression in football, as in all things, by their colonial masters. It was demeaning to play in Japanese colours, but there were also protests that only two Korean players were considered for the Olympics despite the ascendancy of Korean players and teams at that time.

Kim Yong-sik played in both of Japan's matches at the Berlin Games. The first was the historic victory over Sweden when Japan came back from 2-0 down to win 3-2, and the second, an 8-0 hammering by Italy.

Japanese football now felt confident that it could field a competitive team on the world stage. Kim Yong-sik had been central to the team's success and eyes now turned increasingly to Korean talent with a view to making a serious splash at home in Tokyo at the 1940 Olympics.

The formal outbreak of war between Japan and China in 1937 cancelled Japan's World Cup application and eliminated any chance of a Japanese Olympiad. Japan still ploughed on with other football tournaments with a strong Korean flavour.

The Three Nations Games featured Japan, a China side not picked by China, and Manchuria, or Manchukuo. Japan won easily. Taking a cue from the legend that the Japanese Empire began in 660 B.C., Japan organised a competition in the Meiji Shrine Athletic Grounds in Tokyo celebrating the supposed 2600th anniversary of its foundation. The other teams were the puppet state of Manchuria, a Republic of China side the republic again played no role in selecting, and the Philippines.

Japan won all three of its matches with Koreans KimYong-sik, Lee Hoo-Hyung, Kim Song-An, Kim Hee-Soo, Kim Incheol and Min Byung-Dae in their lineups. Kim Hee Soo netted twice in a 7-0 romp against Manchuria and Kim Song-An scored in a 6-0 thumping of China.

In 1942, another dubious tournament, the Manchukuo Founding Anniversary competition took place in Xinjing. Yet another tricked up China team lost 6-1, Japan defeated a Manchuria side 3-1 which had its own contingent of Korean players, and Mongolia were on the end of a 12-0 bashing.

Kim Yong-Sik was recruited by Japan's Waseda University in 1937 but returned to Korea in 1938 to work as a reporter for the Dong-a Ilbo newspaper, one of the media outlets which was also a big sponsor of Korean football. He played for Boseong All-Stars before switching to Pyongyang in 1940.

After the 1942 tournament, there was no longer even a pretence of international football as the war situation became more intense. Football diehards immediately set about reconstructing the game after the liberation of Korea and, for the first time, a team representing the country was finally able to take its place at the 1948 Olympics in London.

Kim Yong-Sik, hero of Korean football, led his side on to the Champion Hill ground at Dulwich in south London along with another Korean former Japanese international Min Byung-Dae. Korea beat Mexico 5-3. Three days later at Selhurst Park, the Koreans were mown down by a Swedish side featuring Gunnar Gren, Gunnar Nordahl and Nils Liedholm who got seven goals between them in a 12-0 hiding.

Sweden went on to beat Yugoslavia 3-1 at Wembley to win the gold medal, and in the years to follow, the Gre-No-Li forward line found its way to A.C. Milan, Scudetto success and a well remunerated domination of Serie A defenders.

Kim Yong-Sik was the first head coach of a South Korean team at the Word Cup in Switzerland in 1954 where Min Byung-Dae was the captain. The Koreans were well out of their depth in going down 9-0 to a Ferenc Puskas led Hungarian wonder team, and were further walloped 7-0 by Turkey.

Kim and Min, these two veterans of the period of co-option by the Japanese, eventually had a brush with the Australian football world through other World Cup campaigns. Australia finished ahead of South Korea and Japan in a World Cup qualifying tournament in Seoul in 1969 with Kim Yong-Sik sitting on the coach's bench for the Koreans.

When Jimmy Mackay's blistering long range drive in Hong Kong settled a three match play-off struggle with South Korea to earn Australia a place at the 1974 World Cup, Rale Rasic punched the air. The glum figure on the opposite bench was Min Byung-Dae.

20.
THE ENGLISH ROLLERCOASTER

The Death of the English Tour Dream, 1934-1938

The Australia - England football relationship lurched clumsily through the storms of the 1930s and showed what the nationalists in sport and politics to Australia's north already knew. Colonial arrangements from a previous century were anachronisms that had to go.

The settlement of the soccer wars in 1932 meant there could once again be a united approach to finding a path forward for the national team, and as ever in the Australian mind, that meant a renewed push for contact with Britain in the form of an Australian tour to the old country.

The Football Association sent a message welcoming the outbreak of peace in Australia and made a gift of £500, a sum originally requested by Ern Lukeman as a loan. The settlement was the point at which Lukeman left the stage with Roy Druery taking on his international duties.

After the interstate series of 1932, Lukeman repeated his familiar call for Australia to embark on a world tour, or at least an extensive tour focused on Britain and continental Europe. By 1934, it looked like this might finally happen.

Australia's Steven Slack told the 1934 annual meeting of the Australian Soccer Football Association that he had conferred with F.A. Secretary Sir Frederick Wall while in London. Sir Frederick told him that the prospect of an English or Scottish tour of Australia was remote but that the chances of an Australian trip to Britain in 1935 were brighter. Slack said Sir Frederick himself suggested a seven week tour.

Other countries would also be included in the tour and to that end contacts had been made with South Africa, Canada, USA, Dutch East Indies, Italy, Switzerland, Hungary, Austria, Czechoslovakia, Belgium, France, Germany, Spain and Portugal. Favourable replies were reported to have been received from all of these countries except Germany, who explained they would be heavily involved with planning for the Olympic Games.

This was a major coup. ASFA's international tour committee would now go on to consider three models for the big trip. The first started with four or five weeks in South Africa before heading to England with a trip to Canada on the way home. The second was a tour of Britain and Europe. The third was an excursion to the Dutch East Indies before heading on to England. It was thought a tour would last for six months and cost £6,000.

Things moved ahead three months later with a cable from England that the matter had been referred to the clubs. Druery also wrote directly to 41 English clubs about the prospect of matches and the *Newcastle Morning Herald* reported that "unqualified support" had been received from West Bromwich Albion, Leicester City, Tottenham Hotspur, Hull City, Stoke City, Sheffield United, Preston North End, Norwich City, Huddersfield Town, Newcastle United, Manchester City, Manchester United and Southampton.

The conditions of the tour were reported to be that the Football Association would pay travelling expenses and allowances, as Australia had done when the English team came to Australia in 1925. There would be 20 people in the touring party, including any managers and trainers deemed to be necessary.

In 1935, selection trials, a series of four matches featuring a combined South and West Australian side, a combined Victoria and Tasmania eleven, Queensland, and New South Wales were scheduled to be held in Sydney and Newcastle in June.

However, just two weeks before the trials were due to start, the F.A. sent a cable asking that the tour be postponed for a year. The F.A. stated that it wanted to make sure the tour would be successful and did not want to make hasty arrangements which might compromise that aim. The request was accepted by ASFA whose leaders put out the spin that this would allow better preparation for what would surely be a stronger and more competitive team.

The prospect of the English trip had been 50 years in the making so maybe another year wasn't such a big deal. The F.A. went quiet on arrangements in the ensuing months to the point where ASFA became nervous. Victoria's member on the national committee, J. Owen Wilshaw, announced that he was heading to London and would help the oil the wheels.

The bombshell came in March 1936. The F.A. cabled Australia to announce the cancellation of the tour which "at the present time would not be a success financially or otherwise." They had decided to seek other ways to support football in Australia. The decision was a devastating blow to Australia's international hopes, the credibility of ASFA as a national association, and to soccer's standing in Australian sporting life.

Not only had the half century cherished dream been dashed once again, it made a mockery of the work of the previous three years. Australia kept the appointments calendar clear for the big date that didn't happen. The F.A.'s conduct had killed Australia's international football life just at the time that is was able to make its strongest unified push.

The cancellation decision was followed shortly afterwards by an announcement that Great Britain would enter a team in the 1936 Olympic Games in Berlin.

Ten years earlier, Australia's hopes of going to the Amsterdam Olympiad crashed in the furore of the International Olympic Committee decision to accept 'broken time' payments for footballers, the pattern of payment prevailing in much of Europe. Australian and British Olympic officials denounced the move as an assault on amateur sporting values.

Despite their high minded denunciation of "professionalism", neither country withdrew entirely from the Games, but neither country would send a football team. They warned of the threat of a kind of contagion by competing with players operating from motives beyond the pure celebration of sport. The hubris of the British football establishment extended only to their withdrawal from FIFA, which controlled the football section of the Games.

By 1936, some sort of miracle innoculation had taken place.

It was now okay to play against players who used to pose such a threat to civilised sport. The F.A. did not see fit to consult or even notify its member nations of the backflip.

A postponed tour, a cancelled tour, and an arbitrary reversal of a long held policy which helped freeze Australia out of world football should surely have been enough to tell even the most obstinate acolytes of all things English that the Football Association did not present any kind of path forward.

During the 1930s, Australian officials hammered away at various schemes designed to drag Britain into the Australian scene, despite their obvious reluctance to do so. In 1932, the first major idea produced by the new powerbrokers was a tri-nation series involving Australia, England and Scotland to be played in Australia.

Then there was a 1936 thought bubble about getting an English second division team to play an entire season in the NSW State League as part of the celebrations of the 150th anniversary of white settlement in Sydney. A second division team was floated because some decision makers in Australia believed their playing standard to be competitive at that level.

Queens Park Rangers manager Billy Birrell said the suggestion was "too ridiculous for words." With wacky ideas like these being communicated to London no wonder the Australians weren't taken very seriously. Then again, the Australians may well have argued that they have tried just about everything else, so why not?

Not that Australian interests ranked very highly anyway. Sir Frederick Wall's 1934 encouragement of an Australian tour was one of his last acts before retiring after almost forty years as Football Association secretary to be replaced by Stanley Rous. The final rejection of the tour plan came after the appointment of Rous.

Upon retirement, Sir Frederick published a reflection on his time in the game entitled *Fifty Years of Football 1884-1934*. It is a revealing description of the values and views of a man who has spent decades at the top of an organisation which guided Australia's international journey, but it is grim reading for an Australian fan.

Wall is not opposed to professionals but is against agents and promoters who might "carry on the game on a private hippodrome basis." He's against the use of substitutes. He is dedicated to policing the line between amateurs and professionals and punishing those who cross it. He praises many fine individuals involved in the European game and notes that FIFA " is now the recognised authority in most parts of the world where the game is played" except, of course, in "Great Britain and her family of nations."

Wall says while FIFA is an excellent organisation it is too unwieldy. Its object is to control world football but that cannot be done successfully. There's scope for covering European countries but is a mistake to attempt to legislate for and govern the United States and South America. Evidently this impractical level of world wide control did not impede the efficient operation of the F.A.'s football empire.

Wall was knighted in 1930 for his services to football. Despite his devotion to the principles of amateurism he had no difficulty in accepting an honorarium of £10,000 from the F.A. when he stepped down as secretary.

After the disgraceful dismissal of Australian interests by the F.A. in 1935-36, Australia did come up with a proposal which might have provided at least a starting point for a more orderly future relationship with headquarters in London.

Roy Druery suggested the creation by the F.A. of an Imperial Fund which would underwrite international tours between the brothers of Empire, a notion he discussed with English officials on the 1937 England amateur tour. Druery framed the tour co-ordination initiative as bringing a greater degree of stability to football in the Empire. The Football Association had also asked Stanley Rous to come up with a three to four year match schedule for England.

The plan was an echo of South Africa's earlier bids to include the dominions of Empire at the F.A.'s top table.

The proposal was heard as part of an Australian six point agenda - including loans to buy grounds in Australia and subsidies for schools football along with an Empire wide international match programme – put to the F.A. in 1938 by Australia's new man in London, the Queensland Agent-General, Len Pike. He had picked up the role once held by the now deceased Arthur Gibbs, but he was not a football man. None of Australia's points gained support.

One of the points was a call for England to provide Australia with coaches. This request was knocked back at a time when the supply of coaching services overseas was gaining support as part of British diplomatic activity. The British Council, a new body set up to promote British cultural values, started to pay coaches to take up positions overseas.

When Greece played 1938 World Cup qualifiers against the players of the British mandate in Palestine who would subsequently come to Australia, they were coached by the former Reading and Bolton inside forward Bill Baggett. His World Cup mission in Greece was funded by the British Council.

British diplomat Eugen Millington-Drake was active in recruiting British coaches in South America that were paid for by the British Council. Millington-Drake was an old Etonian who rowed in a winning Oxford team in the Oxford-Cambridge boat race who became a famous figure in Latin American sport.

He led the Uruguayan contingent at the 1936 Olympics and had a pre-season football trophy in Paraguay named after him, the *Plaqueta Artur Millington-Drake*. He arranged, with funds from the British Council, to bring Scottish coach William Reaside to Nacional in Montevideo, overseeing the first of five championship wins. He went on to an illustrious coaching career including stints with Asturias, Atlante and Guadalajara in Mexico as well as Newells Old Boys in Argentina.

In 1938, the Football Association's priorities did not include Australia or any other part of the Empire. Although this year marked the 75th anniversary of the founding of the organisation, the F.A. chose not to celebrate its growth with its own national association members, such as Australia, but with FIFA, whose role in world football it had opposed for so long.

In October, England played against a Rest of Europe team

selected on behalf of FIFA by Italy's World Cup winning coach Vittorio Pozzo. All eleven starters for Europe had played at the just completed World Cup, six of them in the final. The friendly match at Highbury was won by England 3-0.

The second Empire Exhibition also took place in 1938, this time in Glasgow. The first celebration of the glories of the Empire had taken place in London in 1924-25, and although that event did not include a football tournament, the Exhibition was the reason the Empire Stadium was built. This is the hallowed ground of football we know as Wembley Stadium.

The second exhibition did include a football tournament. It was decided to celebrate global imperial splendour by inviting four English and four Scottish clubs to play in a knockout format. Celtic beat Everton 1-0 in the Ibrox Park final in front of 82,000 fans. Three cheers for the Empire!

The Empire Games in February was the first big sports event of the year, held in Sydney to commemorate the city's sesquicentenary. England, Scotland and Australia were all involved along with twelve other national squads competing for medals in athletics, boxing, cycling, diving, lawn bowls, swimming, rowing and wrestling.

Of course, football was never part of the Empire or Commonwealth Games, so the only faint whisper of Britain's football cacophony to reach Australia came in the person of Sandy Duncan, the skipper of Oxford University's football team, who arrived to captain England's Games squad as a long jumper.

Australia was added to the England Amateurs 1937 tour schedule originally arranged with New Zealand when the bigger Anglo-Australian deal collapsed. England Amateurs lost a series against an Empire team for the first time when Australia ran out winners in two of the three matches.

The tour was very popular and provided some memorable matches. Would Anglo-Australian contests on English soil produce similar drama? We never found out.

The English team of 1925 came to an Australian football community still in the first flush of excitement about international football. The Australians were in awe of the Englishmen and hoped to be able to give a good account of themselves in the company of revered professionals.

The Australians of 1937 had acquired a certain cockiness about their status. The 20s Aussies hoped they wouldn't be embarrassed, the 30s Aussies thought they could win.

Talks about this tour were initiated by New Zealand which played host for the first nine matches. Hopes that the chastening experience of thrashings at the hands of Australia the previous year would at least have stiffened the opposition for England were quickly dashed. England never had to step up from holiday mode.

They started with a 12-0 thumping of Hawkes Bay then cruised through a couple of provincial matches 7-0 over Wellington and 9-0 against Southland and Otago. The first clash with New Zealand in Dunedin was won 12-0. More strolls followed, Canterbury 7-1, a relatively close run thing against Auckland 8-4, then another 12-0. The tour ended with two matches against New Zealand won 6-0 in Auckland and 12-1 in Wellington.

Fans seemed to have lost heart in seeing one sided contests. Crowds were much smaller than expected and the tour ran at a loss of £1,200. New Zealand as an international football venue was as good as dead.

The England squad was a decent quality selection talked up by manager Charles Wreford-Brown as the finest amateur team ever to leave England. Seven of the 18 players had been in the Great Britain squad at the Berlin Olympics a year earlier and only three had never played for their country before.

Seventeen year old full back Bill Pickering was a surprise selection tipped to join the professional ranks at the end of the trip and earmarked for a big career. He did indeed sign for Sheffield Wednesday upon the team's return but war stopped him adding to three appearances for the club. After the war, he became a mainstay at Oldham Athletic.

Winger Bill Parr played alongside pro footballers at Blackpool, as did the star of the show Bernard Joy, who turned out for a high class Arsenal side when available.

The period of the late 1930s was the high point of Joy's career. In 1935, he made his first appearances for Arsenal, the English champions. The Gunners won the FA Cup in 1936, although Joy did not play in the final. As captain of his usual side Casuals though, he led his side to victory in the FA Amateur Cup.

He was that year appointed captain of the Great Britain team at the Olympics and played for England in a 3-2 loss to Belgium at Heysel Stadium. He was the last amateur player to appear for England in a full international. By any stretch, Bernard Joy was a significant player.

In the first match in Australia, over 30,000 fans watched England wear down a New South Wales team which had not had the benefit of a training session together before match day. After a scoreless first half, the visitors ran out 3-1 winners.

There was much comment about the "third back" game built around deep lying centre half Joy, still regarded as an innovation in Australia, and which was credited as the tactical tool which had blunted the threat of Wallsend centre forward Alf Quill. The Australians were said to have developed a plan to deal with this in the first Test.

Northern Districts ran England close in a midweek match before going down 5-4. The Northerners came back from a 3-1 deficit to 3-3 before a controversial penalty gave England the lead, which was quickly stretched to 5-3. Alf Quill, playing well against Joy's replacement John Sutcliffe, narrowed the gap to 5-4 then hit the crossbar in the dying minutes.

An all New South Wales based Australian side lined up for the first Test at the Sydney Cricket Ground, to the vocal distress of Queensland selector Alex Gibb. Sydney and Hunter Valley commentators also whinged about how much weight was given to each other's regions. Parochial bickering was blasted away by a classic match with an historic outcome.

A crowd of over 40,000 was stunned to see Australia kick off, move down the field and set up Bully Hughes to score before England had touched the ball and with only 35 seconds on the clock. Inside five minutes, Billy Price drew defenders and released to Hughes who scored again.

England's Stan Eastham hit the net from the penalty spot after Jack Evans handled, then Lester Finch set up Roy Mathews to square the ledger. Australia went back in front when Roy Crowhurst's cross caused confusion between Joy and goalkeeper Bertie Woolcock with Billy Price on hand to score. Five goals in less than half an hour.

Ted Collins released Eastham to blaze in from outside the box to level again but George Smith restored the lead, emerging from a scramble of players to place past Woolcock. A breathless 45 minutes had Australia up 4-3 at half time.

England piled on the pressure from the kick off forcing a string of saves from Bill Morgan. Australia kicked again with Smith firing over from a couple of chances. A left wing move by Jock Parkes and Harold Whitelaw ended with a cross to Smith who headed Australia further in front. Collins flashed in England's fourth from a Tommy Leek pass.

A furious finish yielded plenty of thrills but no goals. Australia won 5-4 in what was hailed as the first victory over an England team, amateur or professional, by an Empire country.

Newspapers fell over themselves battling for superlatives to describe the Australian success. *Truth*'s alliterative reporter hailing a "preconceived plan of paralysing passing that had the Englishmen petrified" and *The Referee* declaring Saturday July 10, 1937 "will go down as the most famous date in Australia's Soccer history."

The plan to deal with England's third back defensive set up was to introduce the big, heavy, combative and aerially strong George Smith as centre forward and get him to throw his considerable weight at Joy in the England penalty area. Crowhurst and Whitelaw rained in crosses. Australian captain Bill Coolahan moved forward into the vacated midfield space along with deeper lying inside forwards. Australia flooded midfield and had a posse battling for second balls from the bombardment.

The result was a rare defeat for England's amateurs and in Australian eyes was confirmation of a growing status in the football world.

England ground out a 2-1 win over Queensland in midweek before facing Australia for the second time in Brisbane. This time England were in command throughout, Bernard Joy was the man of the match and Australia rarely saw the goal. Mathews headed in a shot from Bill Parr which came back off the crossbar, an Eastham drive made it 2-0 before half time, Mathews sprinted between the Australian full backs to up the advantage to 3-0 with a quarter of an hour to go and Finch converted late for a 4-0 win.

Despite being played on a Tuesday afternoon, the series decider drew a crowd of over 15,000 to the Newcastle Sports Ground which the *Newcastle Morning Herald* reported as the stadium's record attendance for a match of any kind.

Australia made seven changes and loaded up with Hunter Valley players. The English squad was feeling the pinch of a long tour with several players carrying injuries, Bernard Joy not fit enough to take the field, and Lester Finch in hospital with German measles.

George Smith headed in Aub Teece's corner to open the scoring and finished off a passing movement initiated by Coolahan for the second. Fred Riley bustled returning goalkeeper Jim McNabb out of the way to head in a hotly disputed reply before half time.

Wilkinson's cross was hammered home first time by Smith for Australia's third and headed in another Wilkinson ball for his third and Australia's fourth. Collins and Mathews scored in England's fightback but McNabb's late full length diving save from Eastham's penalty meant their efforts fell short at 4-3 for the home team. The series belonged to Australia.

In Melbourne, an Australian XI led 2-0 before losing 4-3, and England had little trouble in their remaining matches, beating Victoria 6-1 and South Australia 10-0.

England manager Charles Wreford-Brown was complimentary about the standard of football his team had met, said his high opinion would be prominent in his tour report, and expressed the view that another tour, home or away, would take place within two years.

There had been none of the rancour that had bedevilled the 1925 tour. At the Sydney farewell for the team, Wreford-Brown noted "There has not been a single incident throughout the tour which created the slightest unpleasantness" and went on without irony "I have no doubt that our association will do all it can to help you develop the game here. We shall do all our best to see that there is another early visit to this country, the alternative being that you send a team to visit us."

Once again, a kind of public fantasising was indulged in by Australian officials based on titbits of encouragement. ASFA Secretary Roy Druery spoke of a European tour with five Test matches in Britain along with matches in Belgium, France and Austria. Late in the year he was quoted as saying tours from South Africa and Scotland were in the bag for 1938. They weren't.

Jack Mathews, who covered the tour for Brisbane's *Telegraph*, reported that he spoke to a group of five England players on the night of Australia's 4-3 win in Newcastle, skipper Bernard Joy and team mates Terry Huddle, Tony Strasser, Horry Robbins and Eric Tunnington.

Mathews led his story "At long last Australia's feet are firmly placed on the roadway which leads to lasting fame in international soccer" but went on to say "The idea of sending a team to England next year must be forgotten."

He conveyed the opinion of the English group that Australia had many promising players but needed more experience before touring. It would be better to invite a a team from South Africa or a nation of equal strength. They agreed Australia might do well in England but only against amateur clubs before comparatively small crowds.

The England Amateurs tour had been hugely successful,

generating over £11,000 in gate receipts, but because the initial capital had been raised privately, much of the windfall profits left the game to swell the wallets of the investors. This was a point Wreford-Brown made plain would be hard to explain to a Football Association which was forever being asked to lend support of one kind or another to Australia.

The F.A. was disinclined to support Australian football if it was so aligned to partnerships with investors. In their eyes this was akin to subsidising private business, the hippodrome merchants so reviled by Sir Frederick Wall. ASFA argued that the absence of investment from the likes of the F.A. left it no alternative.

Druery's public statement that he saw a future where the FA's role in Australia would be to finance tours was certainly thinking outside the box but it was always unlikely that the F.A. would go anywhere near such an idea. It was another indication that the connection just wasn't working. Slapdash conduct in the international domain now had players too complaining in public.

Bill Coolahan, the Australian captain admired by the tourists and the Australian star of the series, expressed his frustration at the way international players were treated by telling *Truth* in December "I will never play anything but club football from now on, and I think every other Australian player is of similar mind." The paper went on to name George Smith, Jack Evans and Jock Parkes as being of the same opinion.

The biggest sticking point was money. Coolahan revealed that the players had met and threatened to go on strike over pay before the first tour match but had been assured by officials that matters would be adjusted before the first Test.

"We finally played on the understanding that we would receive a good bonus at the end of the tour if it was a success. Judging by the way the players were treated it must have been a flop. I'm sorry now that all the players hadn't stuck together at the outset. I'll bet they are too."

As far as playing standards were concerned, it was increasingly difficult to talk about an Australian level. Playing standards were highest in Sydney and the Hunter Valley, Queensland was also strong, but elsewhere? The other states were nowhere near comparable.

The 11,000 crowd at the MCG for the English Amateurs was easily the biggest crowd for an association football match in Melbourne and turned a profit. But ordinarily, anything outside New South Wales and Queensland was likely to make a loss.

Here was the dilemma of the inbound tour in a nutshell. Visitors had to be comparable or better than Australia or people wouldn't go to see them, the tour would lose money, and the players would not get the football education they needed.

Money was only ever made in New South Wales and Queensland. Should profits be used to subsidise visits to other states to broaden the football experience of players and crowds alike? Would national delegates from the smaller states support tour initiatives in the first place if they didn't get a slice of the action?

How would player demands be accommodated? And what about the restlessness of increasingly professional clubs who were uneasy about releasing their stars for national duties? Toiling away unrecognised was frustrating, but growth had its problems too.

For outbound tours, all gaze remained focused on England, so the views of Bernard Joy and his team mates about what kind of international experience was appropriate for Australia got prominent attention, and their first hand opinions would carry weight in England. Australia again contemplated the stale question of whether visiting England or being visited by England was the better idea. In both cases, decisions on Australian progress would be in English hands.

While the English side was on tour, star packed sides representing Western Europe and Central Europe met in front of 50,000 fans in Amsterdam. Central Europe won 3-1, Western Europe's late consolation goal came from former Surabaya forward Bep Bakhuys.

Meanwhile, in Batavia and Tokyo, East Indies and Japanese officials deciding their own fate were planning a trip to the World Cup in France.

21.
ASIA IN PARIS

East Indies and the 1938 World Cup

Dutch East Indies captain Achmad Nawir led his men out at the Velodrome Municipale in Reims as the leader of the first team from Asia ever to play in a World Cup match. FIFA's records show a crowd of around 9,000 saw the bespectacled Nawir march onto the pitch alongside his illustrious Hungarian counterpart Györgi Sárosi.

This was Nawir's debut full international but not the first time he had faced a national team. A regular for many years in the HBS club side, he was picked for a Surabaya regional selection to play the Australian touring team in 1931. He made it to the East Indies long list to play at the 1934 Far Eastern championship in Manila but missed the cut for the final squad.

Two other starters on that historic day in Reims, defenders Tan Hong Djien and Frans Meeng, did get to Manila and play in that tournament, but the other nine were all debutants. The Hungarian side was packed with top class players of impressive pedigree and rated as one of the favourites to win the title.

Sárosi made nearly 400 appearances for Ferencvaros in his one-club career and was half way through a twelve year stint in the national team which produced 42 goals. He was one of the greatest players of the era whose fabulous technique made him able to play at the highest level in practically any position.

In the 1930s, a popular press pastime was to select a best European XI of the day. During that decade, *La Gazetta dello Sport* in Italy picked Sárosi as a defender, Germany's *Kicker* saw him as a midfielder, and *L'Auto* in France had him down in the forward line. After the war he had a long career as a coach in Italy with seven clubs, including spells at Roma and Juventus.

Hungary's firepower featured Marseille centre forward Vilmos Kohut, Ujpest legend Gyula Zsengellér, whose personal tally at this

World Cup was second only to Brazil's Leônidas, and winger Ferenc Sas who went to Argentina after the tournament to star for Boca Juniors. There can have been few bigger mismatches in World Cup finals history.

The Hungarians quickly asserted their superiority going 2-0 up inside a quarter of an hour through Kohut and Géza Toldi. Sárosi and Zsengellér extended the lead to 4-0 before half time. Hungary eased off after half time and the Indies side got a chance to get a hold of the ball but without seriously threatening the Magyars' goal. Zsengellér added a fifth midway through the second period and Sárosi got on the scoresheet with a minute left for a 6-0 win.

There was no shame in losing to a team of this calibre and these players from the Indonesian archipelago will forever be able to lay claim to being the first from Asia to reach world football's highest level. They were the ones to test themselves against the world's best and to witness the emerging grandeur of the World Cup.

This was the last World Cup to be played in a knockout format. Zsengellér and Sárosi each scored in Hungary's 2-0 defeat of Switzerland in the quarter finals, and contributed three of Hungary's goals in beating Sweden 5-1 in the semi finals after going behind in the first minute.

In the final, Italy netted first through Gino Colaussi in the 6th minute, Pál Titkos equalised straight away, strikes by Lazio's Silvio Piola and Colaussi had Italy 3-1 ahead at half time, Sárosi got Hungary back in the hunt with 20 minutes left, but a late second goal from Piola ended the contest at 4-2.

FIFA wanted Asian involvement in the World Cup and allocated a place in the finals. Dutch East Indies were drawn to play Japan in a one-off qualifier on neutral ground in Saigon in January of that year, but the match was awarded to the East Indies side when Japan withdrew.

FIFA wasn't keen however on the idea of teams reaching the finals without having beaten anybody to get there. They arranged a new qualifier to be played between Dutch East Indies and the USA in Rotterdam in late May. USA withdrew in April for financial reasons and the Indies team advanced to the final tournament.

Like the Australians and Chinese before them, the Americans had planned to build a longer tour around an appearance at a major tournament. They hoped the money spinner would be a match against an English team to mark the silver jubilee of the United States Football Association, but England cancelled the match and the Americans did not feel able to continue.

Thirty seven countries entered the qualifying rounds to join hosts France and holders Italy who were given automatic places at the finals, the first time this was done. The gentlemen's agreement that the finals would alternate between Europe and South America went out the window when the FIFA Congress of 1936 at the Opera Kroll in Berlin bent to pressure from President Jules Rimet for his country, France, to be host.

The countries of South America and the Caribbean, led by the likely alternative host Argentina, withdrew en masse although Brazil and Cuba came back to the fold.

A week after the World Cup final, the East Indies side continued its European sojourn with a series of matches in the Netherlands starting with a creditable 2-2 draw with The Hague's H.B.S., namesake of Nawir's Surabaya side.

A 5-3 win over Haarlem was followed by a 4-3 loss to Sparta Rotterdam and a 4-2 victory over Dordrecht. The big match was the meeting with the Netherlands in front of 50,000 fans at Amsterdam's Olympic Stadium.

The Dutch, playing in white as the Indies wore orange, selected a side which included seven players from their own 1938 World Cup squad, six of whom started their sole outing in Le Havre on the same day as the East Indies -Hungary game. Netherlands and Czechoslovakia were level at 0-0 after ninety minutes, but the Czechoslovakians put three past Philippines born keeper Adri van Male in extra time for a 3-0 win.

Things were much easier on this occasion with the Dutch racing to a 5-0 lead inside 25 minutes. Hans Taihuttu and Tjaak

Pattiwael, both from Batavia club Jung Ambon, each scored in the five minutes before half time for a 5-2 scoreline which put a better complexion on the contest. The reprieve was short lived. Netherlands netted twice right after the break and went on to win 9-2. The tour ended two days later with a 2-0 East Indies loss to a Hague selection at the training base for their European adventure, Houtrust.

The level of support given to the East Indies squad by the Dutch football Association, the KNVB, illustrates everything positive in the relationship between these two closely related football cultures. The experience provides the most vivid contrast possible with the dysfunctional relationship between the Football Association and Australia's international ambitions.

KNVB gave every assistance to the East Indies, providing coaching, a training base and the plum of a high profile match against the Dutch national team. In the previous five years, the F.A. had twice cancelled tours to Britain and had ignored its own ban on playing in the Olympics - the ban that effectively ruled Australia out of contention - to play in Berlin in 1936.

Johannes Mastenbroek, chairman of the reconstituted NIVU, the national association recognised by FIFA, led a three man panel which picked the team. When they arrived in Holland after the long sea trip, unable to practice with a ball en route to Europe, the KNVB asked its long serving coach Bob Glendenning to supervise the training of the East Indies squad as well as the Dutch side. The HBS club in The Hague provided the training base.

The East Indies squad comprised players from Java, Sumatra, Molucca and Ambon, others with Chinese heritage, and eight Indo-Europeans, a truly multi-ethnic representation of the archipelago hailed by Dutch language newspapers as an achievement in itself. *Sportskroniek* proudly noted, "It is no coincidence, it is a typical outcome, the very expression of the Netherlands colonial spirit"

But this was far from the view of the Indonesian PSSI, which felt double crossed by the colonial controlling body which PSSI said had reneged on agreements about how the team would be assembled. In August 1937, NIVU and PSSI made an agreement recognising each other as the two top level football organisations. NIVU arranged a series of matches which acted as selection trials for the World Cup but did not directly involve PSSI, which felt the process had been monopolised by NIVU.

A PSSI selection played an international opponent for the first time in 1937, the touring South China side led by Lee Wai Tong, and performed with great credit in a 2-2 draw. PSSI pointed to that result as being better than most other sides facing the Chinese and evidence that their players were at least as good as players in the competitions of the colonial controlling body NIVU, but were still being frozen out.

Soeratin Sosrosoegondo, the Harvard graduate PSSI chairman and co-founder, called for a challenge match between PSSI and NIVU to act as a selection trial. PSSI was further outraged by seeing the team that finally went to Paris playing in orange and standing to attention for the Dutch national anthem. After that, there would be no further deals with any neocolonial administrations. PSSI officially cancelled its co-operation agreement with NIVU in 1939.

These early days of the PSSI are usually portrayed in modern Indonesia as principled and even heroic times for the organisation. It proudly proclaimed itself to be an Indonesian body, one whose struggle for recognition for indigenous players and teams was always part of a broader battle for independence and national identity at a time of Dutch colonial control.

Modern Indonesian football has been beset by upheavals. Corruption scandals, betting and match fixing issues, crowd trouble, rival leagues and suspension from FIFA all give extra nostalgic lustre to the legend of a more purposeful and less muddled historical story. When Lieutenant-General Edy Rahmayadi was campaigning for national football leadership in 2016, he said he wanted to make PSSI more professional and "bring back its 1930s dignity." Rahmayadi was elected chairman of PSSI in November of that year for a four year term.

The match between the Netherlands and the Dutch East Indies

was certainly treated as a very big deal in the Dutch communities at either end of this imperial connection. Dutch newspaper reports were full of hype about the unity of the empire, fifty thousand fans turned up to witness the spectacle, and most of them were reported to be shouting their encourage for the team from the east.

The players were presented to Prince Bernhard at half time and the match was broadcast live on the radio to Java. Despite the crushing scores in the two big games of their European tour, the East Indies players were warmly welcomed home by an enthusiastic crowd when their ship returned to the wharf at Tandjong Priok.

Skipper Achmad Nawir told an interviewer they always knew this venture was not likely to be one with success determined by the scoreboard. "If ever sport lived up to its highest ideals, then it was during the Netherlands Indies tour to Europe. Winning or losing was quite beside the point. This was about the international contacts, about the sport for its own sake, about sport that creates joy in life and is not reflected in the downcast faces of the diehards who are intent purely on success."

First steps have to be taken somehow. In those terms, the Dutch East Indies players achieved their aims and claimed a unique place in Asian football history. To be sure, the late 1930s was a time of increasing instability in the politics of football in the Indonesian archipelago, but the achievements of the 1938 World Cup team are nowadays a source of pride for everyone.

The momentous achievement of playing at the World Cup, playing a leading European country on its own home ground, and being able to eat, drink and sleep football for weeks on end as a national team was in large part made possible by a sympathetic Dutch football establishment which was willing, indeed eager, to lend its support.

That support helped overcome NIVU's problems of limited capital, lack of coaches and alienation from top level competition. Australia suffered from these problems too and did not do nearly enough to take control of the problem and find a solution. Australia also outsourced the big decisions of its foreign policy to a more senior colonial era leader but did not get anything like this kind of encouragement.

22.
INDIA STEPS OUT

The Bengali Tour of 1938

Despite its long history, Indian football had little contact with teams from other countries and had not become a favoured destination of touring teams. India's football history stretches a long way back into the 19th century but its boisterous development happened in relative isolation when compared to other Asian countries.

In 1938, India football spread its wings further than ever before to meet the challenge of playing away on a major tour of Australia.

The Chinese played matches in India on the way to Berlin in 1936 and a great deal of attention had been given to the London amateurs Islington Corinthians as they passed through on their epic world tour of 1937.

Bengal was the undisputed heartland of Indian football, and home to the Indian Football Association, the ruling body of football in Bengal, and by virtue of its domestic strength and membership of the Football Association, the dominant organisation in the years before the advent of the All India Football Federation in 1937. Australia asked AIFF to send a team to Australia but the new body did not feel it was yet up to the task and passed on the invitation to the IFA who selected the team and ran the tour.

The first international experience for Indian footballers came in 1924 when a group of Bengali players travelled to Singapore and Java under the name Bengal Gymkhana but widely referred to as Calcutta Indians. The IFA's Diamond Jubilee history describes subsequent tours to Java in each of the next three years.

The IFA side made an unbeaten five match tour of Ceylon in 1933 which included a 1-0 victory over All Ceylon in Colombo, and in 1934, made a major tour of South Africa but playing only against teams drawn from the country's Indian communities. On the way home, the team played two matches against a Portuguese

XI in Port Beira in Mozambique and the European Sports Club in Mombasa, Kenya.

At home, a representative Indian team played against Lee Wai Tong's China en route to Berlin for the Olympics in 1936, a 1-1 draw, and both All India and an IFA XI played two matches against the touring Islington Corinthians in 1937, each recording a draw and a loss.

The most cosmopolitan figure was tour manager Pankaj Gupta, a leading journalist and sports administrator, prominent in hockey and cricket as well as football. Gupta had experience of the international football trips to Java and had already visited Australia as a manager of an Indian hockey team in 1935.

Gupta was a key figure in the establishment of the All India Football Federation and was co-draughtsman of the rules governing the new national body. He had also been a manager of Indian hockey teams at the Olympics of 1932 and 1936. Along with his prominence in the power structures of Indian sport, Gupta was influential as a journalist, writing in the high circulation and well regarded Indian nationalist paper *Amrita Bazar Patrika*.

This was the first time Indians had left the country to play another national team. Gupta acknowledged that his squad was not an all-India team but one which had been selected from clubs in Bengal, although their players were often from other parts of the country.

A handful of players brought some touring experience. Noor Mohammad had played in Ceylon, Choudhury went to South Africa, and captain Battacharjee was on both tours.

Bhattacharjee, also the captain of the East Bengal club, had played against China and Islington, while Dutt, Rahim, Rosario and Jumma Khan had played in matches against one or the other of those opponents. Nevertheless, the trip to Australia was a major new project.

The departure date of the Indian side was put back more than once and Australian officials worried that the tour might not take place. When the players finally boarded the ship to Fremantle, three of the leading lights selected stayed behind. Rahim, Jumma Khan and Noor Mohammed were all in the Mohammedan Sporting side to play against the British Army team East York in the final of the IFA Shield, the glamour knockout cup fixture of Kolkata's Indian Football Association.

Tour officials on both sides were further tormented by the fact that not only was the final drawn 1-1, the replay also ended in a 1-all draw. East York won the second replay 2-0. The three Mohammedan players made a later voyage to Fremantle then travelled by train across the continent to reach Sydney.

Players from all over the country came to play in Kolkata at the highest level the country could offer. Resentment around the country of the dominance of Kolkata's Indian Football Association was a major factor in the push for the creation of the All India Football Federation in 1937, and even then, the IFA retained its strong influence. Pankaj Gupta, president of the IFA, became treasurer of AIFF.

Mohammedan Sporting won the league for the fifth time in a row in 1938, an achievement which cemented their status as heroes to Muslims in Kolkata and all over India.

The revered poet and anti colonial activist Kazi Nazrul Islam, described as the national poet of Bangladesh, even wrote verse in praise of the team, linking their success to national liberation. *"These feet that have so incredibly woven wonders with the football, May the power of India rise from those very feet, May those feet break our chains, and our fear and our dread. May those feet kick them away.*

The Kolkata scene was dominated by three big clubs - Mohammedan, East Bengal and Mohun Bagan. Mohammedan's rise during the 1930s was resented by a mainly Hindu Kolkata establishment and led to a fight which saw the side excluded from the league in 1939.

East Bengal was a club whose main support drew on migrants who had come to the city from the east, an area spreading to what is now Bangladesh. Their clashes with Mohun Bagan - then as now - drew huge crowds in a local derby as passionately contested as any in the world.

Mohun Bagan is India's oldest team whose legend is built upon its victory in the IFA Shield final of 1911, when they beat the East Yorkshire Regiment 2-1. This was the first victory by an Indian club over a British team and is frequently referred to in India not simply as a sporting achievement but as an assertion of Indian identity and a landmark in the struggle for freedom and independence.

Several prominent players did not make the trip due to work and other commitments. One of them, Mohammedan Sporting winger Mohammed Salim, was the first Indian player to be offered a contract in Europe.

Salim impressed for All India against China in 1936 and despite being selected to line up in a marginally different All Kolkata selection two days later, he did not appear. He had already departed for Britain, where, after a short time in London, he was given a trial in Glasgow by Celtic manager Willie Maley.

The barefooted winger impressed in a 5-1 win over Hamilton and backed up for another eye catching show against non-league Galston, won by Celtic 7-1. The Scottish *Daily Express* reported "Ten twinkling toes of Salim, Celtic FC's player from India, hypnotised the crowd at Parkhead last night. He balances the ball on his big toe, lets it run down the scale to his little toe, twirls it, hops on one foot around the defender."

He was asked to stay but decided to return to Kolkata and Mohammedan Sporting where he retired at the end of the 1938 season.

Despite the release in 1937 of a five year plan for home and away tours, the Indian venture was the product of more ad hockery after the failure of attempts to secure deals with South Africa and Austria. Australia sought advice from London and was assured the Indians would provide a good standard of opposition. For the F.A., this arrangement would keep two Commonwealth supplicants happy without having to despatch a team anywhere.

As ever, the travel arrangements were a strain on the visitors. Arriving by ship in Fremantle on a Tuesday, they boarded a train for Adelaide that afternoon which arrived on Thursday for a Saturday match against South Australia. They caught another train that night for a trip to Melbourne. They arrived the next day, two days ahead of a clash with Victoria then took the night train to Sydney to prepare for their first big game against New South Wales.

Early results would be an indicator of how strong the team was, and how much of a drawcard they might prove to be for the sporting public. After breezing to a 6-1 hammering of South Australia, the Indians fell 4-2 to Victoria on an MCG cut up by a VFL match played the day before.

In Sydney, they went down 6-4 to a bigger and more physical New South Wales side although most accounts of the game held that they were somewhat unlucky. First impressions were that there were some tricky ball playing talents in the side but the defending was well below par.

A crowd of 16,000 showed there was interest in the side, although many may have come to see the well publicised novelty of barefoot football players. Most of the Indian side preferred to play in bandaged feet which left toes and heels exposed than to wear boots.

A hard fought midweek match in Cessnock produced a 2-1 result in favour of Northern Districts. The Hunter Valley players, always among the most physically aggressive of Australian representative sides, left their mark. The Indians were already buffeted and bruised by the time they reached Sydney.

Fears that India might get a drubbing were dispelled by a much tighter defensive display in the first Test where better shooting should have put them in front. The diminutive left winger Prosad and his counterpart on the right, Noor Mohammed, were setting up plenty of chances which were squandered by centre forward Lumsden.

With less than two minutes to go to half time, Alf Quill tricked his way past two defenders before lobbing to Jim Wilkinson to finally open the scoring.

The issue of Australia's acceptance of a level of physical contact frowned upon elsewhere was obliquely referred to in newspaper match reports. Unable to contain the ball skills of the Indians, Australia adopted a more belligerent approach in the second half.

The *Sydney Morning Herald* view was "the result was a triumph for the more robust type of Australian football pitted against the speedy, tricky but more conventional positional play" while *The Sun* explained the relatively timid mood of the first half by pointing out that "the game was played under international rules, which allow only the player in possession to be charged."

Rahim equalised early in the second half, Hughes restored the lead after Wilkinson's shot came back off the post, and a back heel from Quill set up Hughes for number three. A long range Bhattacharjee shot narrowed the margin, but another shot from distance, this time from Quill, made the score 4-2. Lumsden tapped in for 4-3 but Quill punished a fumble by goalkeeper Dutt for a final score of 5-3.

In midweek, India led 5-1 at half time against Queensland but were made to fight for a 7-6 victory in a floodlit goalfest. New Australian call up Cec Brittain got four goals, as did Lumsden.

A squad of six players each from Queensland and New South Wales fronted for the second Test at Brisbane's Exhibition Ground. A disjointed Australian side struggled throughout against an Indian eleven whose ball control and positional play, according to the *Queensland Times* account, enabled it to "run rings around the home side."

After a goalless first half, the two teams could hardly stop scoring. Rahim converted a Noor Mohammed cross for the first, and another Mohammed cross produced a second, this time from Bhattacharjee. A Hughes header got Australia on the board, Mohammed scored India's third, Hughes put away a rebound from the crossbar, Kitching equalised, Brittain put Australia in front for the first time, then Lumsden completed the goal deluge to make it 4-4.

The *Queensland Times* put the failure of the Indian team to win down to poor finishing and the excellent form of Australia's goalkeeper Jim McNabb. The *Newcastle Morning Herald* alluded to darker problems in the Australian camp.

The *Herald* reported "The Australian team is not a happy combination. There seems to be an interstate jealousy barrier which must be broken down if the XI are to play as one unit." The paper went on to say with Queenslanders picked for left flank positions and the New South Wales boys on the right, "opportunities are lost when rival factions keep the ball too much among themselves."

Cec Brittain and 20 year old Lex Gibb, son of 1920s Australian captain Alex Gibb, were the only Queenslanders retained for the third Test in Newcastle. Hughes got Australia in front from Lex Gibb's pass but after that, the home side rarely looked likely to win. Lumsden equalised before half time and scored a penalty after the break. Bhattarcharjee netted for 3-1 and Rahim's drive from the edge of the box went in off the post for a 4-1 result.

Another high scoring midweek match at Woonona saw India defeat Illawarra 6-4 after being two down in the first five minutes. The sides stood to attention before kick off as the Balgownie Brass Band played God Save The King. The band's conductor was former Australian great Judy Masters.

There would be no interstate rivalries in the squad for the fourth clash in Sydney - all twelve would come from New South Wales. In fact, the squad was drawn from just four State League clubs. Six players came from Sydney high fliers Metters, with two each from fellow corporate semi pros Goodyear, and the northern clubs Weston and Wallsend.

Brisbane's *Telegraph* football writer "Junius" blasted the selection as a blatant snub which harmed the code and killed Queensland interest in the match.

The match was a dazzler, won by Australia. Alf Quill scored early, Jim Wilkinson netted Jim Osborne's pass for the second, Prosad scored from an acute angle for India, Hughes headed in Australia's third, Lumsden fired in from 25 metres and Ray Bryant established the 4-2 half time lead.

Wilkinson got the fifth from a corner, Lumsden converted from the spot after Aubrey Mascord's handball, then Lumsden finished off a move begun on India's goal line to make the final score 5-4.

Prominent football writer Jack Mathews was bewildered by the decision to let Wilkinson's goal stand. In his account, Wilkinson "fisted the ball into the net from a corner, laughed, ran into the net, and placed the ball for a free kick which everyone expected - that is, everyone but the referee, who awarded a goal. The Australian forwards and the Indian defence pointed out his error, but he was adamant."

Six Queenslanders were in the Brisbane Test and Hunter Valley players were prominent in the Newcastle match in the manner now well established in Australia. The presence of local players reduced costs and bolstered local fan interest. The fifth and final Test in Melbourne featured four Victorians and two South Australians.

There were more complaints about the selection, particularly from Queensland, which opened up a wider debate about what a national team was all about. Jack Mathews, writing for the *Brisbane Telegraph*, began "One regards this side more in sorrow than in anger. One could pick a team of Queenslanders to beat it hands down."

He went on to claim "the South Australians in this Test team would not get a place in a reserve grade team in New South Wales. The Victorians are not so good either." He took the view that "Queensland and New South Wales must get together to do something, not only for their own welfare, but for the good of Australian soccer." This case would gain traction later in the year.

The squad brought the number of Australian players used in the five match series to 27. Only Metters inside forward Jack "Bully" Hughes and Goodyear full back Jack "Digger" Evans played in all matches.

India had much of the game against a significantly weaker Australian line-up but still lost 3-1. India led through Lumsden, who turned in Noor Mohammed's cross. Hughes put away a long ball played through by the South Australian Evans, then Frank McIver, wearing an Australian shirt for the first time since the 1931 East Indies tour, netted a second. Coolahan scored from Alec Forrest's pass in the final minute to the applause of a miniscule Melbourne crowd.

The Indians had proven to be opponents of a respectable level for most of their matches but, like most touring teams, suffered from having too few players, too many matches, and too much travel. The team was generally complimented for its technical level, speed, positional sense and 'scientific' use of the ball in a short passing game. It was criticised for its lack of ability to withstand Australia's physical challenge and poor finishing.

The Indian wingers, 18-year old Noor Mohammed and the tiny Prosad, proved to be popular with fans and admired for their trickiness. The captain, Bhattacharjee also had a good tour, as did the Chennai born inside forward Rahim.

Although the advocates of international football talked up the qualities of the Indians, another current of opinion was that they were not of sufficient quality to excite the public. Diehards and the curious would pay money at the gate but there would be few converts to the game.

Indian tour manager Pankaj Gupta thought Australia to be at a competitive level but had no players that were at a world professional standard. He rated goalkeeper Jim McNabb highly and believed winger Roy Crowhurst and inside forward Jack Hughes to be the best outfield players they had played.

The IFA's Diamond Jubilee record published in 1953 remembers the Indian experience as "not a very good success from a playing point of view" but of "a very great educative value" in games played against "a good class of amateur football in Australia where the standard of this kind of football compared favourably with that in England."

The Australians had chopped and changed their own team in a way which devalued its currency. In order to cut costs, more

Queenslanders appeared in Brisbane, Hunter Valley stars lined up in Newcastle and Sydney players dominated the squad for local tests. South Australian and Victorian players suddenly became international candidates when Australia played in Melbourne.

There was criticism that the status of winning an international call-up was being devalued by the very people who were promoting international football. Suggestions were made that Australia had run dead in order to make the visitors seem more competitive and thereby keep up interest in the tour and revenue through the gate.

Whatever its composition, Australia was invited to tour India. Gupta said matches could be easily arranged in Burma and Bengal and that he was confident a tour would be a success. The invitation was welcomed but never acted on.

The value of Asian football was not recognised as anything other than to provide potential playing stopovers on the way to the promised land of Britain.

23.
PALESTINE AND THE GATHERING STORM
The Tour from the British Mandate in Palestine, 1939

Australia's last visitors before the war brought men with richly varied experiences in the football world who arrived at a time of high Australian scepticism about travelling teams.

Jewish communities in Europe were under the most dire of threats to their existence. The Jewish footballers who came to Australia promoted Zionism, raised money for Jewish causes, and gave Australian sports fans another chance to see the playing style of central Europe which ran through their veins.

In the now long established Australian tradition, foreign visitors were described by a grander sounding and more marketable title with the biggest appeal to fans. It was also a title which suited the political aims of the guests. The touring team was always referred to as Palestine, a problematic moniker for many reasons, but was really Maccabi Tel Aviv, with a couple of guest players joining in. Or was it?

The fact that other players were added to the mix was, in the eyes of its supporters, proof that this should not be referred to as a club side and was indeed a representative Jewish team of the British Mandate in Palestine. At the very least, it meant the team should not be referred to as Maccabi Tel Aviv. However, the matches against Australia have never been recognised as full internationals by modern day Israel, or its precursor organisation the Palestine Football Association, founded in 1928 and admitted to FIFA in 1929.

The team contained many fine talents, but in the now all too familiar manner, had too few players and a highly demanding schedule of matches which was bound to reduce their strength and popular appeal. The unsuspecting tourists walked in to an increasingly acrimonious domestic dispute about integrating domestic and international football with commentators raising questions about whether "Palestine" had anything at all to contribute to Australia's football development.

The tour kicked off before a few thousand fans at Melbourne's Olympic Park with the Palestine Mandate team scoring early against Victoria and racing to a 4-0 lead inside half an hour. It was 5-1 at half time, 7-1 soon afterwards, then the visitors eased off.

The second match, against a Melbourne metropolitan selection on the same ground three days later was scoreless for the first half hour, then the deluge started. The visitors led 4-0 at half time with a final score of 8-0.

The higher level examination by New South Wales at the Sydney Cricket Ground resulted in a 6-4 victory for the near national team strength local selection. The visitors were praised for their passing and clever combinations but criticised for their lack of muscle and wayward shooting.

Their preference for retaining possession and an unhurried approach to goal was seen by many fans and reporters as pretty but pointless. Australian players were able to unsettle them with tough, bustling defence, and this was seen as exploiting a clear weakness. As ever, an argument about the technical skills of tourists versus the physical challenge of Australians was a constant current of debate for the duration of the tour.

NSW were 3-0 up early in the match and never looked like losing. *The Referee*'s Alec Boyd declared "In 20 years I have not seen an Australian team play as well as the NSW team", and tour guarantor Jack Skolnik observed "no amateur team could have lived with the NSW side."

A good performance, but one which was underpinned by the size and strength of the locals and the acceptance by officials of a level of physical contact tolerated in Australia but in few other places. *Sporting Globe*'s match report concluded that 'the forceful methods of NSW were better than the picturesque style of Palestine."

Coach Egon Pollak was already lamenting that three unfit players had to line up after their buffeting in the otherwise trouble free Victorian matches. This was an ominous sign with 15 games still to go. A solid 3-1 defeat of Northern Districts in Cessnock midweek was the final preparation for the first clash with Australia.

Back at the SCG, 15,000 fans turned up to see this latest test for Australia's best - a starting eleven which listed only players from NSW. A Jim Osborne penalty, a Jack Hughes drive off the post and a Skeeter Wilkinson shot put Australia three goals to the good inside five minutes.

A Wilkinson shot was deflected in by Palestine skipper Avraham Reznik, Werner pulled one back, then Crowhurst and Quill stretched the lead to 6-1 by half time. After the break, Werner got a second, Max Wynn scored Australia's seventh, Werner crashed home a free kick off the post and scored a penalty from Henwood's handball. Makhlis made it 7-5 a couple of minutes from time.

The team billed as Palestine pictured outside the Sydney Cricket Ground in 1939. Two players signed up with the Australian Army and were killed in action during World War II, others played for and coached post-War Israel.

A view gained ground that Australia eased off to stop a slaughter. There were scathing attacks on the contest and on the move to have the tour at all. Alec Boyd had nothing but good words for the home team when NSW played but was now calling for a post-mortem on the tour.

Bill Douglas, the secretary of the powerful Metters club in the NSW State League, was a man already well known as a trenchant critic of the foreign teams brought to Australia. He offered a £100 bet that his club side would beat the Palestine team. "It is an insult to public intelligence to bring a team all this way ... when they cannot keep our lads warm."

Douglas was belligerent and single minded in his promotion of State League club interests but this attack was severe even by his standards. He lambasted state officials for supporting the tour. He maintained that club football would be absolutely ruined if poor footballers from obscure places were foisted any longer upon the long suffering public.

The tourists were untroubled in trouncing Queensland 5-1 under lights in Brisbane and prepared for the second "Test" at the Exhibition Grounds. A changed Australian side including five Queenslanders looked weaker, again a decision some regarded as an attempt to allow "Palestine" to be more competitive.

After a goalless first half, Neufeld ran through the middle of the Australian defence and placed a shot past McNabb to give the visitors the opening goal. Crowhurst equalised midway through the first half and Hughes nodded in a winner when Crowhurst's corner reached him via the crossbar.

Queensland were thumped 8-1 in Ipswich and a weaker state team was taken apart 13-3 at Toowoomba where Neufeld scored seven.

With the credibility of the opposition under attack in Sydney, only five thousand spectators attended the SCG for the next clash with Australia. Ginsburg's goal meant a one goal advantage at half time and Neufeld finished off a sequence of passes to double the lead. Hughes kept Australia in contention, but breaching a defence with as many as five players at the back proved too tough a task.

After the 2-1 win there was some recognition of the visitors more determined showing while maintaining their best technical values. Still, compliments were qualified by questions about the standards applied in picking the Australian team.

The crazy match schedule took the team to Woonona two days later for their eleventh match in 31 days. Kick off against the Illawarra was delayed three quarters of an hour to give morning shift coal miners a better chance to get to the ground. Another gutsy performance earned a 3-2 win in a match that ended in fading light.

The fourth Test at Newcastle saw a return to a home line up stacked with established players, all from NSW with the exception of Melbourne Hakoah left winger Alec Forrest. By now, "Palestine" were fielding the fittest eleven they could find.

A lacklustre match was won 4-1 by Australia and provoked another round of condemnation of playing standards and the value of the tour. *The Sun* characterised the match as drab and disappointing and the *Newcastle Morning Herald* headlined its report as Soccer Test Unworthy of the Name. "The fault for this lies almost entirely with Palestine. Australia was never called on to play real football."

The *Herald* report accused Australia of tanking. "Australia, after ignoring early chances so that Palestine might settle down, put on the pressure, scored a goal, and from then on did not exert itself." The charge was the Australians allowed themselves to be dragged down to the same level as their opponents, a team which had not one chance in a hundred of winning.

When questioned, team manager Shlomo Arazi spoke of fatigue and injuries to explain his side's weaker performances. The 4-1 loss was the tenth match played in July and, despite the evident fatigue, they played again the next day in a fundraising charity match for Hunter Valley hospitals.

The final Australia - Palestine fixture was set down for St

Kilda a week later with the home side fielding six Victorian and South Australian players. George Smith, not in contention for earlier games due to a very public dispute with Metters over his non-selection for State League matches, was recalled to the Australian squad after showing bright form following his transfer to Leichhardt.

Days of rain left the playing surface very heavy and with one report describing the centre of the ground where the cricket pitches were as "like square yards of black porridge." This did not augur well for the ball playing guests.

George Smith headed in Crowhurst's cross inside five minutes but Ginsberg equalised. White headed in Crowhurst's corner to restore the lead, with Zvi Fuchs levelling. Werner got a third and Neufeld a fourth to put the team from Palestine 4-2 up at half time.

Australia pulled a goal back straight from the second half kick off and found another to finish 4-4, Crowhurst and Smith scoring the goals.

In the final tour matches a last minute Alec Forrest goal gave Victoria a 4-3 win, South Australia went down 4-2 then 8-0, and Western Australia drew 4-4 and lost 7-3.

Despite all the forthright criticism, the visitors' tour results compare favourably with those of other teams who were not on the end of vitriolic attacks. The tour guarantor who signed the contract to bring the team to Australia, Melbourne Jewish community leader Benzion Patkin, produced a table showing only the two English tours of 1925 and 1937 had been more successful on the field of play.

Patkin complained of unfair media treatment which he blamed for the tour's financial problems. He said poor attendances at some matches had only one reason, and that was "unsporting and demoralising propaganda."

Patkin also denied that the squad was simply the Maccabi Tel Aviv club side. He stated that it was indeed a national team, containing players from Hapoel Tel-Aviv, Hedera, Ness-Ziona and

Petah-Tikva.

Nevertheless, there was an acknowledgement from another guarantor that he expected a stronger side. Sam Wynn, president of the Zionist Association of Victoria, was quoted as saying he did not know the composition of the team until it arrived in Australia. He said guarantors asked for a more representative group, and although two Hapoel players had joined, two others had declined invitations for personal reasons.

Tour manager Shlomo Arazi told the *West Australian* in the last week of the tour that his side had been the victim of a lot of misfortune through illness and injury. There had been games when the starting eleven were not in the best of condition and in two Tests there had been early injuries which forced them to play a man down.

Asked about the locals, he took the the view that the standard in New South Wales was exceptionally high and compared favourably with that of the European amateur teams. He said the Australians they played were great athletes but lacked positional play in their football. If they could combine accurate passing with their physical power they would be almost unbeatable.

One of the many projects in Palestine mentioned in connection with the team's fund raising activities while in Australia was a good quality sports stadium. Arazi said that during the tour committees had been formed in all state capitals to raise money to buy land for a stadium. Money for a pitch, grandstands and other buildings would be raised in Palestine. The facility would be known as the Australian Monash Memorial Ground, named after the Australian general Sir John Monash.

The touring squad played a type of football reminiscent of the middle European style first seen in Australia during the Bohemians tour in 1927. About half the squad had played high level club football in Austria and Hungary making this another link with that culture and the first substantial contact with a Jewish football world which would enrich and enable Australia's post War football transformation.

Efforts by Australia's Jewish community to bring a football team to Australia date back to at least 1930. Melbourne based Jack Skolnik travelled to Tel Aviv to take part in the first Maccabi Games saying he would be donating a trophy from Australia for the football competition. He said he could bring back a team of the world's best Jewish players for a tour of Australia.

That year, the Jewish Telegraphic Agency reported Australia had invited New York's Hakoah All Stars to undertake a three month tour. This was one of three tours being considered by the club, along with invitations from Europe and South America.

The unnamed writer took the view that the trip to South America seemed the most likely with a purse of US$37,000 accruing to the club, but noted that the club's president, Max Krauss, favoured the Australian proposal. Skolnik seems to have been man who initiated this link.

Various proposals involving Jewish teams surfaced from time to time throughout the 1930s, but they were all regarded as, at best, fallback positions if more attractive opponents could not be secured.

The tour involved very little financial risk for the cash strapped Australian football bodies and was underwritten by men prominent in Melbourne's Jewish community. Along with Skolnik were the likes of wine and spirit merchant Sam Wynn, who was also president of the Zionist Association in Victoria, and Benzion Patkin, the founder of that Association, and a number of other organisations supporting Jewish institutions in Palestine.

In 1898, the Zionist orator Max Nordau called for Jewish sporting groups to embrace a "muscular Judaism", promoting an athletic Jewish identity to counter cliches about Jews as weak and to help prepare, physically as well as mentally, for the challenge of achieving the aims of Zionism.

The sports based Maccabi World Union, formed in 1921, promoted physical and sporting activity. Clubs such as Maccabi Tel Aviv, formed in 1929, progressed the cause further.

Maccabi Tel Aviv's first major tour was to North America via France in 1936. They lost 2-0 to Racing Paris and 3-1 to Lille before successes in Philadelphia and New York, where their match against an All Stars eleven attracted close to 50,000 fans. Matches in Toronto, Boston and St Louis produced draws and narrow losses.

The Palestine team recognised by FIFA played qualifiers for the World Cup starting in 1934 when they lost 7-1 to Egypt in Cairo and 4-1 in Tel Aviv. In 1938, they lost 3-1 to Greece in Tel Aviv and 1-0 in Athens. The Greek side was then humbled 11-1 by Hungary.

Although it is true to say that it could not be described as a national team, the international experience of the touring team's main players should be noted. Of 16 players used by Palestine in the World Cup qualifiers against Greece, nine were from Maccabi Tel Aviv, and seven of those men made the tour to Australia.

Coach Egon Pollak was part of the Hakoah Vienna side which won the Austrian title in 1924-25, the first winners of Europe's first professional league. He was the centre half in a defence that had him dropping to occupy the space between international full backs Max Gold and Béla Guttman.

All three would stay in the United States when Hakoah toured there the following year. Gold and Guttmann were part of the Hakoah All Stars that were invited to Australia in 1930 but elected to go to South America.

Gold got to Australia eventually as the organiser in 1955 of the tour by Rapid Vienna featuring the extravagant talents of Gerhard Hanappi, star of the Austrian semi finalists at the World Cup a year earlier.

Béla Guttmann's later life C.V. is a record of one of the most illustrious of coaching careers. His pinnacle achievements came during a spell as boss at Benfica, where he won two Portuguese titles and two European Cups. The list of clubs he led - there were more than 20 of them - includes A.C. Milan, Sao Paulo, Penarol, Panathinaikos, Honved and Porto. His first full time post was Hakoah Vienna.

Palestine's full backs for the World Cup qualifiers in 1938 were Avraham Reznik and Avraham Beit-Halevi, the Maccabi Tel Aviv pair who came to Australia. At the end of the tour, both asked to stay in Australia. They were recruited by Jack Skolnik for Melbourne Hakoah and in 1941 played for Victoria against the touring Hong Kong club side Eastern.

Avraham Schneiderorwitsch and Gaul Machlis, two forwards on the tour, played in the last recognised international match played by the British Mandate Palestine team in 1940. A 5-1 victory for Palestine over Lebanon in Jaffa four months after they left Fremantle featured first half goals from each of the players.

Avraham Beit-Halevi enlisted in the Australian Army and was killed in action against Japanese forces in New Guinea in January 1944. Menahem Mirmovich also stayed, enlisted, and died in New Guinea in May 1945.

Beit-Halevi's brother Moshe (Jerry), who was also on the Australian tour playing under the name Greenberg, said goodbye to his brother for the last time in Fremantle a matter of three days before the German invasion of Poland which plunged Europe into its darkest days. Jerry boarded the ship to Port Said, Avraham stayed in Western Australia.

Jerry Beit-Halevi succeeded Egon Pollak as coach of Maccabi Tel Aviv, and like Pollak, became the national coach of Israel. He later managed Nigeria. Menahem Mirmovich's younger brother Yosef became a Maccabi Tel Aviv player and later an Israeli international in the 1940s and 50s. He also coached both Maccabi and Israel.

Egon Pollak's talents and contacts were not limited to his sporting endeavours. Apart from his role as a player in the Hakoah championship winning side, and earning international honours for Austria, he also trained as an opera singer and was later engaged as a baritone by the Palestine Opera Company. He took the stage in a performance of "Tales of Hoffmann" in Tel Aviv shortly before the trip to Australia.

He performed as a singer in order to support himself while in exile in Australia, giving his first recital at North Perth Town

Hall in October 1939. The *West Australian* reported favourably on his singing of items from the works of Handel, Mozart and Schubert and a popular rendition of "Old Man River" in a series of performances illuminating the Perth musical world throughout the first half of 1940. His repertoire included songs in English, French, Italian, Hebrew and German, although he explained that he didn't want to sing in German any more.

Arguments about the value of the team raged before, during and after the trip to Australia. Without doubt, the team had talented players and the world from which they emerged is rich with great characters, teams and significant turning points for football in Europe and North America.

Even its greatest supporters would have to admit the team was not successful in Australia. Travel in pre-war Australia was often a major trial, match schedules were always too long, and Australia's robust playing culture left opponents with more bumps and bruises than most places.

But it could be that Australia, for all its isolation from the main stage, had actually built a competitive team well capable of dealing with teams outside the top tier of international competitors.

24.
AUSTRALIA'S EARLY STARS

Australian International Players Before Word War II

The 18 year adventure in international football between the wars featured the skills of Australia's best players at the highest representative level the game was able to provide. These national team stars are now largely forgotten. What kind of players were they? What did they achieve? How did the likes of Judy Masters, Digger Evans or Bully Hughes compare with their contemporaries in other lands?

Our best were certainly good players but they never got the chance to prove themselves at a big tournament.

In the absence of real tournaments, Australia imitated the rugby and cricket practice of the "Test" series, a string of three, four, five or six matches configured as a competition in itself. Only a few scraps of video footage of the players remain, so assessments of their abilities rely on published accounts from their times, the views of their opponents, word of mouth, and club legend.

Australia's football was always physically strong, excessively so in the view of many, and not reined in by a local refereeing regime which was highly tolerant of rough play. The most obvious example was Australia's acceptance of vigorous charges on goalkeepers.

Over the two decades, the reckless aggression which was accepted in earlier times matured at the top level into a kind of physicality based on athleticism. Dominating strength was important, but booting everything that moves gave way to "combination" skills, essentially the teamwork brought about by a positional awareness and an ability to pass.

Long diagonal balls to touchline hugging wingers were a common means of starting attacks, with crosses for the centre forward to follow. Full backs disposed of the ball quickly. An ability to thump the ball a distance was still a noted virtue. Australia was never short of good quality goalkeepers.

The 2-3-5 formation was a template rarely tampered with. Australia saw variations on basic structures through opponents like Bohemians, Palestine and even the second English touring side, but did not see a reason to bring about any fundamental changes.

In a sense this was a practical measure. Selecting a national team which usually had little or no preparation meant everybody had to arrive for match day with a clear understanding of what full backs, wingers, inside forwards or whatever actually did. Over time, increasing recognition and praise was given to the technique of individual players and their ability to perform at a higher level, but within the fixed roles assigned to them. These were skills they seem mostly to have developed by themselves. Training concentrated on fitness.

In this hyperphysical world, smaller men with good close skills really stood out. Chief among those players was the man commonly described as Australia's best pre-war player, Judy Masters.

Speedy and agile, Masters used his pace and technique to skip away from the big men. Football historian Philip Mosely describes him as "an instinctive player who valued teamwork ... a leader." He was short of stature but tough, "all muscle and bone". Like other 1920s captains Alex Gibb and Tom Traynor, Masters was a coal miner who worked hard and expected those around him to do the same. In the tradition of miners' solidarity, he gave back to his team mates through support on the field, and backing for the players cause off the field. He was an early advocate for players' rights and fair pay.

His first grade career started with his local team of Balgownie on the NSW south coast at the age of 15. He spent a couple of seasons playing for Granville and Newtown before the Great War while he was training at the Liverpool army barracks in Sydney's south west.

During the war, he served at Gallipoli and on the western front, where he was wounded in the shoulder at Pozieres. He continued to play football with AIF personnel while in France at the end of the war and resumed his career with Balgownie when he came home.

He was already in his thirties when he made his debut for Australia against New Zealand in 1923. He quickly advanced to be captain in the series against the Chinese later that year and played as a centre forward or inside forward in every home series for the rest of the 1920s.

Masters scored four in Australia's 5-1 victory in the opening Test match of the 1923 series against the Chinese, another four for New South Wales in the opening match of the 1927 Chinese tour, and netted the only goal of the game at the SCG to win the series against Canada in 1924. His most magical moment against international opposition came in 1925 when he scored in the first minute for NSW against the fabled English professionals in front of 45,000 fans at the SCG.

He retired in 1929 but served as Balgownie club secretary until 1953. In a career of over 400 matches he was never cautioned.

In the 1930s, two other inside forwards carried on the role of slightly built tricky players able to use technique to outwit defenders. The left sided Jim Osborne debuted against New Zealand in 1933 and was still in Australian sides to face Palestine in 1939, while Jim "Skeeta" Wilkinson played a similar role in ten Australian sides in the late 30s.

Alex Cameron was another midfielder/forward of note whose 13 match tally of international appearances would surely have been much greater if not for the six year drought of home matches starting in 1928. Cameron was 15 when he made his debut for Adamstown and attracted words of praise from England tour manager John Lewis when he lined up for a Newcastle selection against the English side as a 17-year old.

He was a significant presence on the 1928 Australian tour of the East Indies and the only player from the Australian teams of the 1920s to resume his international career when New Zealand arrived in 1933. He played in more away matches than anybody else having toured East Indies, New Caledonia and New Zealand where, in 1936, he was captain.

In the history of the Australian game, the most consistently high level performing position has been goalkeeper. In the between wars era, George Cartwright and Jimmy McNabb dominated national team selections.

Cartwright was between the posts for Leichhardt Rovers when they won the NSW under-18 championship, the Nurse Cup, in 1912. He played club football for Sydney's Balmain-Fernleigh side when he became the first ever choice for Australia's number one shirt, and went on to play in 16 of Australia's first 21 matches.

Jimmy McNabb started out as full back but after breaking both ankles in an accident decided to switch to goalkeeping. He became a mainstay in lineups of Hunter Valley side Weston and was one of only two players, along with Jack "Digger" Evans, to play in all six of the tour series played in the 1930s.

Australia's two games to one series victory over the England Amateur team in 1937 was a major milestone for local football. In the deciding third "Test" in Newcastle, the Australians had been pegged back from 4-1 to 4-3 when England were awarded a late penalty after a foul by Bert Murray. Stan Eastham, a player who never missed penalties, saw his spot kick parried away by McNabb. Australia won the match, the series, and considerable glory.

Jimmy McNabb was said to have been contacted about playing in England but rejected the approaches because of his ankle problems. It took him most of the week to recover from matches and he believed he would not be able to stand the strain of English style weekend and midweek games.

Leaving aside the second tour of the Dutch East Indies during the domestic political split in 1931, full back Digger Evans started all 23 of Australia's matches during the 1930s. When Hong Kong club Eastern arrived for a tour in 1941, they played five times against Australia. Evans started in all of them too, as captain.

He began his career in the Hunter region with Aberdare and Cessnock before moving to Sydney for spells with Metters, Goodyear and Leichhardt-Annandale, finally returning to Cessnock. At Leichhardt at the end of the war he shared defensive duties with Chinese international Yik Yeung. and the promising new recruit

Joe Marston. For Australia, centre half Jock Parkes was his most regular defensive team mate in matches played on home soil.

Evans was tall, powerfully built, a ferocious tackler and an efficient defensive organiser. At the end of his playing career, was offered the position of national coach of New Caledonia, a country he toured as a player in 1933.

During the 1930s, Jack "Bully" Hughes piled in goals in the NSW State League and was a near automatic selection for home games against the English amateurs and the touring sides from India and Palestine where he averaged better than a goal a game. Fast and elusive, the inside forward packed a shot in both feet and a body swerve which took him away from defenders.

The Referee nominated Hughes as soccer's top man of 1938, describing a player whose "ball control is an object lesson to forwards" who "passes the ball along the floor, is always in position, and has few peers as a shot." Hughes was "the nearest approach we have in Australia to first class overseas standard."

That same year, he was reported to have been approached by an agent acting for English first division high flyers Bolton Wanderers as well as second division sides Bury and Newcastle United, with Newcastle the fancied destination. The agent was said to have followed a tip from England centre half Bernard Joy who played against Hughes on the 1937 tour and picked him as Australia's best.

A year later, former Newcastle United star Tom McDonald, an F.A. Cup and championship winner with the club in the 1920s, was reported to be in Sydney making an offer for both Hughes and international winger Roy Crowhurst, both players with Metters.

Crowhurst was quoted as knocking back the offer, but Hughes was enthusiastic about going, saying he had been asked to name his terms and was looking forward to a chance in the big time. This would have been the first direct transfer from an Australian team to an overseas club but the contact came to nothing.

Crowhurst was the pick of Australia's wingers in the 1930s, playing in all international series except the 1936 away trip to New

Zealand and following in the steps of star 1920s flank men Stan Bourke and Roy McNaughton.

Their goal scoring team mate for much of the 1930s was powerhouse centre forward George Smith, a player fans and team mates alike expected to score whenever he played. He first played for Australia against New Zealand in 1933, scoring seven goals in a three match series including a hat trick at the SCG.

He captained the Australian side on a tour to New Caledonia later that season where the Australians won all three matches against the national team. Smith's personal highlight was a four goal haul in a 7-3 victory in the third of those clashes.

When Australia steamrolled New Zealand in 1936, Smith gorged on goals, netting four in the 7-1 demolition in Dunedin and five in the 10-0 massacre in Wellington. Sterner opposition was provided the following year by the England Amateurs but Smith was crucial in securing Australia's two wins to clinch the series. He scored twice in the 5-4 victory at the SCG and a hat-trick in the 4-3 win at Newcastle.

He had a thunderbolt shot and, although not especially tall, was dominant in the air. He weighed over 80 kilos and threw his weight around with vigour. He physically bullied Bernard Joy out of the match in one clash with the English side and delighted in charging goalkeepers into the net if they collected high balls under the crossbar.

All of these players stood out against the opposition they were provided. England tour manager Charles Wreford-Brown saw Crowhurst as a top player who troubled England's full backs and India's manager Arazi named McNabb, Crowhurst and Hughes as the best locals, but that nobody he'd seen was in an international professional class. He thought the Australians would do well at Olympic level.

Immigration and football have always been closely related and attention has always been given to the higher class import. A Scot who played for Australia, Tom Tennant, brought with him fabulous experiences of Spanish and Latin American football.

Tennant was part of a Motherwell side which toured Spain at the end of the 1926-27 season and beat Real Madrid 3-1, drew with Barcelona 2-2, and thumped Celta Vigo 4-0. The following year, Motherwell accepted an invitation to go to South America.

Motherwell were clouted 5-0 by Brazil at Fluminense's ground but won six of 13 tour fixtures, including a 3-0 victory over an Argentina selection and another 3-0 win over a combined Argentina/Uruguay team at River Plate.

The top players of both countries were away at the Amsterdam Olympics at the time but the opposition was still good. Tennant's goal against *Combinado Argentina/Uruguay* was scored past Quilmes goalkeeper Juan Botasso, who started in goal for Argentina in the first ever World Cup final at the Centenario two years later along with defenders Juan Della Torre and forward Carlos Peucelle.

Ramon Muttis and Mario Evaristo, also in the Argentina World Cup squad in 1930, played for Boca Juniors against Motherwell. Uruguayan World Cup winner Carlos Riolfo was another opponent who appeared for Penarol, and the Rio selection Tennant scored against in a 1-1 draw included Brazilian 1930 World Cup squad members Pamplona and Theophilo.

Tennant moved to Sydney in 1929 to join his parents and two of his brothers who had already emigrated to Australia. The Tennant brothers all played for top club Metters, Tom for ten years during which he played for Australia against New Zealand in a sensational 6-5 victory in 1933.

He captained New South Wales against Queensland and played for New South Wales against the touring teams from India and Palestine.

The 1920s started with losses to New Zealand, victories over China and a narrow series win over a tiring and injury depleted Canada. A squad of professionals of no particular note in England proved too strong here, although there were some good Australian highlights. The goalfests against Prague's skilful Bohemians in 1927 did not provide Australia with a victory but a Chinese squad which supplied half the team that won the Far Eastern championship weeks later had been comfortably beaten.

A much weakened Australia had also been generally better than the teams met on the 1928 tour, despite losing 4-2 to a Singapore selection and 2-1 in extra time to the NIVB side which was effectively the Dutch East Indies

All tours to Australia involved lots of matches and too much travel, factors which clearly wore down visiting teams and which can't be ignored when assessing their merit, and let's acknowledge that teams weren't always able to bring all the players they would like.

There's as much guesswork as method in these comparisons but on the evidence available, it is reasonable to say that at the end of the decade, Australia was as good as, or better, than the countries we now regard as regional rivals.

The combination of unforgiving domestic politics and an inability or unwillingness to consistently engage the non-British football world, particularly through FIFA, was a disaster for the national team and for the status of football in Australian sport. Australia's choices meant no World Cup, no Olympics, and the rejection of invitations to go to China, India, Philippines and Europe. There would be no tournaments of any kind.

The 1930s started with a return to the East Indies with a squad weaker than the first but which still performed well. Tours from New Zealand, and to New Caledonia, showed Australian standards to be well ahead of its Pacific neighbours, and a trip to New Zealand in 1936 was by a decent Australian side no longer challenged by its oldest opponent.

A decade which saw the consolidation of talent in a nascent semi-professional league in New South Wales improved the level of club football in that state to the point that it was difficult to talk about Australian standards since disparities between the states were so obvious.

The Australians were better than the England amateurs of 1937 as well as the teams from India and Palestine that followed. The Australian team was probably better than it had ever been, but how might it have fared if given a chance on the big stage?

Australia had become so isolated by this time that guesswork now overwhelms method in an assessment of their competitive strength. Two of the England touring squad, Bernard Joy and Lester Finch, played in the team that beat China 2-0 in Berlin but lost two of England's three matches against Australia. The general level of the two England squads does not seem to be dramatically different.

Perhaps Australia was still at or near the top of the Asia-Pacific football tree but it was becoming increasingly difficult to tell. Seventeen years on from the first match, Australia had still not played a competitive fixture and had not found a role to play in world football.

The players deserved better.

25.
WHERE DO WE GO NOW?

"What would Brisbane's most ardent Soccer enthusiast do if he received a cheque for £250,000?"

Millions of Australian lottery ticket buyers ask themselves a similar question every week. In 1937, Queensland Football Association secretary Dick Tainton picked up the theme from the Hollywood movie "If I Had A Million" starring Charles Laughton and, for his fellow pipe dreamers in the *Sunday Mail*, imagined the windfall in the lap of Australian soccer.

He talks of the fabled yearning for "the time when an Australian team will go on a world tour, a project now difficult of accomplishment due to lack of financial backing." He dreams on to the destinations, a football holiday brochure filled with a list of countries on all the continents of the world.

Such a tour could be played against 60 fully organised national associations "for such is the membership of the Federation Internationale de Football Association founded in Paris 23 years ago." It was actually 33 years ago, but at least he knows.

Money was of course a big factor, but Tainton's reverie allows him to gloss over football's inability to bring about change. As the real world international contacts of Australian football shrank during the 1930s, officials retired to their rooms like awkward teenagers to fantasise about the relationships they wished they had.

NSW State League President Tom Crawford officially opened the new grandstand at Clyde Oval in Sydney's west in 1933, speaking just after the under-12s curtain raiser and before the big match, Granville versus New Zealand. The *Cumberland Argus* says Crawford peered into the future.

"I have a vision of a big airship coming to Australia in the near future, and in that airship there will be nine international teams from the European countries. The tenth team will be that of

Australia, and we will have one of the biggest Soccer carnivals ever known in the world. That can be done in Australia, because it is the off season for the European countries. You may think it's a Jules Verne idea; but it will come in the near future."

The great French writer, credited by many as the father of science fiction, had been dead for ten years at this point but was only slightly less likely than Crawford to make the airship games happen. In the real world, Italy was twelve months out from staging the second edition of the World Cup. Thirty six countries filled in entry forms and 16 teams from three continents qualified for a tournament to be staged in eight Italian cities. Over 350,000 fans watched them.

Australian leaders knew about the World Cup. Victoria's national committee official J. Owen Wilshaw commented on the likelihood of Australian participation in 1931. He thought that in the absence of subsidies, Australia would most likely not be able to afford to go or to take part in qualifiers.

He didn't know FIFA would offer to cover the expenses of teams participating in future World Cup finals, including their travel bills.

By 1936, the fantasy had evolved. The man responsible for Australia's international contacts was the secretary of the Australian Soccer Football Association, Roy Druery. He wrote a letter to the *Newcastle Sun* urging Australia to consider staging the World Cup in 1938 as part of the sequicentenary celebrations of the arrival of British colonists in Sydney.

He describes the immense spread of football throughout the world and that "an International Federation is already in existence which organises a world championship every three years. At the last contests held two years ago in Italy, 16 nations took part and the championship was won by Italy who defeated Germany by three goals to one."

Again, the knowledge is sketchy. That's every four years actually and Italy beat Czechoslovakia 2-1 in extra time, but once more, at least he knows that these games happened. He goes on to assure us that "organisation does not present great difficulty" because of patriotic corporate support, the financial backing of national associations, and because, shades of Asian Cup 2015, "the occasion would also provide opportunity for the national communities here to perform real service in the furtherance of the celebrations."

Druery invents his own format involving a knockout competition with preliminary matches in country districts of New South Wales and in the other capital cities. He concludes by forecasting the event would pay for itself and provide world wide publicity for Sydney and Australia.

Of course, it is easy to smile at the naivety of a World Cup run by the 150th Anniversary Celebrations Council and played on country showgrounds. Australia had not yet persuaded any European or South American national team to make the journey but now indulged the fantasy of getting 15 to come all at once.

The idea is a view of the world as seen from the isolation of Druery's Wallsend living room, unaided by advice freely available to him should he choose to ask. Maurice Vandendriessche was still around in Melbourne and football mad Sydney businessman Fred Robertson was on first name terms with top figures in Hungary, Austria, Czechoslovakia and elsewhere from his regular trips to Europe, all of which involve football watching and meetings with leading officials, and all of which he regularly reports in the columns of the press.

Australia's friend in China, Lee Wai Tong, would surely share his immense knowledge of international football, and the East Indies football federation, FIFA's designated agent in Asia by this time, would be obliged to help if Australia was a FIFA member.

One Australian we know attended the 1938 World Cup final was cricketer Sid Barnes who was on the Ashes tour to England that year. Barnes broke his wrist on the way to England but kept the injury quiet in case he got sent home. Unable to play due to injury, he took time out to cross the channel and see Italy defeat Hungary 4-2 in Paris.

The likes of Crawford and Druery clearly longed for serious international competition but either didn't know how to get involved or feared the consequences of stepping out of England's shadow. Druery invoked the name of FIFA when talking up soccer to a general audience but did nothing to join the world body.

The Football Association, Australia's international organisation of choice, was not a member of FIFA either and its attitude to the World Cup provided a practical and cultural barrier to Australian participation in a tournament the game's leaders were openly dreaming about.

Australia desperately needed genuine international competition. Without it, all of Australia's efforts were exhibition matches where, because of the precarious nature of game's economy, there was always a temptation to protect the standing of the opposition rather than put the best players forward for the best result.

England's disgraceful treatment of Australia in the mid 1930s crushed the life out of football's international ambitions. Even Druery's left field attempt to snaffle a bigger share of English attention through an Empire wide F.A. funded tour schedule went nowhere. By the late 1930s, touring teams from India and Palestine struggled for credibility and non-British international football was being attacked as second rate by an emboldened club culture in New South Wales and Queensland.

Questions of Australian identity and a place in the football world have been constant themes in the game's history. Once Australian representative teams took the field, specifically Australian interests started to be identified - an opportunity for international competition, a chance to measure themselves in Britain, British investment in coaching and football grounds.

The F.A. had little or no interest in these aims. Australian officials pointed to their lack of money to explain the retreat from the big thinking of the 1920s, but their 1930s timidity was just as much due to a lack of imagination and failure to find the political courage to pursue what were now clearly identified as their dream aims - world tours and the World Cup.

The desire for international contact and tournament play was also strong in Asia. Major Asian powers had a high level of exchange with each other during the 1920s and 1930s and the presence of a regional championship providing a measuring stick for progress, a point of contact for the communication of ideas, and a venue for competition.

They tried to involve Australia in that world, a community of international development, but Australia was dubious about the value of Asian football. Australia was invited to China, Dutch East Indies, India and the Philippines, played in Singapore on a tour which included a match against Malay opposition, and was reported to have received an approach from Siam.

Asia's rising football powers dealt with each other as neighbours with mutual interests. This bred a regional sensibility and a certain confidence in their thinking. Australia believed, despite the weight of evidence, that England would provide the path to salvation. England wasn't even thinking about the question. Where Asia considered regional practicalities, Australia simply longed for better times.

China and Japan were keen to establish football and other cultural profiles emphasising their modernity and independence. Dutch East Indies became the Asian hub of touring football action and had a highly productive relationship with Dutch football culture. This enabled Batavia to eventually be the regional contact point for FIFA during the 1930s. Deeper in the Javanese scene, PSSI pressed for a much more explicit expression of national independence which broke the mould of Dutch colonialism.

They all pursued one or another form of national expression. To its immense cost, Australia simply chose dependence.

It is true that the new regime running the game in the 1930s endured the heavy burdens of tough economic times, and on the international front, was treated outrageously by London. But it is equally true that the new regime was so inept at producing a way forward for the national team that the very idea of international football started to fall into disrepute.

England's treatment of Australia was high handed, tin eared and disrespectful, but Australia could have walked away from the

F.A. at any time. They had the evidence the link wasn't working but they did not develop an alternative path to progress. Faith in the *just maybe* possibility of a dream tour was thought solid enough to seem better than a leap into the unknown.

Ten years after the disastrous 1928 split which brought Australian home matches to a screeching halt, another split loomed, with international football a major issue of contention.

Clubs in New South Wales and Queensland were dismissive of the playing standards in the rest of the country and felt they were overrepresented at the game's top level. Their argument was that small states were dragging the chain on playing levels, crowds and investment, so why were they given equal weight with the two big states at ASFA?

Furthermore, the practice of incorporating much weaker local players into the Australian team just because it is playing in, say, Adelaide or Melbourne, had to stop. Let's just have quality opposition facing the best players Australia can provide, the argument ran. If smaller centres can't produce players or crowds that are good enough, other regions shouldn't expect to see international matches at all.

In December 1938, the presidents of the state football bodies in both New South Wales and Queensland, Sid Grant and Bill Elson Green, jointly called for a complete overhaul of the national association. They released a statement that New South Wales and Queensland provided the money, the players and the crowds, yet policy was determined by states which provided none of these things. If a meeting to reshape the organisation was not held by the end of January, the two states would withdraw and set up a new Australian Council.

National secretary Roy Druery, also on the NSW committee, quickly slapped down the move which he said had not even been endorsed by his home state. Grant had no authority to speak and anyway everybody knew New South Wales effectively held the right of veto over any tour plan. The breakaway fizzled, Grant continued in office, Elson Green resigned from Queensland football, but the critique of dysfunctional national team arrangements went on.

Grant, a member of the national selection committee, told guests at a dinner for the visitors from Palestine that it was impossible to feel that teams which had taken the field for Australia were representative of the game's strength. Small states must accept Australia's best and not seek teams in which their own players were given positions for which better men could be found.

The very next day, Australia announced the lineup for the fifth Palestinian match in Melbourne which contained four Victorians and two South Australians. The *Sydney Morning Herald* complained that "no Australian team can be considered full strength which does not contain at least 10 New South Welshmen."

The most vociferous critic of the national team agenda was Bill Douglass, the sharp suited cigar smoking boss of the country's richest club, Metters. Douglass was a Scot who was reported to have worked as an agent for English professional clubs before coming to Australia.

His first big clashes with the national set up came in 1936 when Metters initially refused to release players for the tour of New Zealand, then relented, but with a warning to the players that their off field employment could not be guaranteed. Metters was the best paying team around and by 1938 had signed so many representative players that they couldn't all get into the first team, a source of widespread resentment.

Douglass was a supporter, and probably the originator, of the secession proposal taken up by Grant and Elson Green. His motivation was to stop international matches disrupting the progress of club football. In his view, the clubs provided the players, so why should they postpone their matches to play inferior teams especially in states not pulling their weight?

Douglass loudly criticised the Palestine tour, saying his Metters side was better and he was prepared to up a £100 stake for a challenge match, a comment promoter Jack Skolnik regarded as offensive. Douglass said the Palestine team had taught Australia nothing and charged that Australia had fielded teams below maximum strength to even up the contest.

Speaking in support of a review by the State League of international tours, he argued that postponing club matches to accommodate poor touring teams made no sense, clubs were upset, fans lost interest and player training went awry. Clubs needed to reassert themselves even at the cost of putting the whole business of internationals on ice.

His remedy was severe." I do not think that we should agree to a tour for at least two years, *even if the world's best team can come to Australia.* It will take at least two years for us to recover position and prestige." This was stern stuff from the team providing more top players than any other.

The 'world's best team' reference meant even the British sides we had always been told were the key to Australian advancement should now be discouraged. Douglass and some others in the State League camp did not regard international football as a priority. It was a threat to the clubs' business model, disrupting the fixture list and taking players, fans and public attention away from their domain. International football was just too hard.

Four days after most of the Palestine footballers boarded their ship at Fremantle on the 28th of August to go home, Germany invaded Poland and World War II was under way. Sporting arguments were now minor concerns, and among their backwaters, Australia's international rivers ran dry without Douglass's radical proposition being tested.

Football in Australia made enormous progress between the world wars. The helter skelter years of the 1920s exploded with international matches involving teams from what we would now describe as four of the world's six confederations.

Australia played as many or more matches than any country in the world against national teams, clubs, regional selections and others. There were big matches, huge crowds and exciting players. A national interstate championship emerged, although it never included all states. In the New South Wales heartland at least, competition went from suburban amateurism to state wide semi professionalism.

At the end of the 1920s, Australia might reasonably regard itself as at least the equal of any football nation in the Asia Pacific region. In the 1930s, Australia probably had even stronger teams at national and club level but its international compass was broken. While its neighbours forged ahead, Australia lost its way.

Subservience to English leadership in international affairs was ultimately disastrous for Australia's ambitions. English views on player payments, the Olympics, FIFA and the World Cup all went in a direction which did not favour Australia's best interests.

At the end of the 1930s, the individual and collective actions of our Asian neighbours projected them on to the world stage. The Far Eastern Games gave China, Japan and the Philippines the discipline of competition and a mutually acknowledged measuring stick to regularly assess their progress. This ladder enabled China and Japan to reach the heights of the Olympics.

Australia's national team played opposition from Asia more times than any national team in the world and stimulated the growth of football in Asia. Then, as now, Asia provided more paths to success than Australia realised. The footballers of long ago stuck with the track they felt they knew. The barriers of poor communication, lack of money and the absence of administrative skills explain a lot about the their world and the decisions they made.

Some of these issues remain but cannot credibly be used to account for the cultural gap that still bedevils Australia's Asian relationships. Mainstream media coverage of Asian football is abysmal and Asian faces or voices are conspicuously absent in Australian discourse.

The best visiting teams at A-League grounds are usually from Asia playing Champions League matches and yet they are likely to draw among the lowest crowds. Once Australian teams are knocked out of the ACL, reporting on the competition practically disappears. The variety of Asian football and the opportunities it provides are still ignored by a public gaze which still dwells on England, now via the Premier League and marketing driven exhibition matches in Australia.

As match commentators never fail to remind us, if you don't take your chances you will be punished. The scoring rate from chances still needs to improve.

Australia's future is intimately bound to Asia in football as in so many other aspects of life. Our mutual progress is an exciting prospect which will be made better by a higher level of understanding of our respective football cultures.

One obvious lesson from the earliest days to now is that national teams have always been more powerful than any other factor in unifying and advancing Australia's football cause. They must take priority over all other aspects of the game. We also know that all of our international life is invested in Asia. That alone means we must do everything we can to make Asian competitions as strong as possible.

Australia is closing in on 100 years of football contact with Asia and has entered a decade which will see a string of centenaries of hugely important events in the life of the game. Commemorations on and off the field provide a chance to revisit our history and bring about better relationships with important partners, especially in Asia.

There are centenaries of the birth of the Socceroos in 2022; international football on Australian soil and the first encounter with Asia in 2023; the clashes with England in 2025; and the inaugural trip to Asia in 2028.

Among all the lost and fumbled opportunities along a bumpy and challenging track, Australia's football pioneers still achieved so much. Marking the coming centenaries of their efforts will mean reconnecting with old friends, celebrating shared histories, and re-committing to building ever stronger bonds in the future.

We can take pride in our football culture and its uniquely multicultural history. We know what it means to be playing for Australia.

ACKNOWLEDGEMENTS

The challenge of bringing to attention the life of Australia's pre-World War II football is both frustrating and a deep pleasure. The absence of much of the documentary record, and the survival of just a small number of flickering frames of actual playing time, brings the risk of uncertainty to the detail of many stories.

However, entry to the football environment of bygone days through published records, correspondence, club legend and family history is an immense pleasure. Some issues, such as the status of amateurs, seem remote and arcane, while others, such as states' rights and the power balance between club and national teams, are vividly familiar.

The biggest information base I have drawn upon is that provided by Australian newspapers. The quality of football coverage in the between wars years varied from state to state, and sometimes from year to year. Nevertheless, the general standard of reporting is not bad at all and is a lot more plentiful than a modern reader might expect to find.

I have read thousands upon thousands of words in match reports to build as reliable a record as I can of what the football action actually looked like. Seekers of more match details should check out the range of reporting online.

The National Library of Australia's *Trove* search engine is, as the name implies, a national treasure. It is the best newspaper archive service in the world and I commend it to anyone looking a broader range of writing on specific events at particular times, football or otherwise.

The French Bibliothèque Nationale enables access to French language publications, including France's rich history of sports journalism, through its *Gallica* portal. The National Library of Singapore operates a similar service, as does the excellent Dutch language *Delpher* through the Nationale bibliotheek van Nederland, the National Library of New Zealand's *Papers Past*, and the British

Library's *British Newspaper Archive*. All of these services have revealed information on Australia's early international football life.

The Mitchell Library in Sydney has been a valuable help. I have draw on annual reports and other documents from New South Wales and national associations, particularly through the E.S. Marks Collection. The City of Sydney Library's Haymarket branch is home to much expertise on Australian Chinese language publications, and the Australian Chinese Museum in Melbourne has also provided information on Australian Chinese cultural life. The Australian National University library holds Nick Guoth's thesis *Kangaroos and Dragons: The 1923 Chinese Football Tour of Australia*, the most comprehensive account of that first contact with Asia.

The Japanese Football Museum in Tokyo is not only as good as sports museums get, it offers a valuable information asset through Hiroshi Kagawa's excellent Japan Soccer Archive. RSSSF, the Rec. Sport. Soccer Statistics Foundation, has exhaustive accounts of early international football, and in Karel Stokkerman, the best authority on the course of the Dutch East Indies game. OzFootball, the Australian football website, is a valuable source of information on Australian international matches.

Alex Jackson at England's National Football Museum has been of great assistance in pointing to some excellent reference material. Football Association Council minutes held by the museum in Preston proved to be most illuminating. Michael Schmalholz at the FIFA Library and Dominik Petermann at FIFA Archives have also been immensely helpful.

Very many individuals have been generous with responses to my enquiries. Jacqueline Dwyer, author of *Flanders in Australia*, patiently fielded my questions on the social and political scene the wool buyer and footballer Maurice Vandendriessche inhabited. Likewise, Nadia Wright, author of *The History of Armenians in Singapore and Malaysia*, helped me understand the world of the Armenian community in south east Asia.

Hanyang University's Professor Jong Sung Lee, who wrote the fascinating *History of Football in North and South Korea*, confirmed some Korean details, and Canadian football historian Colin Jose also aided my research of his country's football. The South China club's Li Jimay and theatre writer/director Anthony Chan helped my efforts in Hong Kong.

Allard Doesburg has given lots of time to my Dutch language research, translating newspaper and other texts as well as freely offering the expertise of his own football history research. I thank him for his passion. Tito Ambyo has translated Indonesian texts, giving me access to R.N. Bayu Aji's *Tionghoa Surabaya Dalam Sepak Bola 1915-1942*, an account of the Chinese community influence on football in Surabaya. The ABC's Beijing correspondent Bill Birtles has translated important details of 1920s Chinese matches.

Descendants and other family of the players of old have shared information, stories, and clues to other lines of inquiry. The ever gracious Kay Hunter has been invaluable in helping me discover the story of Tom Traynor; Richard Boothman and Peter Lukeman greatly enhanced my understanding of Ernest Lukeman; Poppy Fogarty and Anne Lemon both shone lights on the life of Harry Millard.

Balgownie Rangers is a fabulous source of information on Judy Masters and other NSW south coast football figures, and the football communities of Maitland, Newcastle and Ipswich head a long list of regional centres keeping a flame alight in honour of the contributions of players and teams outside the capital cities. Andrew Howe, responsible for the *Encyclopedia of Socceroos* (also published by Fair Play Publishing), is an ever reliable guardian of the national record.

For all of that, I alone accept responsibility for any errors in this book.

TREVOR THOMPSON

Trevor Thompson has reported on football in Australia since the 1980s when he wrote and presented a documentary for Radio National on Australia's national football competitions. He covered the National Soccer League for ABC Radio's Grandstand program for over ten years and wrote A weekly review of A-League matches for ABC Online.

He covered the World Youth Cup for Triple Jay in 1993 and went on to report on Australian World Cup qualifiers for tournaments between 1994 and 2006. He reported from the World Cup finals in Germany in 2006 and South Africa in 2010. His history of football in Australia, *One Fantastic Goal*, was published in 2006.

He produced and presented Match Night Asia, a weekly program on Australian and Asian football, for Radio Australia in 2007, and wrote about Asian football history for the Asian Cup 2015 website.

He has been a freelance contributor on football for BBC's Radio Five Live, CBS Radio, and Radio New Zealand.

Trevor Thompson was born in England and spent the Saturdays of his childhood watching Newcastle United at St James' Park. His last game as a suburban player was for Arncliffe Scots in a grand final win in the St George Association's over-35s league.

In a long career in journalism, he has also been a specialist reporter on communications and industrial relations as well as sport. He served for more than ten years as Chief of Staff in the ABC's Sydney newsroom and has been heavily involved in the training of young journalists.

Want some more really good football books from Fair Play Publishing?

Encyclopedia of Socceroos – Every National Team Player
by Andrew Howe

The World Cup Chronicles – 31 Days that Rocked Brazil
By Jorge Knijnik

Coming Soon:

Encyclopedia of Matildas – Every National Team Player
by Andrew Howe and Greg Werner

Support Your Local League
by Antony Sutton

From our US partners, Powderhouse Press:

Whatever It Takes – the Inside Story of the FIFA Way
by Bonita Mersiades

www.fairplaypublishing.com.au

www.ingramcontent.com/pod-product-compliance
Lightning Source LLC
Chambersburg PA
CBHW051938290426
44110CB00015B/2029